Teaching America

The Case for Civic Education

Edited by David Feith

ROWMAN & LITTLEFIELD EDUCATION

A division of
ROWMAN & LITTLEFIELD PUBLISHERS, INC.
Lanham • Boulder • New York • Toronto • Plymouth, UK

Published by Rowman & Littlefield Education
A division of Rowman & Littlefield Publishers, Inc.
A wholly owned subsidiary of The Rowman & Littlefield Publishing Group, Inc.
4501 Forbes Boulevard, Suite 200, Lanham, Maryland 20706
http://www.rowmaneducation.com

Estover Road, Plymouth PL6 7PY, United Kingdom

British Library Cataloguing in Publication Information Available

Library of Congress Cataloging-in-Publication Data

Feith, David.
Teaching America : the case for civic education / David Feith.
p. cm.
Includes bibliographical references and index.
ISBN 978-1-60709-840-9 (cloth : alk. paper) -- ISBN 978-1-60709-841-6 (pbk. : alk. paper) -- ISBN
978-1-60709-842-3 (electronic)
1. Citizenship--Study and teaching--United States. 2. Civics--Study and teaching--United States. I.
Title.
LC1091.F45 2011
372.890973--dc23
2011026696

♾™ The paper used in this publication meets the minimum requirements of American
National Standard for Information Sciences Permanence of Paper for Printed Library
Materials, ANSI/NISO Z39.48-1992.

Printed in the United States of America

To my parents—with love, admiration, and thanks

Contents

6 Civic Literacy and No Child Left Behind: A Lesson in the
Limits of Government Power   51
Eugene Hickok

7 A Failure of Leadership: The Duty of Politicians and
Universities to Salvage Citizenship   61
Senator Bob Graham, with Chris Hand

8 Forgetting Martin Luther King's Dream: How Politics Threatens
America's Civil Rights Memory   69
Secretary Rod Paige

9 Revolutionary Ignorance: What Do Americans Know of the
Original Tea Party?   81
Bruce Cole

10 Core Curriculum: How to Tackle General Illiteracy and Civic
Illiteracy at the Same Time   89
Andrew J. Rotherham

III: In the Classroom—What Works, What Doesn't

11 Fighting Civic Malpractice: How a Harlem Charter School
Closes the Civic Achievement Gap   99
Seth Andrew

12 The KIPP Approach: Be the Change You Wish to See in the World   111
Mike Feinberg

13 The Wisdom of Twenty Thousand Teachers: Strengthen State
Requirements, Stop Marginalizing the Founders   119
Jason Ross

14 Teaching Political Sophistication: On Self-Interest and the
Common Good   127
Charles N. Quigley and Charles F. Bahmueller

IV: Among the Ivory Towers—Fighting Civic Neglect on Campus

15 Good History and Good Citizens: Howard Zinn, Woodrow
Wilson, and the Historian's Purpose   141
Michael Kazin

16 Talk Is Cheap: The University and the National Project—A
History   151
John R. Thelin

Foreword

Civic Education, Devalued

Frederick M. Hess

In the past decade—roughly since the enactment of the No Child Left Behind Act in 2001—we have become used to describing education as the new front in promoting civil rights. This has necessarily and usefully focused educators, advocates, and policymakers on test scores and on whether schools are preparing students for college or careers.

But this healthy emphasis has also had less reassuring consequences. A prominent one is the devaluing of preparation for citizenship. Going back to the earliest days of the Western tradition, schooling was celebrated for its ability to produce good citizens. Plato's *Republic* depicted schooling primarily as a means to cultivate the right kinds of attitudes and a proper attachment to the state. For America's founders—particularly those like Benjamin Rush, Noah Webster, and Thomas Jefferson, who played outsized roles in shaping thinking about education—the crucial mission of schools was to form good democratic citizens. In Rush's telling phrase, the first purpose of schools was to mold "republican machines" who would support and defend their new nation.

In recent decades, though, as education has come to be seen as the path to lucrative professional success, the private purposes of schooling have gained increasing prominence. We have seen this crystallized by President Obama's oft-repeated goal of ensuring that all students are "college or career ready" by 2020. Whatever the merits of that emphasis, it is clear that as schooling has become more economically central, the stuff of citizenship has become increasingly peripheral.

* * *

When we do deign to speak of citizenship today, it is increasingly in transactional and practical terms—with citizenship understood as the basket of skills and attitudes (how to shake hands, speak properly, be punctual) that will help students attend prestigious colleges and obtain desirable jobs. The exception to this state of affairs was the burst of attention to citizenship after September 11, when politicians, teachers, and parents deemed it important to remind students of their privileges and responsibilities as American citizens. But aside from some thoughtful commentary and attention to instructional materials, that energy amounted to little. And it was quickly swept away by the tide of attention devoted to proficiency and graduation rates, among other measures of college and career readiness.

In short, we have entered the twenty-first century—an epoch defined by profound debates over the state's authority in areas such as health care and the economy, and the propriety of US efforts to combat Islamist radicalism on the world stage—with schools devoting remarkably little intellectual energy to questions of citizenship or the formation of democratic citizens. A focus on academic performance, along with concerns about being branded controversial or intolerant, have in many places demoted talk of citizenship to assemblies, ceremonies, or the occasional social studies lesson.

For all the rivers of studies and data that flood schooling today, one has to go back more than a decade—to 1998's Public Agenda study, "A Lot to Be Thankful For"—to find a serious effort examining what parents think public schools should teach children about what it means to be an American. The annual Phi Delta Kappan/Gallup poll has not asked questions about citizenship or the purpose of schooling for a decade. When these questions were last addressed in 2000, respondents indicated that to "prepare people to become responsible citizens" was the least important purpose of schooling—behind such goals as to "enhance people's happiness and enrich their lives" and to "dispel inequities in education among certain schools and certain groups." Perhaps it's no great surprise, then, that respondents gave schools low marks on this task, ranking school performance between 2 and 4 on a 10-point scale (where 1 signaled that schools were not at all effective and 10 that they were highly effective).

Even in schools that make forthright efforts to impart socially desirable habits of mind, there has long been a trend toward what might be termed "vocational citizenship." Vocational citizenship is characterized by its focus on behaviors typically considered part of good citizenship, but with primary emphasis on the practical benefits that they can provide to the individual student. Thus, when we look at high-performing district schools or charter schools—including the charter schools so deftly profiled in David Whitman's *Sweating the Small Stuff: Inner-City Schools and the New Paternalism* (2008) or Jay Mathews's *Work Hard, Be Nice: How Two Inspired Teachers Created the Most Promising Schools in America* (2009)—we see a celebrated devotion to citizenship that plays out almost entirely in terms of sketching a path of individual success. Schools use chants, ceremonies, signs, and strong discipline to forge a culture defined by college going and career success rather than attachment to America as a civic enterprise.

Is this a bad thing? Not necessarily. It is indeed difficult for schools to engage disaffected youth, especially those from at-risk populations. Emphasizing the practical and personal is both sensible and effective. Paternalistic schools that "sweat the small stuff" are just what many students need. And one can certainly make the case that teaching students habits of respect, self-discipline, perseverance, and delayed gratification—whatever the justification—will make them better citizens. I would heartily concede the point.

Questions about vocational citizenship, then, are not intended as an indictment. They are, rather, intended to prod us to wrestle with what we can and should reasonably expect schools to do when it comes to teaching civic values and shaping young citizens.

* * *

Although vocational citizenship fosters some essential social values, it often ignores other values that are crucial to civic health. These include such "subversive" habits as questioning authority and searching for one's own truths. Whereas lessons on the civil rights movement or the internment of Japanese Americans during World War II routinely celebrate the need to question majoritarian views and even legal authorities, schools (understandably) do not invite that kind of critique of school organization, routine, or operations.

Various values coexist under the banner of citizenship. Students require a grasp and appreciation of their nation's history, fundamental tenets, and democratic processes—including the Bill of Rights and esoteric topics such as judicial review and federalism. If students are unfamiliar with the Fourteenth Amendment, the Civil War, and slavery, they will have difficulty making sense of contemporary debates—for example, regarding proposals to amend constitutional language in order to deny citizenship to children born of illegal immigrants. Students must learn enough to be able to obtain and analyze the information that underlies our public debates.

It is also crucial that schools help students understand the sacrifices and efforts of previous generations of their countrymen so that they judge their nation with appropriate sympathy and respect for its struggles and traditions.

The challenges on this score fall uniquely on schools and educators. For one thing, schools are the only institutions with the capacity and mandate to reach virtually every young person in the country. Schools are also, by design, the institutions best equipped to teach civic and political knowledge and skills such as critical thinking and deliberation.

As a matter of course, schools are communities in which young people learn to interact, argue, work together, and begin to learn the norms of social interaction within the larger society. And, for good or ill, many nonschool institutions that used to provide venues for young people to participate in civic and political affairs have weakened in recent decades, for reasons ranging from personalized technologies to changing family dynamics.

And yet the civic education problem extends all the way from grade school through higher education and into the schools that train our teachers. At so many colleges of education, teacher-education programs adopt a reflexive skepticism toward American institutions and traditions. They enact policies such as the one proposed in 2009 by the University of Minnesota's duly deputized Race, Culture, Class, and Gender Task Group, which stipulated that prospective teachers should be required "to discuss their own histories and current thinking drawing on notions of white privilege, hegemonic masculinity, heteronormativity, and internalized oppression," and to have an understanding of US history that takes into account the "myth of meritocracy in the United States."[1]

Meanwhile, K–12 schools now increasingly focused on state assessments have deemphasized traditional sources of knowledge related to citizenship, including foundational documents. While many fourth graders today are tasked with writing a letter to the president, rare is the classroom in which those students will spend much time discussing what it means to be a good American citizen.

* * *

Fortunately, given the urgency of these matters, David Feith has here gathered a superlative set of thinkers to tackle them and so many related ones. They provide a thought-provoking and moving review of the challenges and opportunities we face.

Happy reading.

NOTE

1. Mark Bauerlein, "Heteronormativity, White Racism, Etc. at Minnesota," *Chronicle of Higher Education*, January 25, 2010.

Preface

Keeping the Republic

David Feith

As the wigged revolutionaries completed their negotiations in the Pennsylvania State House that September day, they had been through four months of drafting and debate, which followed on more than fifteen years of anti-imperial protest, revolutionary war, and fitful state building. Now, to form a more perfect union, thirty-nine men would sign a new accord, which they called the Constitution of the United States.

The men, grouped by state delegation, filed toward the quill and parchment at the front of the hall. As they did, Benjamin Franklin turned to a few and pointed out the chair in which George Washington, president of the convention, had sat quietly for months. An image of the sun was painted on the back of the chair. During the vicissitudes of the summertime convention, Franklin said, he had often looked at that image "without being able to tell whether it was rising or setting."

"Now," said the eighty-one-year-old polymath, "at length I have the happiness to know that it is a rising and not a setting sun." It was, Franklin might have said, morning in America.

But only a few minutes later, leaving the building that would come to be called Independence Hall, Franklin issued a warning. Asked by a woman he was passing on the street what kind of government the convention delegates had given the people, Franklin is said to have replied: "A republic, madam— if you can keep it."

It was a sober rather than celebratory reply. The delegates had concluded their hard work, but Franklin was cautioning that an even harder task lay ahead, with every American responsible for taking it up.

And so it still is today. Since Franklin's admonition in 1787, Americans have kept and in many ways improved our republic. But today we are failing in a fundamental part of that task: civic education—teaching students about American history and government. To remain America, our country has to give its kids a civic identity, an understanding of our constitutional system, and some appreciation of the amazing achievement of American self-government, including the work of Franklin and his founding brothers.

Yet American schools often do no such thing. US history—in contrast to math, reading, writing, and science—is the only subject in which more than half of high-school seniors can't demonstrate even basic knowledge: not about our founding, not about the First Amendment, not about the civil rights movement.

That is the subject of this book, authored by an extraordinary and politically diverse collection of public officials, scholars, and educators. In these pages, they describe our nation's civic education problem, assess its causes, offer an agenda for reform—and explain the high stakes at risk if we fail.

* * *

Ask an American why the United States is a great country, and you're apt to hear: Because it's the land of the free. That phrase incorporates various aspects of American life, from our freedoms of speech and religion to free elections, free enterprise and the freedom to pursue happiness in relative economic comfort. In popular understanding, "freedom" is the theme—and for good reason. But for America to endure and flourish, freedom alone is not sufficient.

"The effect of liberty to individuals is, that they may do what they please." So wrote Edmund Burke in 1789, adding: "We ought to see what it will please them to do, before we risk congratulations, which may soon be turned into complaints." The British statesman was writing about the then-unfolding French Revolution, but his message remains relevant to Americans today, even as our experiment in liberty has a two-hundred-year record of success.

That record is not grounds for complacent self-congratulation. It is negligent to assume that the American civic order will perpetuate itself, let alone grow stronger, without conscious effort from political and cultural figures, teachers, parents, and others. Americans in every generation are free to choose what it pleases them to do—what virtues to honor, what behavior to condemn, whether to vote, whom to vote for. That's our blessing. But it also means that in every generation we have to encourage sound, informed choices.

In our republic, responsible citizens know their rights and how to exercise them. They also know their civic responsibilities and are willing, even keen, to meet them. Such citizens tend to be grateful for their political good fortune, their liberties and those who fight to preserve them. In the political sphere, they may do battle vigorously among themselves, but they appreciate that America is a community and they are respectful of the ebb and flow of the electoral tides.

Citizens lacking civic education are none of these things. They are, in crucial respects, disenfranchised. They are not part of America's common civic culture, and they often view its political, social, and economic systems with contempt. In discussing politics, they often characterize their opponents as evil, not just wrong. Such incivility goes hand in hand with a lack of historical and moral perspective—the kind shown by Americans of all stripes who poison political debate by regularly accusing rivals of being latter-day Stalins or Hitlers.

These are the roots of civic discord.

* * *

It is worrisome that, as this volume shows, American schools are providing children with grossly inadequate civic education. Some observers have made this case before, but never has a group of such diverse and deep expertise come together in a single work to address the problem.

The alarm sounded by this book's authors is not just an old-fogy lament about "kids these days." Rather, it is a thoughtful warning that America's civic education problem is now particularly acute.

American schools today are too often mediocre and stagnant, yet in recent decades they have become increasingly responsible for cultivating civic identity, as institutions like the military, labor unions, and places of worship have diminished in cultural influence. The Internet has made information plentiful and accessible, yet it may be fostering more polarization in our culture than harmony. In addition, digital technologies will require Americans to reckon with unprecedented threats to our civil liberties, yet they may also erode our capacity to do so in responsible, thoughtful ways.

This volume studies these issues and many more—from immigration and assimilation to the remarkable influence of the radical historian Howard Zinn. It poses crucial questions, such as "What role do politics and ideology play in shaping civic education?" and "What distinguishes education from indoctrination?"

In assessing all this, authors draw on lessons and innovations from the Supreme Court, the White House, America's best inner-city schools, immigrant life in 1960s New York, and elsewhere. They lay out how political reform, digital tools, charter schools, strategic philanthropy, teachers, and parents nationwide can advance civic renewal. Their message addresses parents concerned with their children's education, teachers and education reformers, policymakers at all levels of government, activists and philanthropists looking for the cutting edge in civic health, and scholars concerned with citizenship and democracy.

Like Benjamin Franklin on September 17, 1787, this book offers messages of both optimism and warning. Its aim is to play at least a small part in keeping our republic.

New York
May 2011

Acknowledgments

This book is the centerpiece of the Civic Education Initiative, which began in a Columbia University dorm room in 2008. Originally called the Columbia Civics Project, its mission from the start has been to tap the best thinkers to answer a great national question: How to sustain America's experiment in government of, by, and for the people.

Present at the creation—fueled by mozzarella sticks—were Evan Daar, Dov Friedman, Eliav Bitan, and Allon Brann. We had worked together on *The Current*, a small Columbia student magazine that punched above its weight, and all were great company as this effort was born. Dov's insights informed the project for months thereafter. Evan, my esteemed roommate, was an invaluable cocurator, always game to work through a political question, a new idea, or the fourth draft of an email.

In September 2008, I wrote an op-ed about civic literacy for the Taste page of *The Wall Street Journal*, edited by Naomi Schaefer Riley. In the process I met several experts who taught me a great deal and later joined this project, including John Bridgeland, Bruce Cole, and Chuck Quigley.

They and all their coauthors—busy public officials, scholars, executives—were generous to join an amateur project and work hard over many months to see it through to a rigorous conclusion. It was an honor to collaborate with such eminent thinkers. Seth Andrew, Mark Bauerlein, Peter Levine, Harry Lewis, Admiral Mike Ratliff, and Andy Rotherham were particularly committed, devoting time not only as authors but as advisers.

Also crucial to the writing and compilation of this volume was the assistance of Jeff Curley, Annie Hsiao, Jeremiah Kittredge, Steve Mancini, William Packer, Victoria Thorp, Larry Scholer, and Delise Williams.

This project's original board of advisers included Bill Bennett, William Galston, Judge Joseph Greenaway, Robert McCaughey, and Barbara Perry. Others who lent valuable strategic advice included Elizabeth Ames, James Basker, Daniel Brujis, Jonathan Cannon, John DiIulio, Gardner Dunnan, Jon Gould, Linda Johnson, Neal Kozodoy, Seth Leibsohn, Michael Weiser, and Reed Werner. And among those who kindly helped me spread the word were Mallory Factor, David Fine, Justin Rydstrom, Lila Prounis, Elizabeth Tretter, Trish Rubin, and David Smith.

This book got immeasurable help from Rick Hess and his staff at the American Enterprise Institute, including Raphael Gang, Jenna Schuette, and Juliet Squire. I appreciate their bringing this project to the attention of their colleagues Gary Schmitt and Cheryl Miller, and especially to Tom Koerner at Rowman & Littlefield. I've benefited since from Tom's support and guidance, along with that of his colleagues Lindsey Schauer and Lynn Weber.

It has been a privilege to work at two publications, *Foreign Affairs* and *The Wall Street Journal*, that exposed me to serious writing on public policy for a general audience. I hope I applied to this book some lessons learned from the support and mentorship of *Foreign Affairs*'s Jim Hoge and Gideon Rose and *The Wall Street Journal*'s Paul Gigot, Melanie Kirkpatrick, and Bret Stephens.

Greatest thanks go to a few. David Bruce Smith and his family helped support the production of this volume. Bari Weiss (visionary founding editor of *The Current*), Dave Aldrich, Scot Faulkner, and Matt Swift gave their entrepreneurial wisdom to the board of the Civic Education Initiative. Jordan Hirsch (another alumnus of *The Current*) offered his sharp editor's eye to this project. And Sarah Morgan, most of all, lent insight, care, and good cheer to every word of this volume and to its grateful editor.

Finally, my father was my chief counselor on this project as on so many others. My mother was the reader to whom I was most eager to send each chapter and whose positivity was most encouraging. This book is dedicated to them.

I

Making the Case

Chapter One

The Democratic Purpose of Education

From the Founders to Horace Mann to Today

Justice Sandra Day O'Connor

At its inception, American republicanism was a highly experimental form of government that depended for its success on the participation and self-government of its citizens. The experiment had its fair share of skeptics who believed that self-rule was not possible in a society so heterogeneous and geographically expansive. Thomas Jefferson, James Madison, John Adams, and other Founding Fathers believed that the answer to these skeptics was public education. [1]

In the preamble to his 1779 bill for free schools in Virginia, Thomas Jefferson argued for public education as a way to preserve self-rule:

> Experience hath shewn, that even under the best forms [of government] those entrusted with power have, in time, and by slow operations, perverted it into tyranny; and it is believed that the most effectual means of preventing this would be, to illuminate, as far as practicable, the minds of the people at large, and more especially to give them knowledge of those facts, which history exhibiteth, that, possessed thereby of the experience of other ages and countries, they may be enabled to know ambition under all its shapes, and prompt to exert their natural powers to defeat its purposes.

Jefferson further asserted that education would allow Americans to draw from the widest possible pool of citizens to find wise and honest lawmakers. And since educating citizens would benefit society at large, he reasoned, all should share the cost of this education. [2]

Noah Webster and Benjamin Rush were also advocates of public education as a means of strengthening republican government. Webster believed
that bad legislative decisions rarely result from bad intentions, but rather
"generally proceed from ignorance either in the [legislators] themselves, or
in their constituents." Thus "the more generally knowledge is diffused
among the substantial yeomanry, the more perfect will be the laws of a
republican state."[3]

In 1798, Benjamin Rush created a rigorous curriculum to teach youth how
to fulfill the "new class of duties" required of every American by the recently
adopted republican form of government. Students were to be instructed in
history, not only of the American republic, but of the various governments of
Europe and of ancient civilizations. They were also to learn "the nature and
variety of treaties," the roles played by ambassadors, and the obligations of
individuals and states.[4]

Rush believed that every student should be "directed frequently to attend
the courts of justice, where he will have the best opportunities of acquiring
habits of arranging and comparing his ideas by observing the secretion of
truth in the examination of witnesses and where he will hear the laws of the
state explained." The curriculum would also include instruction in "elo-
quence," which Rush saw as crucial in bringing about the American Revolution and as a catalyst that "often sets the whole machine of government in
motion." Finally, Rush included subjects seemingly unrelated to civic participation, especially the sciences, since improvements in agriculture, naviga-
tion, and manufacturing would promote "national prosperity and independence."[5]

Although the founders supported the idea of robust civic education, widespread public education systems did not gain broad support for some time.
For the first decades of US history, public schooling was extremely limited
across the country (Massachusetts, Connecticut, and New York were notable
exceptions), and where public schooling was available, few members of the
lower classes partook.[6]

The founders' vision began to gain traction during the antebellum period,
when reformers such as Horace Mann led the "common school" movement,
building systems of free and compulsory public education across the country.
Rapid social change—precipitated by accelerating economic growth, urban-
ization, industrialization, and immigration—cultivated a sense of urgency for
the movement. Reformers saw universal education as a solution to the growing class strife that threatened to undermine the founders' republican vision.[7]

Mann, the educational pioneer who became secretary of the Massachu-setts State Board of Education in 1837, wrote that common education was "the great equalizer" that would help unify and promote understanding be-tween rich and poor, immigrant and native. Common schools, he envisioned, would provide a fair opportunity for all to gain the education necessary to participate actively in government.

Leaders of the common school movement echoed Jefferson, Webster, and Rush, seeing public schools as the "nurseries of a free republic."[8] As Mann said, "however elevated the moral character of a constituency may be; how-ever well informed in matters of general science or history, yet they must, if citizens of a Republic, understand something of the true nature and functions of the government under which they live."[9] Mann went on to conclude that, without a citizenry educated in the roles and responsibilities of the different branches of government, a republic is merely a "political solecism."[10]

By 1850, the states' combined investment in public education exceeded that of any other Western country.[11] Still, although the founding of public schools was an important step toward ensuring an educated citizenry, robust civic education programs did not take hold. Due to the schoolhouses' limited resources, most early public school curricula focused only on the three R's: reading, writing and arithmetic.

In the early twentieth century, however, political leaders and educators recognized civic education as a way to assimilate a massive wave of new immigrants.[12] As a result, civics curricula and initiatives proliferated.[13]

These curricula were based on what the historian Jeffrey Mirel has called "American civil religion."[14] To inculcate new immigrants with "the Anglo-Saxon conception of righteousness, law and order, and popular government, and to awaken in them a reverence for our democratic institutions," schools offered courses in civics, American history, English language, and Anglo-American literature.[15] This notion of civic education as a means to promote a common culture rooted in democratic ideals persisted into the 1960s.

Civic education remained on the rise with the onset of the Cold War,[16] which was often seen as a war of ideas that demanded education about the qualities of democracy. The baby boomers, who received fairly comprehen-sive civic education, would grow up to play a large and active role in civic discourse throughout the 1960s and early 1970s, a period often noted for an abundance of civic engagement.

Until the 1960s, three courses in civics and government were common in American high schools. Two of them ("civics" and "problems of democracy") explored the role of citizens and encouraged students to discuss current issues. [17] The third ("civics and government") took a more abstract view of government. This course, which addressed the concepts of government but not necessarily their applications or the role of the citizens, most closely resembled today's government courses.

* * *

Today, forty state constitutions mention the importance of students' civic literacy and thirteen cite civic education as the primary purpose of schools. [18] But civic education has declined in the past decades. Many factors led to this downturn. First, in the wake of the Vietnam War and the Watergate scandal, the public increasingly lost faith in traditional government institutions and leaders. [19]

In addition, educators had difficulty reconciling the American population's increased diversity with the ethnocentric values that formed the foundation of early civic education. [20] Critics assailed the traditional approach to civic education for imposing a common culture rather than preserving elements of the diverse cultures that students brought with them to the classroom. [21] These critics argued that the imposition of majority values made it harder for students from minority and immigrant backgrounds to perform well and that it therefore constituted "an educational inequality." [22] In response to these challenges, many school leaders have attempted to avoid controversy by excising civic education from the curriculum. [23]

To make matters worse, the training of teachers in civics, political thought, and government became increasingly inadequate. The National Center for Educational Statistics reported in 1996 that more than 50 percent of students in history and world civilization classes had teachers who neither majored nor minored in history. The results of this lack of training are evident. According to a study by the Center for Civic Education, more than 50 percent of high school government teachers could not adequately explain key concepts such as popular sovereignty, habeas corpus, judicial review, federalism, and checks and balances. [24]

The No Child Left Behind law and other recent educational initiatives have unintentionally contributed to the problem by assessing schools mainly according to students' performance in reading, math, and science. This approach pressures teachers to focus on subjects that are tested at the expense of others, such as civics and history.[25] Today, many students' only exposure to civics comes through a one-semester government class in high school.[26] Although approximately 80 percent of high school students take at least one semester of American government, only 50 percent of students have a senior-year course on the subject and of the remaining 50 percent, most take their last American government course in ninth grade, if at all.[27]

On the nationwide civics assessment administered by the federal government in 2006, more than two-thirds of students scored below proficiency, not even a third of eighth graders surveyed could identify the historical purpose of the Declaration of Independence, and less than a fifth of twelfth graders could explain how citizen participation benefits democracy.[28] On the 2010 test, the overall performance of eighth graders was essentially unchanged, while that of twelfth graders actually declined slightly.[29]

As troubling is the large civic achievement gap between poor, minority, and immigrant students and their middle-class, white, and native-born counterparts. From the fourth grade to the twelfth grade, African American, Hispanic, and disadvantaged students score significantly worse on the National Assessment of Educational Progress civics test than do white, Asian, and middle-class students.[30]

Poor and minority students are also at a disadvantage in learning skills necessary for effective civic engagement, such as leadership and communication. These skills are often learned in the workplace and in voluntary associations, but poor and minority youth typically have lower-status jobs and are less likely to participate in voluntary associations.[31] Such youth are also most likely to face civic problems, such as crime, and to live in neighborhoods most in need of effective civic engagement.

There is a direct correlation between civic knowledge and "political participation, expression of democratic values including toleration, stable political attitudes, and adoption of enlightened self-interest."[32] It is therefore unsurprising that "by almost every measure, Americans' direct engagement in politics and government has fallen steadily and sharply over the last generation,"[33] or that the victims of the civic achievement gap show the most troubling lack of democratic participation.

In the 2004 presidential election, citizens with an annual household income of less than $15,000 were about half as likely to vote as were those with household income over $75,000. This disparity extends also to involvement in political campaigns, membership on organizational boards, participation in protests, and communication with elected representatives.[34]

* * *

Another result of civic illiteracy is that citizens come to see judges as politicians in robes who should be controlled by popular opinion.

Forty percent think that the Constitution permits the president to ignore a Supreme Court ruling if he believes that doing so will protect the country from harm.[35] When citizens are thus misinformed about the role of the judiciary, it is not surprising that nearly half of Americans (48 percent) believe that "it is essential or very important to be able to impeach or remove a judge from office if the judge makes an unpopular ruling."[36] Citizens who are less knowledgeable about the judiciary are more likely to believe that judges are biased and less likely to believe that courts act in the public interest.[37]

In recent years, attacks on the judiciary have escalated far beyond productive criticism.[38] Disagreement with judicial decisions has led to calls for impeachment, the recall of judges, increasingly negative advertising in judicial campaigns, the slashing of state court budgets, and the curbing of state court jurisdiction by state legislatures.[39] In some instances, judges and court officials have been subject to physical threats and violence. According to a recent report by the Department of Justice, threats and other inappropriate communications to federal judges, US attorneys, and assistant US attorneys more than doubled between 2003 and 2008.[40]

The problem is particularly acute for state judges, who generally have less job security and are more vulnerable to political forces than are their federal counterparts. Recent attacks include a proposal in South Dakota to eliminate judicial immunity and one in Oregon to institute a district-based system of judicial elections that would oust particular judges based on their views.[41]

Civic education is the best way to combat the erosion of public confidence in the judiciary and the threats to judges' independence and integrity. Our independent judiciary will only survive if the public understands it and works to preserve it as a meaningful part of our constitutional framework.

* * *

Despite the decline in civic education, Americans still believe in the civic mission of public schools. But we cannot continue to teach civics as it was taught in the nineteenth and twentieth centuries.

Civics and history courses may have been more common in the past, but they often provided a one-sided view, failing to adequately address controversies and conflicts that citizens must confront.[42] The common school reformers, concerned about the potential for classroom treatment of divisive political issues to derail the fledgling public education system, often directed teachers not to address controversial topics.[43]

Civics and history textbooks in the late 1950s and early 1960s taught students "that the United States was the wealthiest, most productive, most classless society known to man, and that this was what made America distinctive and great."[44] At the same time these books ignored or downplayed poverty, women's rights, and African Americans' struggle for equality.[45] This sugarcoated view of American history and government not only deprived students of the opportunity to understand and address the problems facing their society, but it also rendered civics textbooks and classes dull.

Although today's civics curricula do, to an extent, incorporate diverse viewpoints and controversial topics, students continue to be bored by civics and social studies and to rate them among their least favorite subjects.[46] Civics is an active subject. It is about engaging in political action to accomplish results. But civics courses often fail to equip students with an understanding of the history and practice of republican government.

Rather, schools attempt to teach civics by having students read textbooks and then memorize disjointed facts. The average civics textbook is 844 pages, surely an unappealing length for a middle school or high school student.[47] If schools fail to inform students about issues that are interesting and relevant to them, they not only bore them but also weaken their capacity to participate in our democracy. Without an understanding of how to employ civic processes to her advantage, the student citizen is more likely to become frustrated with government than to try to effect change.

Educators must engage the twenty-first-century student in ways that are problem based, interactive, and tied to relevant issues. For guidance, educators can look to the ways in which youth are already engaging in civic life. More Americans aged eighteen to twenty-nine voted in the 2008 presidential election than in any election since 1972, when eighteen-year-olds first had the right to vote.[48] In 2009, 36 percent of college freshmen surveyed by

University of California, Los Angeles's Higher Education Research Institute said that keeping up with politics was a "very important" or "essential" life goal, and about 33 percent indicated that there was a "very good chance" that they would participate in community service during college, which represents an increase of 82 percent in less than 20 years.[49] During the 2008 election, two-thirds of Internet users under the age of thirty had a social networking profile, and half of them used social networking sites to get information and share opinions about politics.[50] As the first generation of digital natives, today's youth have demonstrated the potential of digital media for civic education, organizing, and decision making.

Effective civic education initiatives will prepare students to navigate new pathways for finding information and engagement. Although the Internet offers endless civic opportunities, it can be difficult to distinguish good information from bad. Students, therefore, need guidance about how to use these new pathways to gather information and engage effectively. Otherwise, their participation will be at best ineffective and at worst counterproductive.

For my part, I have had a team of experts in education and technology at Georgetown Law School and Arizona State University develop iCivics (http://www.icivics.org)—a free, interactive, online civics curriculum for middle school and high school students. Our goal is to offer teachers and students civics learning portals including online games, social networking, and other pathways to civic participation. We are using problem-based approaches to facilitate students' exploration of public responses to several pressing issues. After students use persuasive and informed arguments to effect change in the games and simulations offered by iCivics, they will be able to take these skills into the real world.

Our hope is to bridge the gap between classroom time and recreation. A 2005 study by the Kaiser Family Foundation found that children spend forty hours per week using media, including computers, television, videogames, and music.[51] That is more time than they spend in school or with their parents.[52] If students thought about government and civic engagement for just a small portion of that time, it would be a substantial step in the right direction.

To encourage this, iCivics is leveraging the synthesis between teens' interest in Internet gaming and the potential civic value of games. The Kaiser study found that "teens with the most (top 25%) civic gaming experiences are more likely to report interest and engagement in civic and political activities than teens with the fewest (bottom 25%)."[53] This finding is particularly significant since 97 percent of teenagers play some kind of computer, web, portable, or console game.[54]

iCivics' games include "Executive Command," "LawCraft," and "Do I Have a Right?" In "Executive Command," students act as the president to encourage Congress to pass new laws, build support for those laws among the citizens, delegate enforcement of the laws to different executive agencies, and deal with threats to national security. In "LawCraft," students assume the role of legislators responding to citizens' concerns by proposing laws that must get the support of members of both political parties and both houses of Congress. In "Do I Have a Right?" students play lawyers determining if fictional complaints have any basis in the Constitution.

iCivics also offers special resources for teachers, including lesson plans for interactive learning and civics units that can be integrated with our online games. The website gives students a chance to discuss the issues they care about and to ask me questions about civics-related topics.

* * *

The founders may not have lived to see widespread public education take root, but they did establish the enduring notion that it is meant to foster informed participation in society—to make students understand the political foundations of our nation, appreciate different perspectives, and gain the skills to advocate their views in the public sphere.

Today, as the schools are not meeting their founding promise of educating the next generation of active and informed citizens, reinvigorating the civic mission of public education should be a top priority for anyone concerned about the future health of our government and our society. Students must be given the tools to participate in, lead, and perfect our system of self-rule.

NOTES

1. R. Freeman Butts, *The Civic Mission in Educational Reform: Perspectives for the Public and the Profession* (Palo Alto, CA: Hoover Institution Press, 1989), 64–76.

2. Thomas Jefferson, "A Bill for the More General Diffusion of Knowledge," 1779.

3. Noah Webster, "On the Education of Youth in America: A Collection of Essays and Fugitive Writings on Moral, Historical, Political and Literary Subjects," in *The Founders' Constitution*, ed. Philip B. Kurland and Ralph Lerner (Chicago: University of Chicago Press, 1987).

4. Benjamin Rush, "Of the Mode of Education Proper in a Republic (1798)," in *The Selected Writings of Benjamin Rush*, ed. Dagobert D. Runes (New York: Philosophical Library, 1947), 87.

5. Rush, "Of the Mode," 87.

6. Carl F. Kaestle, *Pillars of the Republic: Common School and American Society, 1780–1860* (New York: Hill and Wang, 1983), 9–12.

7. Kaestle, *Pillars of the Republic*, 62–74.

8. William J. Reese, *America's Public Schools: From the Common School to "No Child Left Behind"* (Baltimore: Johns Hopkins University Press, 2005), 26.

9. Horace Mann, "Twelfth Annual Report to the Secretary of the Massachusetts State Board of Education," 1848.

10. Mann, "Twelfth Annual Report."

11. Reese, *America's Public Schools,* 28.

12. Jeffrey Mirel, "The Decline of Civic Education," *Daedalus* 131, no. 3 (2002): 49, 51.

13. Charles N. Quigley, "Civic Education: Recent History, Current Status, and the Future" (speech to a symposium of the American Bar Association, "Public Perception and Understanding of the Justice System," Washington, DC, February 25–26, 1999).

14. Mirel, "The Decline," 51.

15. Mirel, "The Decline," 51, quoting Ellwood P. Cubberly, *Changing Conceptualizations of Education* (New York: Houghton Mifflin, 1909).

16. Quigley, "Civic Education."

17. Nathaniel Leland Schwartz, "Civic Disengagement: The Demise of the American High School Civics Class" (senior honors thesis, Harvard College, 2002).

18. John Doyle and Stephen C. Shenkman, "Revitalizing Civic Education: A Case Study," *Florida Bar Journal* 80, no. 10 (2006): 31.

19. Quigley, "Civic Education."

20. Quigley, "Civic Education."

21. Mirel, "The Decline," 54.

22. Mirel, "The Decline," 54, quoting Sonia Nieto, *The Light in Their Eyes: Creating Multicultural Learning Communities* (New York: Teachers College Press, 1999).

23. Mirel, "The Decline," 54. Mirel argues that this policy of avoiding controversy has a long history. He points to the early concerns of leaders of the common school movement— namely, that addressing controversial issues or appearing to take a political stance could undermine support for public schooling. Other examples include the removal of references to evolution in biology textbooks at the time of the Scopes trial and the general move away from even neutral references to the religious motivations behind figures in American and global history.

24. Quigley, "Civic Education."

25. David Feith, "Don't Know Much about History," *Wall Street Journal*, September 5, 2008.

26. Doyle and Shenkman, "Revitalizing," 31.

27. Richard G. Niemi and Julia Smith, "Enrollments in High School Government Classes: Are We Short-Changing Both Citizenship and Political Science Training?" *PS: Political Science and Politics* 34, no. 2 (2001): 281–83.

28. US Department of Education, National Center for Education Statistics, "The Nation's Report Card: Civics 2006—National Assessment of Educational Progress at Grades 4, 8, and 12," May 2007, http://nces.ed.gov/nationsreportcard/pdf/main2006/2007476.pdf.

29. Sam Dillon, "Failing Grades on Civics Exam a 'Crisis,'" *New York Times*, May 5, 2011.

30. Meira Levinson, "The Civic Achievement Gap," CIRCLE Working Paper 51, January 2007, 5, http://www.civicyouth.org/PopUps/WorkingPapers/WP51Levinson.pdf.

31. Levinson, "The Civic Achievement Gap."

32. William A. Galston, "Civic Education and Political Participation," *Phi Delta Kappan* 85, no. 1 (September 2003): 29–33.

33. Robert D. Putnam, *Bowling Alone: The Collapse and Revival of American Community* (New York: Simon & Schuster, 2000).

34. Levinson, "The Civic Achievement Gap," 6.

35. Levinson, "The Civic Achievement Gap," 6.

36. Kathleen Hall Jamieson and Michael Hennessy, "Public Understanding of and Support for the Courts: Survey Results," *Georgetown Law Journal* 95, no. 4 (April 2007): 899, 901.

37. Jamieson and Hennessy, "Public Understanding," 902.

38. Burt Brandenburg and Roy A. Schotland, "Justice in Peril: The Endangered Balance between Impartial Courts and Judicial Election Campaigns," *Georgetown Journal of Legal Ethics* 21, no. 4 (Fall 2008): 1229, 1249–50.

39. Alfred P. Carlton Jr., "Justice in Jeopardy: Report of the American Bar Association Commission on the 21st Century Judiciary," American Bar Association, 2003, http://www.abanet.org/judind/jeopardy/pdf/report.pdf, 31-33.

40. US Department of Justice, Office of the Inspector, General Evaluation and Inspections Division, "Review of the Protection of the Judiciary and the United States Attorneys" December 2009, http://www.justice.gov/oig/reports/plus/e1002r.pdf.

41. Brandenburg and Schotland, "Justice in Peril," 1249–50.

42. Quigley, "Civic Education."

43. Mirel, "The Decline," 50. See also Mann, "Twelfth Annual Report": "Those articles in the creed of republicanism, which are accepted by all, believed in by all, and which form the common basis of our political faith, shall be taught to all. But when the teacher, in the course of his lessons or lectures on the fundamental law, arrives at a controverted text, he is either to read it without comment or remark; or, at most, he is only to say that the passage is the subject of disputation, and that the schoolroom is neither the tribunal to adjudicate, nor the forum to discuss it."

44. Andrew L. Yarrow, "Beyond Civics and the 3 R's: Teaching Economics in the Schools," *History of Education Quarterly* 48, no. 3 (August 2008): 397.

45. Yarrow, "Beyond Civics."

46. John J. Chiodo, "Do They Really Dislike Social Studies? A Study of Middle School and High School Students," *Journal of Social Studies Research* 28, no. 1 (Spring 2004).

47. Rob Walker, "Macgruder's American Government," *Slate*, September 9, 2002, http://www.slate.com/id/2070583/.

48. CIRCLE, "Young Voters in the 2008 Presidential Election," December 19, 2008, http://www.civicyouth.org/PopUps/FactSheets/FS_08_exit_polls.pdf.

49. Higher Education Research Institute Research Brief, "The American Freshman: National Norms Fall 2009," January 2010, http://www.heri.ucla.edu/PDFs/pubs/briefs/brief-pr012110-09FreshmanNorms.pdf.

50. Aaron Smith and Lee Rainie, "The Internet and the 2008 Election," Pew Research Center, June 15, 2008, http://www.pewinternet.org/~/media//Files/Reports/2008/PIP_2008_election.pdf.pdf.

51. Victoria Rideout, Donald F. Roberts, and Ulla G. Foehr, "Generation M: Media in the Lives of 8-18 Year Olds," Kaiser Family Foundation, 2005, http://www.kff.org/entmedia/7251.cfm.

52. Rideout, Roberts, and Foehr, "Generation M."

53. Rideout, Roberts, and Foehr, "Generation M."

54. Amanda Lenhart Sr. and others, "Teens, Video Games, and Civics," Pew Research Center, September 16, 2008, http://pewresearch.org/pubs/953/.

Chapter Two

My Immigrant Tale

Assimilation and the Road to Success

Juan Williams

Most naturalized American citizens can recall the exact moment they proudly held up their hand to swear allegiance to their new nation.

It is an emotionally powerful moment, a personal declaration of independence, the public display of a conscious decision to join the American experience. It is also a dream come true for those who see it as the initiation into a select group—membership in a free nation that ranks high among the world's military and economic superpowers. It's impossible not to delight at pictures of happy immigrants at naturalization ceremonies, dressed in their best clothes, waving those little red, white and blue flags as they become citizens.

But here is a twist on the all-American immigrant story: I'm a naturalized citizen, but I don't recall any emotional ceremony. I'm not even sure how old I was when I became an American.

I do know that my mom, Alma Williams, got her naturalization papers inside Rockefeller Center, on Fifth Avenue in New York City—the building with the awe-inspiring statue of Atlas, his muscles bulging, holding the world on his shoulders. When my mom became naturalized, so did I, by virtue of being her dependent child.

That was my moment, the instant I became certified as an American kid. There was no ceremony. I was nine or ten years old at the time—but, having been in the United States since I was four, it had never occurred to me that I was anything but an American. In fact, this poor immigrant kid with a single mom always wanted to be an American and be accepted as such.

That meant working to assimilate.

Now I am in my fifties, and my success as a writer and political commentator is a result of family support, hard work—and America's capacity to use a newcomer's burning hunger for success. This miracle is only possible, though, when immigrants open themselves to the American experience.

Unfortunately, the idea of assimilation is under strong attack today.

* * *

In 2006, California Governor Arnold Schwarzenegger remarked that Mexican immigrants should "assimilate" by learning English and becoming "immersed" in American culture.[1] For this, he drew some intense criticism.

Nativo Lopez, then president of the Mexican American Political Association, castigated the governor for demonstrating "total ignorance and prejudice." Immigrants should assimilate "into what?" Lopez challenged, questioning the basic validity of Schwarzenegger's comment. Because Mexican immigrants have long contributed to American culture and history, Lopez argued, all recent or new immigrants from Mexico are already necessarily intertwined with American life.[2]

Lopez's approach brings to mind another leading Latino activist, the late Mario Obledo, who was California's secretary of health and welfare from 1975 to 1982, ran for governor in 1982, and led many organizations including the Mexican American Legal Defense and Education Fund, the League of United Latin American Citizens (the country's largest Hispanic American organization), and the National Rainbow Coalition.

Obledo was celebrated for his prioritization of ethnic identity in politics. At the 1984 Democratic National Convention, he threatened to boycott voting to protest the candidacy of Walter Mondale, declaring "I am a Democrat and I love my party, but I love my community more!" Similarly, in 1998— the year he received the Presidential Medal of Freedom from President Bill Clinton—Obledo predicted that Latinos would soon dominate California politics. His forecast had less to do with demographics than with his idea that Latinos' ethnic heritage would trump their status as Californians and Americans. "It's inevitable that Hispanics or Mexican Americans are going to control most of the state of California in the not too distant future," he said. "If people don't like that, they can leave." As the *New York Times* explained, Obledo "suggested that people who did not like it go back to Europe."[3]

Such approaches to politics reflect a view that is commonly heard at academic conferences and in some neighborhood centers—one that equates assimilation into the American mainstream with subordination and inferiority. It disparages as phonies any immigrants who immerse themselves in American schools, culture, and business, as if they are betraying their true identity. By that standard, the only authentic immigrants are those who remain rooted in their native land and choose to emphasize their ethnic and racial background over their ties to America.

* * *

This trend of opposition to assimilation represents a big break from the past, when generations of American immigrants pushed against anti-immigrant bias at school and at work, changed their names to fit in, and tried to drop their accents as they rushed to learn English.

In my childhood home, my mom insisted on speaking to me only in English. Everyone spoke English in the New York City public schools I attended. There were no English-as-a-second-language classes. Schools sought to help students assimilate by teaching them to read, write, and speak effectively in English, whether their native language was German, Italian, Polish, or Spanish.

My assimilation also included American heroes. The stars I looked up to were athletes such as Willie Mays, Muhammad Ali, Y. A. Tittle, and Walt Frazier. The superstars of my fantasy life included Spider-Man, Alfred E. Neuman of *Mad Magazine*, and the Hardy Boys.

I internalized the desire to assimilate for several reasons. First, because my mom and dad wanted my siblings and me to be Americans—so much so that they risked breaking apart the family, with my mom taking the children to the United States while my dad stayed behind to send us money. We came in August of 1958, so that my sister could start high school the next month.

My mother brought three kids to America on a slow banana boat—really, a banana boat—that took more than two weeks to get from Panama to New York City. It was a cheap ticket for a hard trip with anxious, seasick young children. She got on board only because that old, broken-down boat was going to the United States. In doing so, she left behind more than forty years of family and friends.

She wanted her children to live in an affluent, politically stable country which, despite being majority white, offered the chance of success to black immigrants who had no money or political and social connections. Having just a fourth-grade education, my mom cherished the dream of her children graduating from college and making it based on merit and education. The singular appropriate place was the United States.

My mom did not consider being American an entitlement, but a prize earned by joining in the full experience of speaking English, competing for grades and beauty pageant crowns, playing in baseball games and rock-and-roll bands, participating in democratic institutions from the voting booth to the courts, and being openly patriotic. The reward was to be accepted by other Americans as worthy fellow Americans despite our immigrant origins and dark skin.

That's why I was baffled by the meaning of being naturalized. To me, the confirmation of my American life was not some document, but a daily process of assimilation.

* * *

An unprecedented 38.5 million foreign-born people now live in the United States.[4] Over the past decade, the annual number of legal immigrants to the United States has been between 700,000 and 1.25 million. When my family immigrated in 1958, by contrast, that figure stood at 250,000.[5] In addition, there are now 500,000 illegal immigrants arriving in the United States each year, according to the Pew Hispanic Center's estimates.[6] The biggest contributors to the immigration surge—both legal and illegal—are arrivals from Mexico and Latin America.[7] It is among these populations that assimilation is most crucial and, unfortunately, most in doubt.

A 2009 report by Jacob L. Vigdor, an economist at Duke University, concluded: "Recent immigrants—especially Mexican Americans—are acquiring English-language skills more slowly than their predecessors in the early twentieth century." Moreover, in analyzing data from 1900 to 2007, Vigdor found that "as the immigrant population grows, the English skills of newly arrived immigrants tend to decline. . . . Immigrants don't have as great a need to learn English when they have an extensive network of fellow immigrants on whom they can rely."[8] This is significant given the growing size of immigrant communities, especially those hailing from Spanish-speaking countries.

Another troubling trend within these communities is the number of immigrants who do not identify themselves as American. According to a 2007 report of the Pew Hispanic Center, 52 percent of Latinos in the United States between the ages of sixteen and twenty-five identify not as "American" but as "Mexican," "Salvadoran," or "Dominican," for example. Only 24 percent call themselves American.[9] A study of the Russell Sage Foundation from the 1990s found similar habits. Tracking five thousand children of immigrants over their crucial high school years, the longitudinal study found that after the four years, the children of Mexican and Filipino immigrants were 50 percent more likely to identify as "Mexican" and "Filipino" than as "Mexican American," "Filipino American," or "American."[10]

Such attitudes among immigrants relate to the current prevalence of identity politics, which undermines assimilation and challenges the American tradition of becoming one people out of many—*E pluribus unum*. A politics based on groups' ethnic identity and country of birth is proliferating. It is visible on college campuses where, for example, ethnic studies programs have an unprecedented volume of professors, students, and financial support. Similarly, the last twenty-five years have seen a boom in political advocacy groups that act for specific ethnic and racial groups.

Of course, the United States has always had politicians—Irish, Italian, German, black—who represented certain neighborhoods or ethnic groups. But their goal was typically to promote integration and assimilation—to bring their constituency into the American mainstream, not to enforce its separateness. Today, by contrast, politicians and advocacy groups often seek support and funding—from the government, nonprofit organizations, and individuals—based on their status as outsiders explicitly separate from the mainstream. Thus they scorn integration and accentuate their distinct group identity, pressuring immigrant constituents to consider themselves outsiders in the American system.

The outsider mindset is disabling to all essential citizenship roles. As Woodrow Wilson once said, "You cannot become thoroughly Americans if you think of yourselves in groups. A man who thinks of himself as belonging to a particular national group in America has not yet become an American."[11]

Also threatening the idea of a common American political community is that a record number of US residents do not get on the path to becoming citizens. According to the Census Bureau, more than 8.0 million of the 12.6 million legal permanent residents in the United States are eligible to become naturalized citizens but have chosen not to do so. According to Vigdor, the Duke economist, Mexican immigrants today "become [US] citizens at a lower rate than other immigrant groups," and at a lower rate than did Mexicans who immigrated in the 1970s. [12]

In part these figures reflect the high proportion of immigrants, especially from Mexico, who are in the United States illegally and are therefore ineligible for citizenship. According to estimates by the Immigration and Naturalization Service, the illegal immigrant population has doubled since 1996, from five million then to more than ten million today. [13] (Over six million illegal immigrants are from Mexico, according to Census estimates—more than twelve times the second-largest group of approximately 530,000 from El Salvador.) [14]

For so many people to reside in the United States without progressing toward naturalization devalues the idea of American citizenship. It treats the nation as just another port in the global economy and risks undermining a civic order based not on the mere provision of jobs and education, but on principles of participatory democracy and rule of law.

* * *

For immigrants today, the act of becoming American is much more a matter of choice than of necessity. Upon arriving in the United States, an immigrant can turn on the television—whether in Philadelphia, Indianapolis, or Phoenix—and find channels exclusively for Mexicans, Japanese, Russians, or Indians. The top-rated television and radio stations in cities such as Los Angeles, Houston, and Miami are Spanish-language stations. [15] And thanks to the Internet and calling cards, all immigrants have easy access to distant relatives and to news and entertainment from their native countries. These are invaluable conveniences, of course, but they decrease the need to speak English and to seek out social networks beyond one's own ethnic community.

Immigrants are especially concentrated in so-called gateway states, such as California, Texas, and New York. In California, more than 25 percent of residents are foreign born, including 4.3 million naturalized citizens, 3.5 million legal permanent residents, and 2.6 million illegal immigrants. In New York, almost 22 percent of the population is foreign born. In Texas, the proportion is 16 percent. [16] In these states and elsewhere—from Minneapolis, which has a large population of Somali immigrants, to rural Hamblen

County, Tennessee, where Hispanic immigration has doubled since 2000 and now accounts for more than ten percent of the population[17]—it is increasingly easy for immigrants to stay among fellow newcomers and avoid assimilation.

Indeed, having found that "by historical standards, the assimilation of immigrants in the United States in the early twenty-first century is low," Vigdor noted how the rapid increase in immigration had created large pockets of newcomers slow to make their way into the American mainstream.[18] As the University of California, Los Angeles, sociologists Vilma Ortiz and Edward Telles found in a 2008 study, "among fourth-generation Mexican Americans"—that is, US-born great grandchildren of someone who immigrated from Mexico—"many live in majority Hispanic neighborhoods, most marry other Hispanics, [and] most frequently think of themselves as Mexican."[19]

* * *

As ever, immigrants still bring new blood, hustle, and can-do energy to America. And it is with pride that Americans, unlike the people of any other nation on Earth, call themselves a "nation of immigrants." But successful immigration does not happen willy-nilly.

Immigrants, like native-born Americans, must learn English and adopt a body of values including fidelity to democratic principles, legislative compromise, judicial independence, and the sanctity of law. These are the basic ideas of America, a place of opportunity based on a free market in ideas and goods, and freedom from political monarchs and tyrants. A logical—and, more than ever, necessary—place to learn about these ideas is in school.

If American schools treated civic education as a staple, they could speed assimilation by bringing immigrants into the American family more quickly. Immigrants need to know not only how to open a bank account and avoid being ripped off by check-cashing stores. They must also understand the checks and balances between the City Council and the police department, for example, and come to appreciate the power of being a registered voter or a campaign contributor. Having such knowledge allows one to think like an American and be as powerful as Norman Rockwell's iconic everyman standing up in the town hall meeting. Correctly conceived and executed, civic education can be the most potent antidote to the self-segregation that fosters separate values for immigrants and distorts American history and politics along the way.

But schools cannot provide such an antidote if they continue to approach the teaching of immigrants unwisely—in ways that, for example, reinforce immigrants' preference for retaining their native tongue. The federal Department of Education estimates that 5.1 million students in public schools are now classified as "English-language learners"—a 60 percent increase since 1995.[20] As of 2004, English-language learners made up 10.5 percent of the K–12 student population, an increase of more than 100 percent since 1990.[21]

The two main approaches to teaching such students are immersion, in which immigrant students read and write exclusively in English, and bilingual education, in which immigrant students are taught in English but also use their native tongues. In both types of schooling, immigrants are too often kept separate from their native-born counterparts on the grounds that it is tougher to master English while surrounded by fluent English-speaking students. This is understandable, but it can be a harmful framework for educating young immigrants.

The *New York Times* provided a case in point in 2008, when it profiled Cecil D. Hylton High School in Woodbridge, Virginia. The article quoted one teacher celebrating that 100 percent of her English-language learning students had passed Virginia's state writing exam. But such seemingly positive results stemmed from preparing the immigrant students for their exams with strategies that hid their inadequate language skills. "You don't really need to know anything more about the Battle of Britain, except that it was an air strike," the teacher explained. "If you see a question about the Battle of Britain on the test, look for an answer that refers to air strikes." In another instance, the school required native English speakers to write essays in science class but asked immigrant students only to draw posters.[22]

Such approaches ignore the fact that immigrants seeking academic and professional success need to master English by the standards of native-born Americans, not by the standards of their fellow immigrants. The challenge for immigrants is to learn to speak English well enough to engage with native-born speakers (and all others). Yet too many popular teaching methods require immigrant students to be pulled away from their school's mainstream, diminishing their contact—and ability to integrate—with their native-born peers.

"If you ask whether our [English-language learning] program is successful at getting our students to pass tests, the data would indicate that it is," Hylton High's assistant principal told the *Times*. "But if you ask whether we are helping our students to assimilate, there's no data to answer that question."[23]

This is an unfortunate state of affairs. As Susan Eaton of the Charles Hamilton Houston Institute for Race and Justice at Harvard Law School has said, "Increasing linguistic and cultural diversity enriches our society. A modern integration movement must incorporate immigrant students and English-language learners. The sharp segregation of these groups from mainstream opportunity limits their chances for social mobility and encourages prejudice against them."[24]

* * *

Immigrant students can learn American values outside of the civics classroom, just by mixing with American students and teachers in school. Good schools demonstrate to immigrants how to play politics, write a resume, dress for work, be on a team, build a network, and cooperate with people from different backgrounds. They can also demonstrate a culture of rising on merit—conveying that in this country, success is possible no matter the financial or social standing of one's parents.

When my mom first immigrated, she worked as a harried seamstress in a New York sweatshop. She turned out thousands of dresses under tight deadlines with needles and overheated industrial machines that turned her fingers bloody. The pressure of the work gave her a stomach ulcer. Thankfully, my sister found out about a night school where my mom could learn to type fast enough to qualify as a secretary.

It was there, at Prospect Heights High School, that Alma Williams learned how to apply for a job, and also that speaking Spanish was a valuable skill when applying for secretarial work with the New York City government. She eventually got that job, earning a bigger paycheck, health care, and the right to go to the bathroom without being threatened by some ogre in the factory. Prospect Heights High School had taught her a lot about how America works, even outside of civics class.

But civics class is where much of the puzzle of a new country can come to make sense. And during this age of immigrant groups' increasing isolation, schools should place particular emphasis on civic education. That includes cultivating a sense of patriotism, pride in American values, and gratitude for the sacrifices made by others to make America a beacon of democracy.

It also means introducing students to role models who personify success through assimilation. The idea of the poor immigrant boy or girl embracing American life and making it big is both representative and powerful. Figures such as Madeleine Albright, Sergey Brin, Deepak Chopra, Gloria Estefan, and Michael J. Fox—all immigrants to the United States—show how hard work and assimilation open doors of opportunity.

Assimilation remains the proven path for any immigrant seeking to take full advantage of what America has to offer. Immigrants who avoid the American mainstream, using only old-country customs and language, hurt not just their own chances to succeed but those of their children also. When young people are encouraged to value citizenship—to speak English, study US history, and engage with American news and politics—they are empowered to enter the mainstream and take advantage of, as well as enrich, the institutions of the United States.

NOTES

1. Katherine Corcoran, "Schwarzenegger Encourages Mexican Immigrants to Assimilate," *San Jose Mercury News*, October 5, 2006.

2. Nativo Lopez, interview by Bill O'Reilly, *The O'Reilly Factor*, FOX News Channel, October 6, 2006.

3. Douglas Martin, "Mario Obledo, Hispanic Rights Leaders, Dies at 78," *New York Times*, August 20, 2010.

4. Thomas A. Gryn and Luke J. Larsen, "Nativity Status and Citizenship in the United States: 2009—American Community Survey Briefs," US Census Bureau, October 2010, http://www.census.gov/prod/2010pubs/acsbr09-16.pdf.

5. Office of Immigration Statistics, "Yearbook of Immigration Statistics: 2009," US Department of Homeland Security, August 2010, 5, http://www.dhs.gov/xlibrary/assets/statistics/yearbook/2009/ois_yb_2009.pdf.

6. Jeffrey S. Passel and D'Vera Cohen, "Trends in Unamortized Immigration: Undocumented Inflow Now Trails Legal Inflow," Pew Hispanic Center, October 2, 2008, http://pewhispanic.org/files/reports/94.pdf.

7. Jeffrey S. Passel and Robert Suro, "Rise, Peak and Decline: Trends in US Immigration 1992–2004," Pew Hispanic Center, September 27, 2005, http://pewhispanic.org/reports/report.php?ReportID=53.

8. Jacob L. Vigdor, "Measuring Immigrant Assimilation in the United States," Manhattan Institute Civic Report No. 59, October 2009, http://www.manhattan-institute.org/html/cr_59.htm.

9. "Between Two Worlds: How Young Latinos Come of Age in America," Pew Hispanic Center, December 11, 2009, http://pewhispanic.org/files/reports/117.pdf.

10. John Fonte, "To 'Possess the National Consciousness of an American'" (remarks at the Cantigny Conference Series on Immigration and Citizenship in America, Wheaton, IL, July 2000), http://www.cis.org/articles/cantigny/fonte.html.

11. Fonte, "To 'Possess.'"

12. Vigdor, "Measuring Immigrant Assimilation."

13. Robert Warren, "Estimates of the Undocumented Immigrant Population Residing in the United States: October 1996," US Department of Justice, Immigration and Naturalization Service, Office of Policy and Planning, August 1997, http://pewhispanic.org/files/other/overstayers.pdf.

14. Michael Hoefer, Nancy Rytina, and Bryan C. Baker, "Estimates of the Unauthorized Immigrant Population Residing in the United States: January 2009," US Department of Homeland Security, Office of Immigration Statistics, Policy Directorate, January 2010, http://www.dhs.gov/xlibrary/assets/statistics/publications/ois_ill_pe_2009.pdf.

15. "Hispanic Fact Pack 2010," *Advertising Age*, July 26, 2010, http://adage.com/whitepapers/whitepaper.php?id=26.

16. Nancy Rytina, "Estimates of the Legal Permanent Resident Population in 2008," US Department of Homeland Security, Office of Immigration Statistics, Policy Directorate, October 2009, http://www.dhs.gov/xlibrary/assets/statistics/publications/ois_lpr_pe_2008.pdf.

17. Julia Preston, "A Slippery Place in US Work Force," *New York Times*, March 22, 2009.

18. Vigdor, "Measuring Immigrant Assimilation."

19. Edward E. Telles and Vilma Ortiz, *Generations of Exclusion: Mexican Americans, Assimilation, and Race* (New York: Russell Sage Foundation, 2008), 265.

20. Ginger Thompson, "Where Education and Assimilation Collide," *New York Times*, March 15, 2009.

21. Lee Hoffman and Jennifer Sable, "Public Elementary and Secondary Students, Staff, Schools, and School Districts: School Year 2003–04," National Center for Educational Statistics, February 2006, http://nces.ed.gov/pubs2006/2006307.pdf.

22. Thompson, "Where Education and Assimilation Collide."

23. Thompson, "Where Education and Assimilation Collide."

24. Susan Eaton and Steven Rivkin, "Is Desegregation Dead?" *Education Next* 10, no. 4 (Fall 2010): 50–59.

Chapter Three

The Right to Know Your Rights

Civic Literacy, the Miranda Warnings, and Me

Alan M. Dershowitz

No right is more fundamental to a democracy than the right to know your rights. No matter how powerful they may appear in print, rights are mere parchment pronouncements unless informed citizens are fully aware that they have them and are sufficiently knowledgeable to exercise them.

It is said that a Roman tyrant wrote wonderful laws for his people, but he wrote them in a hand so fine and placed them in a place so high that no citizen could read them. Today's laws are not written in that manner, but they are often written in language so obscure and incomprehensible that the average citizen cannot understand what they mean. At the time when the US Constitution was enacted, a widely used metaphor held that laws must be capable of being understood by a person who "reads them while running." Many of today's laws cannot even be understood by scholars who read them while sitting.

I was first exposed to this issue as a young law graduate clerking for Supreme Court Justice Arthur Goldberg in the 1963–1964 term of the high court. We had a controversial case assigned to our office called *Escobedo v. Illinois*, which involved a twenty-two-year-old man who had been convicted of murder based on his confession. The evidence seemed clear that he had done it, but the process by which his confession was elicited raised grave constitutional questions. He had a right to remain silent under the Fifth

Amendment, but the police deliberately failed to inform him of his right. They also kept his lawyer, who was there to advise him of his right to remain silent, from speaking to him.

Five justices were in favor of reversing the conviction, but they could not agree on the grounds. Some thought the case should be decided on the basis of the Fifth Amendment right against self-incrimination. Others thought that the relevant provision was the Sixth Amendment right to counsel. Justice Goldberg assigned me to write an opinion that would bridge the gap. I came up with yet a third right that seemed implicit in both the right to remain silent and the right to counsel—namely, the right to know about these rights in order to exercise them effectively.

Accordingly, I drafted the following paragraph:

> We have [learned the] lesson of history that no system of criminal justice can, or should, survive if it comes to depend for its continued effectiveness on the citizens' abdication through unawareness of their constitutional rights. No system worth preserving should have to fear that if an accused is permitted to consult with a lawyer, he will become aware of, and exercise, these rights. If the exercise of constitutional rights will thwart the effectiveness of a system of law enforcement, then there is something very wrong with that system.

The phrasing may have been awkward, but the germs of an important idea were plain. The Constitution implicitly recognizes the right to know about one's rights, and it certainly recognizes the right not to be willfully and deliberately denied the opportunity to be informed of one's rights. The majority decision in *Escobedo* adopted my formulation.

Unfortunately this right to be advised about one's rights has never really taken hold in Supreme Court jurisprudence. Over time, the rule announced in *Escobedo* has been whittled away. Indeed it is fair to say today that our system of criminal justice relies heavily on suspects not knowing their rights and not being properly informed of them.

* * *

Shortly after the *Escobedo* decision, the Supreme Court decided the famous *Miranda v. Arizona* (1966), which required policemen to give the following warning to confined suspects who are being interrogated: "You have the right to remain silent. Anything you say can and will be used against you in a court of law. You have the right to speak to an attorney, and to have an attorney present during any questioning. If you cannot afford a lawyer, one will be provided for you at government expense."

This warning, as the late Chief Justice William Rehnquist wrote in deciding *Dickerson v. United States* (2000), became "part of our national culture." Indeed, it is probably the best-known set of words to emanate from our Constitution. Every school child, moviegoer, and television viewer knows that Americans have a right to remain silent. As that most reliable barometer of American culture, Jerry Seinfeld, jokes:

> Aren't you a little surprised that cops still have to read that whole "You have the right to remain silent" speech to every criminal they arrest? I mean is there anybody who doesn't know that by now? Can't they just go, "Freeze, you're under arrest. You ever seen *Baretta*?"
> "Yeah."
> "Good, get in the car."

Writing in 1998, Justice Antonin Scalia agreed with Seinfeld that "In the modern age of frequently dramatized 'Miranda' warnings, [it] is implausible [that a] person under investigation may be unaware of his right to remain silent."

The problem, as I demonstrated in my 2008 book *Is There a Right to Remain Silent?*, is that there is no real right to remain silent. An individual may be compelled to testify against himself in civil cases, and his silence may be used against him in a variety of ways that can result in his being deported, disbarred, fired, or subject to considerable financial losses. Moreover, the Supreme Court has said in a long line of cases that individuals can be coerced into disclosing information so long as that information is not used against them in their own criminal trial.

Accordingly, in the context of terrorism, suspects can be compelled to disclose information to be used by authorities to prevent future acts of terrorism. Even in the ordinary criminal context, if a suspect is given "use immunity," he may be compelled to incriminate himself as long as his compelled testimony is not used to convict him of a crime.

Nor is there a right to counsel in the Miranda situation, despite what the mandatory warning says. I know of no case in history where a lawyer was actually appointed to represent a suspect during his interrogation. An arrested suspect, by asking for a lawyer, can require the police to stop interrogating him, but he will not actually be given a lawyer, as the Miranda warning seems to require.

Thus the Miranda rights are not just commonly known but commonly misunderstood. And which is worse: not being informed at all about one's rights or being misinformed about them?

I teach criminal law and constitutional procedure to first-year law students. By reading cases, my students learn about their rights in the abstract. They learn, for example, that they have no obligation to speak to the police when stopped on the street. They learn that racial profiling is illegal. They learn that it is not a crime to express opinions critical of the police.

What they don't learn is that if they exercise those rights, they may end up arrested or even shot. Consider what happened to my colleague Henry Louis "Skip" Gates when he exercised these rights in his own home, in 2009. I had another case many years ago in which an individual who tried to exercise his rights cannot today record what happened—because he was shot dead by the police. He was a law student who insisted on exercising his right to complain about how the police were treating him. The police shot him and made up a story about him reaching for one of their guns.

As a result of these and many other cases that I have experienced over my long career as a teacher and practitioner of criminal law, I now advise my first-year law students that exercising their constitutional rights can sometimes be hazardous to their health and freedom.

This is not to say that students should be denied information about the scope of their rights, but teachers must understand the difference between rights in theory and rights in practice, between rights written on paper and rights as implemented on the streets.

* * *

Teaching rights is a complicated and difficult matter. It requires extensive knowledge not only about history and theory but also about reality and practice.

Teachers must be taught how to teach young students about their rights. It is not simply a matter of going through the first ten amendments to the Constitution. There is little relationship between the words written near the end of the eighteenth century and the current meaning given to these words by our courts. Moreover, these rights are very much in flux.

Take the First Amendment. That important statement actually establishes very few rights. What it does is impose limitations on the power of government. It forbids Congress from making certain kinds of laws, including those that abridge the freedom of speech, the free exercise of religion, and the right to petition government. It also forbids Congress from making any law "respecting an establishment of religion." These terms are anything but self-defining, and they require constant reinterpretation in light of new contexts and technologies.

Or consider the Fourth Amendment, which protects the right of the people "to be secure in their persons, houses, papers and effects, against unreasonable searches and seizures." What do these words mean in the age of the computer and the Internet? Are emails secure from government intrusion? Are they more like sealed letters or open postcards? Can entire computers be seized by the government? Can the government intrude upon the privacy of the home by using modern technology that can see and hear through walls?

Memorizing the words of the Bill of Rights is a far cry from knowing what your actual rights may be in practice. And television and movies today are probably better guides, when it comes to rights, than are many teachers in the classroom who have little sense of how rights operate in practice.

We need to develop sophisticated curricula that can educate children, of different ages and backgrounds, about how rights affect their lives. These curricula cannot be devised solely by teachers. Others—lawyers, policemen, social workers, journalists, community organizers, housing experts, civil rights activists—must be involved in constructing such curricula.

Today everyone talks about rights. Kids tell their parents that they have a right of free speech or a right of privacy. The language of rights permeates our society. That is a good thing. But it is not enough. An educated citizenry requires more than lip service to rights. Rights must be understood. After all, rights are somewhat counterintuitive, since they are restrictions on the power of the majority.

Students must not only understand why the rights of the minority are essential to the operation of a democracy, but they must also understand that rights may deprive them, at least in the short run, of a desired outcome. "Rights for me but not for thee" are not rights at all. Bad people have rights as well as good people, and they tend to exercise them even more often. (As H. L. Mencken observed, "the trouble with fighting for human freedom is that one spends most of one's time defending scoundrels. For it is against scoundrels that oppressive laws are first aimed, and oppression must be stopped at the beginning if it is to be stopped at all.")

The right of free speech means that those exercising it may say deeply offensive things. The right to petition government may be interpreted to allow corporations to use their money to undercut democratic outcomes. The right of privacy may deprive citizens of essential knowledge. Striking the appropriate balance between the democratic powers of the majority and the essential rights of the minority is never easy—and neither is teaching about the subject.

Chapter Four

Safeguarding American Exceptionalism

An Uninformed Citizenry Risks Ceding Excessive Power to Government

Senator Jon Kyl

One in two Americans today thinks that our country is in decline. Half the country, according to a *CBS News* poll taken in 2010, believes that "the future for the next generation of Americans will be worse than life today."[1]

A key driver of Americans' pessimism is the belief that the future is out of their hands. Many Americans worry that future generations will be burdened with insurmountable debt, unable to recover from all of our spending. Americans are aware that the longer the government waits to act, the more the corrective action will hurt, and the more future generations will have to pay for our policies. More basically, many Americans see the government exercising powers that they don't remember ever ceding to it.

Worried about their future and the loss of important aspects of individual freedom, many Americans are turning to history and learning more about our founding principles. I believe that the health of our union in the long run is directly proportional to our citizens' sustained interest in the principles that underpin America. This interest is overdue, as proven by the grim findings of numerous surveys of civic knowledge among students in elementary school, high school, and college.

When Americans learn about their country, they learn about the idea that animates our government: that, as Thomas Jefferson wrote in the Declaration of Independence, we are all equal—that is, morally equivalent—and endowed by our Creator with certain rights that no one can take from us. Coming from God, the rights are natural to man, not given to man by government. The colonists memorialized this idea as the basis for their liberty, a moral foundation for political rights.

There's a second, related idea expressed immediately afterward in the Declaration of Independence: "That to secure these Rights, Governments are instituted among men, deriving their just powers from the consent of the governed." Thus, the declaration explains the source of and limitations on the government's power, after explaining the source and nature of the people's power.

Our second founding document, the Constitution, begins with the words "We the People." This certifies that we have a government from the bottom up—one created by the people, who predated it and would limit its powers. For this reason, it is an enduring challenge—for our generation and all others—to stress that any effort to transfer our God-given rights to the government demands judicious consideration from all citizens.

This idea has taken on new meaning in recent years, as many Americans have come to see government as too big and powerful—as threatening to liberty, even to our right to care for our families as we want to. Consider the health-care law passed in 2010, which represents a breathtaking cession of power to the government. Under the law's web of government regulations, families will have to obtain care as dictated by a new bureaucratic system that will ultimately impose rationing. A greater diminution of freedom is hard to imagine.

The Founding Fathers gave us the right to cede our freedoms to the government, but the health-care law is an example of the consequences—maybe irreversible—of unwise decisions. The broader lesson is that if people don't understand the limits set forth in the Constitution, they may cede to government powers that challenge the very liberties that the Constitution is supposed to protect.

* * *

When young Americans learn the founding principles of our country, they are more likely to understand what is unique about it and what is, therefore, worth defending, preserving, and passing on to the next generation.

If young people don't learn about their country, they will be citizens only in the technical, legal sense. But true citizenship is about understanding, believing in, and uniting around the country's first principles. These principles are not passed down from generation to generation automatically. They aren't hereditary. Each successive generation must learn them anew.

The United States is different than those countries whose creation was the result of an accident of history. Citizenship is not just another word for nationality. Nationality binds people together, but that bond is not as strong as that of a people who share common ideals about their natural rights.

In our country, citizenship connotes something more meaningful that no law or naturalization process can confer. This kind of citizenship is captured by the motto *E pluribus unum*. Americans are "out of many, one" because we share the values that underpinned our country's founding. Unlike any other country, even those of Europe, our basic rights did not come from the state. They are inherent in each of us. Our rights are endowed by our Creator, and our government derives its power from the people.

In challenging times, Americans have called on the ideals set forth by our founders. The Declaration of Independence inspired Abraham Lincoln's Gettysburg Address in 1863, just as it inspired Martin Luther King Jr.'s "I Have a Dream" address one hundred years later.

President Lincoln and Reverend King understood that we are united by shared beliefs in our founding principles. And the significance of their words underscores how Americans' appreciation for those ideals must be perpetuated from generation to generation. That's where civic education comes in.

As young people learn about America's history, founding documents, leaders, and important ideas, they build a store of knowledge not only about their country but about themselves. They begin to develop the answer to the question: Who am I as an American?

To address this question, students need to learn not just about our civic ideals but also about how they themselves fit into our nation's story. Teaching that empowering lesson is a central way to ensure that *E pluribus unum* holds true today and into the future.

It is also a way of ensuring that the United States remains exceptional. I believe in American exceptionalism—not because Americans are better than anyone else, but because of the ideas that animated our founding and the way they have influenced us ever since.

A few years ago, the American Enterprise Institute scholar Charles Murray described American exceptionalism as encompassing a certain uncommon optimism, a general lack of class envy, and the enduring "assumption by most Americans that they are in control of their own destinies."[2] He commented that "underlying these symptoms of American exceptionalism" are two apparently conflicting dynamics described by Alexis de Tocqueville in the early nineteenth century: Americans' passionate pursuit of individual interests, and their passionate formation of voluntary associations to address community needs.

The cause of all this, explained Murray, isn't "something in the water." It is "the cultural capital generated by the system that the Founders laid down, a system that says people must be free to live life as they see fit and to be responsible for the consequences of their actions; that it is not the government's job to protect people from themselves; that it is not the government's job to stage-manage how people interact with each other."

"Discard the system that created the cultural capital," Murray said, "and the qualities we love about Americans can go away." Those are the high stakes involved with civic education.

If Americans cease to understand who they are as citizens, our country risks losing the qualities that make it exceptional. It risks finding itself in the position of Europe, a continent that has witnessed harmful shifts in its civic personality. Many Europeans today have no faith in anything except their government.

The European economist John Maynard Keynes famously said: "In the long run, we are all dead." He might have been making a point about macroeconomic analysis, but the remark captures a broader cultural point. It presaged a dismal view, unguided by faith or deeper social principles, about society's purpose—or lack thereof. Europe's model today, said Murray, "stifles human flourishing and erodes the civic and cultural institutions and habits that make for a vibrant, sustainable, and satisfying way of life."

If the United States loses what makes it exceptional, it will also lose what has made it successful.

* * *

The recognition that Americans have a civic literacy deficit is not new, and many committed individuals have undertaken noble efforts to educate young Americans. Yet students' progress has not matched this outpouring of effort.

One reason for that is the too-common view that civic education is just another subject, no different than algebra or biology. That is, it may be part of a standard curriculum, but it is not really necessary to one's daily life. There is also a view that civic education is merely indoctrination, so therefore it warrants suspicion, if not outright opposition. According to this view, it is politically incorrect to teach about the virtue and positive influence of our founding principles and their authors.

Another challenge is that the story of our country is not always easy to find. Many of today's textbooks don't relate the drama of our nation; they are lifeless and boring. Our schools are not filling in the gaps. Many other books don't deal with history in an accessible way. Academic works are often inscrutable, catering to the narrow and obscure interests of university faculties.

Americans do find ways to fight through the muddle. The Government Printing Office reported in 2010, for example, that sales of the Constitution had reached highs. That coincided, of course, with Americans taking a serious look at their government, as they asked hard questions about our constitutional system and the powers that the government has assumed.

The majority of Americans still recognize that the government gets its powers from the people. They still ask, did we intend to cede to government these various rights and freedoms? Did the government accrue all of its powers through the consent of the governed, and did the governed make wise decisions?

* * *

At this moment, a new American is being born into a country that has a wonderful story to tell and unique opportunities to offer. Our challenge is to ensure that this young person learns that story and grows into an active, thoughtful citizen of our nation. Civic education is more than teaching US history or the intricacies of our government's operations. It is about preparing Americans to be engaged citizens who can add to our nation's story as prior generations did. That begins with protecting the liberty bequeathed to us.

NOTES

1. *CBS News*, "Where America Stands: Economic Worries Persist—Dissatisfaction with Washington Runs High, May 20–24, 2010," *CBS News* poll, May 25, 2010, http://www.cbsnews.com/htdocs/pdf/poll_052510.pdf.

2. Charles Murray, "The Happiness of the People," 2009 Irving Kristol Lecture, the American Enterprise Institute for Public Policy Research, March 11, 2009, http://www.aei.org/docLib/Murray-Happiness.pdf.

II

From the White House
to the Statehouse—
Policymakers' Lessons Learned

Chapter Five

Civic Nation

My White House Mission after September 11

John M. Bridgeland

The attacks of September 11 changed the focus of the United States as a nation and of my job as director of the White House Domestic Policy Council. Across the country, citizens responded to the attacks with acts of kindness and decency. The tragedy changed the national mood, as signified by American flags on houses, prideful bumper stickers on cars, and emotional tributes to first responders and other heroes. A patina of civility covered Washington, with Senate Majority Leader Tom Daschle and President George W. Bush showing a new camaraderie, embracing on national television at the 2002 State of the Union address. As Bush said that night, we "looked into a mirror and saw our better selves."[1] Americans liked getting a glimpse of what the country could become.

While most Americans exhibited great patriotism after September 11, some demonstrated a disturbing blame-us mentality. On the right, a few leaders said that the attacks were the work of American groups aiming to secularize the country; on the left, some argued that al Qaeda's attack was justified by American imperialism. Others, including many students, exhibited what Supreme Court Justice Anthony Kennedy called a lack of "moral outrage." (Seeing this, Kennedy partnered with the American Bar Association to create the Dialogue on Freedom series to educate young Americans on core American principles and ideas.) Although they did not represent the dominant sentiment, these responses to September 11 were troubling and caught the attention of policymakers.

Shortly after September 11, the White House launched an effort to sustain the country's renewed culture of citizenship and service. As I was briefing the president in the Oval Office one day in October 2001, he asked me "to develop an initiative to foster a culture of service, citizenship and responsibility." I recorded those precise words that day as a reminder to myself that the president did not want a mere public relations campaign or an initiative with only momentary appeal. Rather, the goal was to capture the spirit of service and citizenship and make institutional changes that would sustain it.

This was no simple task, especially in the face of the civic disengagement and disconnectedness that Harvard political scientist Robert Putnam had described in his 2000 book *Bowling Alone: The Collapse and Revival of American Community.* The United States had experienced a thirty-year decline in most indicators of civic health: charitable giving, community volunteering, social and institutional trust, and civic knowledge, among a host of others.[2]

The centerpiece of the Bush administration's initiative was the USA Freedom Corps, a new policy council on par with those dedicated to national security, domestic affairs, economics, and homeland security. Like the other policy councils, the USA Freedom Corps reported directly to the president and could marshal the resources and personnel of all federal departments and agencies to support a renewed culture of service. Having begun the administration as director of the White House Domestic Policy Council, I became the first director of the USA Freedom Corps and its fifteen-person office. Immediately, we commissioned a review of what every previous president had done to promote active service and citizenship among Americans.

Building on the traditions of Franklin Roosevelt's Civilian Conservation Corps, John F. Kennedy's Peace Corps, Lyndon Johnson's VISTA, Richard Nixon's Senior Corps, Ronald Reagan's Private Sector Initiative, George H. W. Bush's Points of Light, and Bill Clinton's AmeriCorps, the USA Freedom Corps made unprecedented investments in national and community service. First, it expanded existing programs, such as the Peace Corps and its domestic counterpart, AmeriCorps, which supports nongovernmental programs including Teach For America, City Year, Habitat for Humanity, and LIFT. In addition, it created new programs to fit the times, including the Citizen Corps and Medical Reserve Corps (to strengthen disaster response and homeland security) and Volunteers for Prosperity (to deploy skilled Americans abroad to address urgent issues such as HIV/AIDS and malaria).

The USA Freedom Corps set out to marry national service with traditional volunteering in creative ways. By creating the online clearinghouse Volunteer.gov (now called Serve.gov), we connected Americans to local service opportunities according to their interests and zip codes. The USA Freedom Corps also encouraged more than one thousand CEOs to deploy their workforces to meet civic needs. One result, among many others, was that Wachovia gave its seventy-two thousand employees six days of paid leave for mentoring and tutoring youth in the communities where they worked. Citigroup, meanwhile, worked with Habitat for Humanity to build homes in communities across the country, and The Home Depot provided sixty thousand jobs for returning veterans. We also gave unprecedented support to faith-based organizations helping the poor and vulnerable, launching competitions for billions of dollars in federal funding and publishing guidance on how faith-based groups could apply.

In 2008, then-presidential candidate Barack Obama used powerful words to capture the relationship between individuals' service and the country at large. "Through service," he said, "I found a community that embraced me; citizenship that was meaningful; the direction I'd been seeking. Through service, I discovered how my own improbable story fit into the larger story of America."[3] That was how I felt after September 11. But that convergence could hardly happen if people did not even understand the basics of the American story—of American history. That was why, in the months after September 11, the government's vision for igniting a new generation of engaged citizens involved strengthening the public's knowledge of American history, values, and civic traditions.

* * *

When my colleagues and I set out to understand the state of civic literacy in the United States, what we found was not encouraging. Studies showed large and disturbing gaps in young people's knowledge of their own history. As President Bush would note, nearly one in five high school seniors thought that Germany was an ally of the United States during World War II; more than one-fourth of eighth graders did not know why the Civil War was fought; and even graduating seniors from leading colleges and universities could not recognize words from the Gettysburg Address or identify James Madison as the father of the Constitution.[4] Communities were not making

history and civic education a priority, even though nearly every state constitution in the country declares it to be one.[5] This was not just an academic, but
a national failure.

To begin addressing this problem, I reached out to someone who was
making American history come alive for millions of Americans: David
McCullough, whose books populated airports, schools, and bestseller lists
across the United States. In a phone call (which led, later, to more phone
calls, some letters, and a lunch in the White House Mess), I asked McCullough what one thing he would do to promote American history if given the
platform of the White House, with its advantages and constraints alike.

Without hesitation, McCullough said, as I recorded in my notes that day,
"I would connect young teachers to master teachers who could ignite a passion in them for telling stories from American history, and connect those
young teachers to summer seminars and institutes that could place them in
historic sites, and connect them to original documents and resources that
bring our history to life." Having just written the book *John Adams*, McCullough offered to teach one such seminar from the home of John and Abigail
Adams in Braintree, Massachusetts. McCullough's ideas were brilliant and,
more importantly, were within the power of the federal government to pursue.

I then contacted another leader who understood Washington's bureaucra-
cies and led an institution especially qualified for the task: James Billington,
the top official of the Library of Congress, which bills itself accurately as
"the largest repository of knowledge in the history of the world." Billington
argued that the key to cultivating civic knowledge was connecting more
students to the original record of American history. Young people should not
read the Declaration of Independence only as it is commonly printed, he
argued, but should study original drafts which show additions and deletions
that students can debate in classrooms. For students to do so would, among
other things, diminish the effect of debates over political correctness, which
often focus students' attention on competing interpretations of history without first equipping them with basic information. Billington's advice led me to
think about how the government could make the original record of the country more widely available to teachers and students.

My next stroke of luck was to meet William Galston, who had been
deputy assistant to President Clinton for domestic policy from 1993 to 1995,
and later created CIRCLE, the Center for Information and Research on Civic
Learning and Engagement. When we met in the White House Mess in 2002,

Galston was working with Peter Levine of CIRCLE (a contributor to this volume) and Cynthia Gibson of the Carnegie Corporation of New York to issue "The Civic Mission of Schools," a landmark report. In it, they stressed that schools must not simply transmit knowledge, but help students develop habits and skills that enable them to absorb information about current affairs, cooperate with others in civil dialogue, and participate actively in the democracy they will inherit.

My final blessing was to have the extraordinary leadership of Amy Kass, a professor at the University of Chicago who studied how great literature and political theory inform American civic participation. On the Freedom Corps staff, Kass was responsible for developing the White House Summit on American History, Civics and Service, which ultimately included President Bush, Laura Bush, Lynne Cheney, and educational leaders such as E. D. Hirsch, who argued that common knowledge of American culture, traditions, and values is fundamental to social equality and citizens' full participation in American life.

After deliberating with these and other advisors, I concluded that the federal government had three comparative advantages regarding the promotion of civic literacy. First, it could collect national data and publicize reports on civic knowledge that drew revealing comparisons across states, regions, and demographic groups. Second, it housed—in the Library of Congress, the National Archives, and elsewhere—resources that could be tapped for extraordinary educational use in the Internet age. And, third, it had both a bully pulpit and significant funding to jumpstart efforts that could, in turn, invigorate civic learning at the state and local levels.

* * *

In September 2002, eight months after creating the USA Freedom Corps, President Bush stood in the Rose Garden to announce a series of new efforts to improve education in American history and civics, and to link civic learning to the tradition of volunteer service.[6]

The National Endowment for the Humanities, the president announced, would administer We the People, a new initiative with various facets. Under the great leadership of National Endowment for the Humanities Chairman Bruce Cole (another contributor to this volume), We the People encouraged curriculum-development through a grant competition that saw scholars, teachers, filmmakers, curators, librarians, and others conceive of creative means to explore American history and culture. It also conducted seminars for teachers guided by distinguished scholars and educators, and it created residential academies offering school principals and teachers intensive two-week programs in American history, culture, and institutions. Another element of We the People was a project called Landmarks of American History, which supported summer enrichment programs at important historical sites such as battlefields and presidential homes. David McCullough's idea had taken life.

The Education Department directed another part of the administration's effort by renewing support for Teaching American History grants, which it first distributed in 2001 after Senator Robert Byrd wrote the grant program into the No Child Left Behind bill. (Byrd also mandated that all schools receiving federal money read and discuss the country's founding documents on Constitution Day, September 17, every year.) These grants encourage schools to teach American history and connect them to a variety of civic organizations such as the Smithsonian, the Library of Congress, the National Archives, the National Park Service, and presidential libraries and museums. Partnerships with such organizations—and with local ones, including universities, museums, and historical societies—often allow schools to sustain their history education efforts even after their specific grant has expired. In 2010 alone, the Teaching American History grant program provided over \$118 million to more than 120 recipients.[7]

Other aspects of the administration's effort took advantage of the fact that, as the president noted, the government "conserves and protects some of our greatest national treasures, and we need to make them more readily available to Americans in their schools and local communities."[8] He therefore announced Our Documents, a program—eventually turned into a best-selling book—that provided teachers and students with facsimiles of one hundred important original documents held in the National Archives, from the Lee Resolution of 1776 to the Voting Rights Act of 1965. The program also offered lesson plans to schools, workshops to train teachers on how to integrate the documents into their lessons, and a competition that allowed students, teachers, and the public to vote on the most important documents in our history.

Although conceived and developed separately, Our Documents built on existing efforts, including the Library of Congress's American Memory program, which made available online nearly eight million original documents from American history. The National Park Service, meanwhile, had since

1992 used parks as classrooms (as one program is called) to teach students about national treasures in places such as Mesa Verde, Jamestown, Thomas Edison's Laboratory, historic battlefields, the Statue of Liberty, and Kitty Hawk.

Finally, in 2003, the Freedom Corps and the White House domestic policy staff worked with the Department of Education to revise the process by which the US government measured student proficiency in American history and civics. Whereas the National Assessment of Education Progress had previously assessed those subjects only every eight years, the assessment now does so every four years, providing every state, and the nation at large, with more regular data on the civic learning of students in the fourth, eighth, and twelfth grades.

Since the federal government plays a relatively small role in American education, my colleagues and I believed we were pulling appropriate institutional levers to give history and civic education attention and visibility commensurate with its importance. And the development of these programs after 2002 was encouraging. Support for the We the People initiative exceeded $93 million, with $75 million from the federal government and an additional $18 million from nongovernmental sources.[9] Funding for Teaching American History grants, meanwhile, grew to more than $118 million per year by 2010.[10] And the Our Documents initiative continues to thrive, and it was joined recently by "docsteach," a collaborative site, launched by the National Archives, through which teachers can develop and share lesson plans based on primary documents.

Of course, these were not the only governmental efforts that affected civic education over the past decade. A major initiative of the Bush administration was the crafting and implementation of the No Child Left Behind (NCLB) law, which fostered a new era of accountability and has boosted student achievement in reading and math. One premise of NCLB was that what gets measured is what gets taught. And having basic reading skills is, of course, fundamental to studying American history and civics.

Unfortunately—as many educators, policymakers and others have rightly complained—focusing on reading and math alone can lead schools to abandon other subject areas, including civic education. Given the unintended consequences of NCLB in further crowding out subjects that are important to a complete education, policymakers should take advantage of the law's reauthorization process to reform it accordingly. Specifically, they should attempt to foster civic learning across the curriculum, enabling students to develop civic skills not only in history and government classes, but in science, social studies, English, foreign languages and other subjects. Leading nonprofits and foundations—not the government—should devise creative ways to integrate civics across the curriculum and to train teachers accordingly. In turn, the government should begin including civic learning in its assessments of schools' yearly progress.

* * *

Since leaving the administration in 2004, I have been gratified to participate in and learn more about various nongovernmental efforts to promote civic education, chiefly through the National Conference on Citizenship. A nonprofit chartered by the Congress in 1953, the National Conference on Citizenship published the first annual national Civic Health Index in 2006. The index measures various indicators—including civic knowledge—across demographic categories and all fifty states. The US Congress found the data so important that it included funding for the index in the 2009 Edward M. Kennedy Serve America Act that became law in April 2009 and was the first major bipartisan legislation of the Obama presidency.

Today the National Conference on Citizenship is directing Civic Nation, an effort by leading institutions to devise policies, programs, and initiatives that will enable a quantum leap in civic understanding. Civic Nation is developing a pamphlet—a modern-day "Common Sense," echoing Thomas Paine—articulating why civic literacy is so vital, which we will distribute to educators, policymakers, and others. Civic Nation is also examining how the reauthorization of NCLB can advance civic learning across the curriculum without creating new federal mandates. And we are reviewing the federal government's record of promoting civic learning and engagement, assessing how best to collect and sort data on students' civic knowledge, and how to highlight the most innovative local educational models so that they can be adapted for broader use. We intend for Civic Nation to culminate in policy changes at both the federal and state levels (akin, perhaps, to the Serve America Act), so that schools and communities will have incentives to prioritize and improve civic learning.

In this and all other efforts, policymakers and educators should remember that civic literacy does not automatically result in greater attachment to country. Stories, songs, emblems, holidays, and service—which appeal to hearts as well as to minds—are essential to creating active, proud citizens. Civic education is not meant to inspire blind patriotism, but to remind more Americans of our system's noble values and beliefs. They include equality of opportunity, adherence to the rule of law, freedom of speech and worship, and civilian control of the military—and they enable the human spirit of Americans to flourish.

Without effective efforts, young Americans may grow up not knowing America's story, values, and ideals—or the role that an individual, inspired by those who came before, can play in shaping a civic nation.

NOTES

1. George W. Bush, "State of the Union Address," January 29, 2002.

2. Robert D. Putnam, *Bowling Alone: The Collapse and Revival of American Community* (New York: Simon & Schuster, 2000).

3. Barack Obama, "A New Era of Service," remarks at the University of Colorado, July 2, 2008.

4. George W. Bush, "Remarks of the President on Teaching American History and Civic Education Initiative," September 17, 2002.

5. Kenneth W. Tolo, "The Civic Education of American Youth: From State Policies to School District Practices," Policy Research Project Report No. 33, Lyndon B. Johnson School of Public Affairs, University of Texas at Austin, 1999, http://www.civiced.org/pdf_archive/ceay_civedpolicyreport.pdf.

6. Bush, "Remarks of the President."

7. US Department of Education, "Teaching American History: Funding Status," http://www2.ed.gov/programs/teachinghistory/funding.html.

8. Bush, "Remarks of the President."

9. National Endowment for the Humanities, "About 'We the People,'" http://www.wethepeople.gov/about/index.html.

10. US Department of Education, "Teaching American History."

Chapter Six

Civic Literacy and No Child Left Behind

A Lesson in the Limits of Government Power

Eugene Hickok

It is ironic and disappointing that Americans' civic literacy is so weak even though education reform has been a high national priority for decades. At the federal level, multiple administrations have spent billions of dollars on hundreds of reform proposals to improve schools and raise student achievement. George H. W. Bush ushered in a national agenda for education reform with his Goals 2000 effort, which gathered the nation's governors together to encourage broad-based improvement. Under Bill Clinton, education reform earned further emphasis with the 1994 Improving America's Schools Act, which helped launch the school accountability movement at the national level. George W. Bush went even further with the very visible and still controversial No Child Left Behind Act in 2001, which introduced unprecedented measures for testing and accountability. And Barack Obama has pursued a strong education reform agenda, using his "Race to the Top" program to channel significant federal funds to reform-minded states, among other measures.

These efforts have come alongside many warnings about a coming (or existing) crisis in American education. And yet the evidence suggests that Americans continue to be out of touch with their country's past and principles—and, therefore, possibly with its future too.

The weakness of history and civic education is a symptom of the United States' larger education malaise, which the government has had only a very limited ability to address effectively. In general, students achieve when they come from certain families (where parents value education and were well educated themselves) and are taught by good teachers. Public policy might help produce good teachers (though I have my doubts), but it can neither take the place of caring and responsible families nor force students to pay attention.

Government does, of course, play a big role in education. Most obvious is that local, state, and federal dollars significantly underwrite American public education, an almost trillion-dollar industry that ranks high in state priorities and has increasingly gained Washington's attention over the years.

This was never more evident than in the first term of President George W. Bush, when I served as under secretary and deputy secretary at the US Department of Education, helping to steer the landmark No Child Left Behind (NCLB) effort. Prior to that, I had served as Pennsylvania's secretary of education—a position that gave me broad oversight for both K–12 and post-secondary education—and as a college professor. Seeing the education world from these various vantage points has shaped my understanding of how to improve history and civic education in America. Public policy surely has a role to play, but the decisive factor is always what teachers do in their classrooms.

* * *

NCLB was intended to ensure that each US state had a school accountability system that included annual testing in reading and math for every student in grades 3 through 8, with additional testing in high school. Through annual testing, education officials can monitor student progress, detect gaps in achievement, and tailor efforts to address them. NCLB also included provisions for improving instruction in reading, boosting teacher quality, providing options for families with children enrolled in persistently poor-performing or dangerous schools, and ensuring transparency in systems for reporting school performance.

Notable among NCLB's requirements was that every state provide students with "highly qualified" teachers of core academic subjects. The law recognized English, reading, math, science, foreign languages, civics/government, economics, the arts, history, and geography as core academic subjects.

New teachers of these subjects needed to be fully certified by the state to teach the subject; provisional, temporary, or emergency certification was no longer sufficient. In addition, new teachers needed to have majored in college in their subject or completed a curriculum that mirrored a major. And veteran teachers needed to be able to demonstrate competence in their subjects based on a high, objective standard of evaluation established by each state. If states did not put policies in place to comply with NCLB's standards, they risked losing substantial federal education funds. [1]

These teacher qualification provisions might seem like common sense since, as policymakers often remark, "You can't teach what you don't know." But the reality is that many teachers, especially in elementary and middle schools, teach disciplines that they are not certified to teach. Many elementary school teachers possess certificates in elementary education, not an academic discipline; special education teachers often possess certificates in special education, not an academic discipline; some teachers have only provisional teaching certificates; and many graduates of teacher preparation programs in schools and colleges of education have only limited academic background in the subjects that they are hired to teach, so they possess degrees in history education, for example, but not in history. NCLB sought to require all these teachers to be certified in all of the disciplines they teach.

Enforcing the teacher quality provisions has proved very difficult. First, rigorous certification requirements present many practical problems, especially for veteran teachers. Second, given that most states already have difficulty ensuring that all teachers have at least some certification, Washington was in no position to ensure that all teachers were certified in the subjects they teach (let alone that they had majored in them or received equivalent training). Most states did revise their certification policies to emphasize teachers' subject knowledge, but it remained impractical for states to impose the requirements of NCLB. In most states, that would have entailed restructuring not only certification requirements but teacher preparation programs as well. It would have meant rethinking how individuals prepare to become teachers.

The teacher quality provisions of NCLB reflected Washington's attempt to get at a very nettlesome problem in American education. The difficulties of implementing those provisions were understood by policymakers in the White House, the Department of Education and on Capitol Hill; we knew it would be difficult to achieve what NCLB required. We chose to keep the provisions in place anyway because it was important to make a strong statement about teacher quality being a key component of student achievement. Indeed American students' understanding and appreciation of history and civics will remain disappointing as long as teachers of these subjects lack adequate knowledge and states lack adequate means for measuring quality and enforcing standards.

NCLB also included a more direct attempt to improve American history and civic education: the Teaching American History grant program. An initiative of Senator Robert Byrd, the program has awarded millions of dollars for the training of teachers in "traditional" American history (a term the law did not clearly define, unfortunately, other than to note that American history should be a distinct discipline apart from social studies).

Congress enacted the program partly out of concern that NCLB's focus on reading and math might narrow curricula and squeeze out other disciplines, especially American history. Another motivation was lawmakers' sense that the field of American history had been politicized by historians, educators, and others.

Textbooks and curriculum standards have indeed become political footballs on state and local boards of education. It is good that members of school boards care deeply about what constitutes American history, but it is troubling when their views are shaped more by contentious contemporary political debates than by sound scholarship. The Texas State Board of Education's recent debate concerning American history standards illustrates the problem. Minimizing Thomas Jefferson because of his role in establishing the idea of a "wall of separation between church and state" reflects the politics of today more than serious regard for the history of our past. [2]

The problem of politicization reaches far beyond school boards. Many of the nation's college campuses are hothouses for faculty who promote all kinds of political agendas in their teaching of, and research in, literature, history, political science, international affairs, and even the sciences. Since future teachers are molded on college campuses, the politicization of the academy—illustrated by campus speech codes and sensitivity training for faculty and students, as well as undue emphasis on political correctness—means that many teachers enter their profession with politicized understandings of the subjects they teach.

In American history, the problem is aggravated by textbooks that leave out significant facts and events while emphasizing others that, though surely a part of the nation's history, do not merit such extended discussion. Many authors of textbooks write their personal political interpretations into them.

And whereas there is legitimate debate over how much attention to devote to the founding of the republic or to the antiwar movement during the Vietnam era, for example, to dismiss the founders' relevance because they are "dead white guys," many of whom owned slaves and were wealthy, is to distort history, not teach it.

The Teaching American History grant program sought to help address this problem by funding teacher development efforts rich in academic content. Among the goals of the program was to encourage partnerships between schools and museums, historical associations, universities, and other institutions with strong track records of solid content and programming in American history. In one case, for example, a grant allowed teachers from the Charlottesville, Virginia school district to receive professional development training through the University of Virginia, the Gilder-Lehrman Institute, and other reputable institutions.

The grant program has been well financed, having dispensed close to a billion dollars in the nine years since its inception.[3] Yet it is difficult to determine how much impact it has had on student achievement. Unfortunately, almost no serious analysis of professional development efforts has been done. As such, although it is one thing to note how many teachers have been affected by Teaching American History grants, it is quite another to measure how they have affected student achievement.

Another federal effort, one which predates NCLB and continues today, is the Department of Education's Character and Civic Education program (located, curiously, within the department's Office of Safe and Drug-Free Schools). This effort underwrites programs that focus on character education and civic responsibility and are implemented by schools and nonprofit organizations such as Boys & Girls Clubs and local historical societies.

Since 1987, a major portion of the funding has gone to the Center for Civic Education, located in California, which is dedicated to helping students understand America's political and constitutional institutions, develop skills needed for responsible citizenship, and feel driven to active participation in the political process. It does this through a number of programs focusing on curriculum, professional development, and community involvement.

The Center for Civic Education's "We the People" program has for years received federal support for its work with students in all grades. At the high school level, the program allows classes to enter a competition, structured like a public hearing, which tests their knowledge and understanding of the Constitution. According to the center, approximately thirty million students and teachers have participated in the program since its inception, it receives favorable reviews from students and faculty, and various studies have linked the center's programs to increases in students' knowledge of American history and civics.[4] But, although it serves about two million students per year, We the People is still a relatively small program considering the number of students enrolled in this nation's schools.

Our various initiatives aimed to raise student achievement (especially among low-income, at-risk, and minority populations) and to promote academic accountability. Although our efforts indeed pushed American education toward those goals, critics have offered some valid criticisms of our work. For example, some argue that NCLB's emphasis on testing has prompted teachers to teach to tests and that, since testing focuses on reading and math (and science, increasingly), history and civics are left behind.

This and other arguments speak to the political and bureaucratic limitations facing policymakers in Washington as they try to promote American history and civic education. The federal government is forbidden by statute from getting engaged in matters relating to K–12 curricula, as education— including what is taught and how—remains primarily a state issue.

This local approach to education yields both costs and benefits, of course. But elements of national uniformity can be helpful, so a number of state governors have recently laid out a promising set of "Common Core Standards" that states may apply voluntarily in order to increase achievement and accountability.[5] Of course, having standards in place does not ensure that they will be met. That challenge is primarily going to remain in the nation's classrooms.

* * *

Since NCLB and other federal reform efforts seem to have produced only modest results, we must examine how other strategies and institutions might better improve historical and civic knowledge.

One way to improve students' civic knowledge is to begin distinguishing more clearly between history and social studies. In far too many states, history teachers are trained and certified in what is called social studies, which typically includes a mix of history, economics, sociology, geography, and political science. These are important disciplines, but a teacher certified to teach all of them is likely to lack real depth in any one of them. History should be a distinct discipline for teacher certification, as should civics.

Accomplishing this change—through action in state legislatures, governor's mansions, or boards of education, depending on the decision-making process of each state—would establish the importance of these disciplines within the school system.

Doing so, however, would be politically difficult. University-based schools of education would likely balk at such action, since it would challenge their long-held dominance over issues of teacher preparation and certification. That dominance is a big part of the larger problem. Until schools of education are done away with or radically reformed—so that, among other things, they no longer emphasize pedagogical theory and classroom management over mastery of subject matter—the problems plaguing the teaching of history and civics (and many other subjects) will continue.

Another strategy to consider for improving instruction in history and civics is to borrow a model that has had some success in postsecondary education: adjunct instructors. Postsecondary institutions have long relied on adjunct faculty to fulfill a variety of instructional needs. For K–12 education, where quality teachers are lacking, local professionals with certain relevant backgrounds could be hired as teachers. For years, reformers have suggested bolstering K–12 instruction in disciplines such as math and science by employing professionals in those fields as adjunct teachers. The same logic applies to history and civics, which could be taught well by lawyers or others with relevant knowledge. Of course, such professionals need to be competent in the discipline and able to manage a classroom, but schools need to find talent wherever it exists—and be empowered to deploy it to help students achieve.

There are substantial political obstacles to adopting this strategy, too. For one, school districts will need to break the convention of all teachers being members of the local bargaining unit; there is no reason why every teacher in every classroom must be party to a contract negotiated by the school district and the local union. Schools will also need to be allowed to hire individuals to teach particular courses, rather than whole subjects or disciplines. This will likely require some sort of state action to adjust teacher certification procedures, or at least to issue waivers from state codes. Powerful teachers unions will probably oppose such proposals, seeing them as a threat to their monopoly in the profession. Still, the adjunct model holds great potential for addressing weaknesses in classroom teaching.

Professional associations can help the cause by encouraging their members to become adjunct teachers. For example, bar associations—long ardent supporters of history and civic education—might encourage their members by providing some sort of credit for adjunct teaching. Members of state bar associations already receive "Continuing Legal Education" credits for various activities, such as judging student mock trial competitions. Surely teaching civics and history is also creditworthy.

There are many ways in which institutions other than schools might further civic knowledge and appreciation. Indeed, schools appear poorly suited for this task and many other social, community, and religious institutions have historically provided means for instilling a civic sense in youth. Churches and synagogues, Boy Scout and Girl Scout troops, Key Clubs and other organizations continue to connect young people with the world beyond their homes and classrooms, teaching them about the operations of government, the political process, and the democratic tools available to citizens.

Alexis de Tocqueville wrote of such organizations and associations in *Democracy in America*, his seminal 1835 survey of American life. Tocqueville argued that, in bringing people together to accomplish things they could not accomplish as individuals, civil society organizations helped the United States possess the size and power of a great nation while retaining much of the character of a smaller one. Tocqueville was quite impressed with this aspect of American democracy, writing that, "Americans of all ages, all conditions, and all dispositions constantly form associations." He observed the effect of associations on the way citizens related to one another: "Feelings and opinions are recruited, the heart is enlarged, and the human mind is developed only by the reciprocal influence of men upon one another."[6]

What Tocqueville was talking about is how civic and religious associations, organizations, and societies promote a sense of civic community that is essential to a vibrant republic. Such organizations exist today in the form of Kiwanis Clubs, Chambers of Commerce, and myriad town and neighborhood associations. But whereas they once were a primary focus of community life—providing opportunities for fellowship and entertainment, bringing people together and fostering civic participation—Americans today spend their leisure time in innumerable other ways. As more than one commentator has argued, we have become a nation of observers rather than participants.

It may be impossible for such organizations to regain the role they once played in civic life, but they can still help highlight the importance of civic literacy and participation. Their challenge is to excite young people through programs and competitions that recognize achievement in history, civics, and community engagement—much the way that spelling bees generate interest at the local, state, and national levels. Although the civic role of such organizations looks different today than it did in the past, its importance to the health of the nation is as great as ever.

* * *

Contributing to the weakness of civic education is a lack of public attention to the subject by political, educational, and cultural leaders. Oratory and rhetoric still matter—as evidenced by the election of Barack Obama, among other things—and schools tend to reflect what society values. Public figures have an opportunity to exert influence on this important issue. This means going beyond sound bites and speaking in detail about the value of understanding history and participating in public life, of knowing the nation's history and helping to shape it going forward.

Although Americans didn't sustain the deep civic sentiment that emerged in the immediate aftermath of September 11, the good news is that such sentiment exists and can be tapped. It might seem unconventional for governors, congressional leaders, or the president to put aside the issues of the moment to discuss civic health, but that is why doing so could be compelling to audiences.

In their desire not to politicize education, politicians too often shy away from discussing anything that might link educational matters to seemingly political ones, including the teaching of history and civics. This is understandable, especially since the academy has politicized history, civics, and much else. But serious public officials (and scholars, and others) should not avoid addressing the civic literacy challenge facing their communities. Indeed, if leaders more often discussed politics and government in nonpartisan terms, they would likely spark interest in students who otherwise are turned off by a seemingly hyperpartisan political world.

Outside of government, a potential source of leadership is the higher education establishment. The world of higher education has only a limited relationship with the world of K–12 education, but the two sectors need each other. They differ in many ways, of course—culturally, financially, managerially, and otherwise—but both are failing to educate students in American history and civics. It would make sense, then, for them to develop strategies together. Students might become more interested in studying the American past if, for instance, the president of the college they hope to attend talked publicly about how important the subject is and how students' knowledge of it might help them gain admission.

University presidents were once public intellectuals who contributed to local and national discussions of important issues. In doing so, they encouraged broader conversation on campuses and in classrooms. Today, however, concerns of fundraising and day-to-day management tend to overshadow just about anything else a university chief executive might want to do—even though there is a real need for the leaders of American higher education to contribute to the broad education of the American public.

In the end, public policy can only do so much when it comes to improving Americans' knowledge of history and civics. It can offer general incentives and broad structures that might move things forward, and it can raise awareness of the huge gap in popular understanding of the nation's history and institutions. But sound policies will require unusual political willingness to challenge convention and entrenched interest groups. And it will require various types of institutions to tap citizens' spirit and soul so that they might recognize the importance of history and civic engagement. In this country, that must remain among our most important purposes.

NOTES

1. Text of the No Child Left Behind law is available at the US Department of Education website, http://www2.ed.gov/policy/elsec/leg/esea02/index.html.

2. For detailed analysis of the Texas State Board controversy and its political significance, see chapter 8.

3. US Department of Education, "Teaching American History: Funding Status," http://www2.ed.gov/programs/teachinghistory/funding.html.

4. Center for Civic Education, "We the People: The Program," http://new.civiced.org/wtp-the-program.

5. National Governors Association Center for Best Practices and the Council of Chief State School Officers, "Common Core State Standards Initiative," http:// www.corestandards.org.

6. Alexis de Tocqueville, *Democracy in America* (1835; repr., Ware, UK: Wordsworth Editions, 1998), 218.

Chapter Seven

A Failure of Leadership

*The Duty of Politicians and Universities
to Salvage Citizenship*

Senator Bob Graham, with Chris Hand

In 1974, I was a state senator in Florida and chair of the State Senate's Education Committee. Early that year, in order to gather suggestions for bills we might introduce in the upcoming spring legislative session, my committee colleagues and I held a series of hearings in public schools throughout the state. One such hearing was at Samuel Wolfson Senior High, in a middle-class area of Jacksonville.

Our practice was to reserve a portion of each hearing for student comments. When the time came on this particular morning, a group of students came to the microphone to ask for our help with a serious problem: bad food in the Wolfson cafeteria.

Their complaint didn't shock me. What was concerning was that these students, so close to receiving their high school diplomas, thought that the Florida State Senate was the place to seek redress.

I asked the students if we were the first authority to whom they had taken their concerns. To my relief, they reported that we were the third—but then I was distressed to hear who the first two were. The students had first gone to the Jacksonville mayor, who agreed with them that the food was bad but told them that it was out of his jurisdiction. The students then went to the Duval County sheriff, who also sympathized but said that while the food was bad, it wasn't criminal. Having heard this, I had to inform the students that the State Senate didn't control cafeteria menus either.

Less than a month later, a group of civics teachers invited me to speak to them in Miami. I related the Wolfson experience and expressed my dismay with the students' lack of knowledge about the roles and responsibilities of government. Perhaps not diplomatically enough, I told the teachers that the students' ignorance was a strong indictment of civic education in our state.

The teachers reacted with controlled outrage. "I am sick to death of you politicians telling us how to do our job better," one seethed. "You don't know what you're talking about. You need to get in the classroom and see what it's really like—prepare the lesson plans that are intended to stimulate uninterested students, make outdated textbooks interesting, deal with all the hassle of paperwork and school bureaucracy, and try to implement politicians' nutty ideas." To loud applause, she challenged me to come into the classroom and experience public education firsthand.

Figuring that I could afford to give up an afternoon—and reluctant to appear like a coward in front of this important constituency—I accepted her challenge. She called three days later. "I have worked it out," she said. "You are to come to my school, Miami Carol City Senior High, on the day after Labor Day and report to room 207. I have arranged for you to teach a semester—eighteen weeks—of twelfth-grade civics."

It wasn't what I had bargained for, but that semester transformed my life. With a coteacher, Donnell Morris, I taught civics through a structured curriculum of required knowledge and skills—and, crucially, through hands-on activities too. To demonstrate how government could be made to work for them, Morris and I exposed our twenty-five students to political practitioners: candidates, officeholders, journalists, civic activists, campaign professionals, pollsters.

On the first day of class, we asked the students to organize themselves into groups of three. Each group selected an issue about which it was dissatisfied—and which government at some level could address. The students could select any topic, but there was a caveat: At the end of the semester, one-third of the students' final grades would be based on their effectiveness in solving the problem they had identified at the outset.

The results were startling. One team tackled the long-standing suspicion that their school received less funding per student than did Dade County public high schools in higher-income neighborhoods. After the school's business faculty gave the students a basic lesson in reading and understanding budgets, the students pored over financial spreadsheets at the headquarters of the county school district. They proved that the funding disparity was more than a myth. And thanks to their work, the schools superintendent recognized the inequity and vowed to correct it in the next budget cycle. That team of students received a very high grade.

That semester at Miami Carol City Senior High taught me how learning by doing differs dramatically from learning by listening, how active learning drives home a subject's relevance and contributes to a sense of self-confidence that can last a lifetime. It was clear by semester's end that students, having worked in the classroom to solve civic problems, felt empowered to do so in the real world, for themselves and their families.

* * *

For young Americans to feel empowered to operate within our political system, they need three aptitudes: knowledge of the system, competence to exercise their rights as citizens, and confidence in the system. That's one reason why the civic health of our country is particularly concerning today: Americans often demonstrate not only limited civic knowledge, but also minimal understanding of how to flex their civic muscles and great feelings of cynicism about, and alienation from, democratic institutions.

In its 2009 annual Civic Health Index, the National Conference on Citizenship found that only 26 percent of Americans believe that "Government in Washington generally does what is right."[1] The Gallup polling organization found in 2010 that only 11 percent of Americans say they have "a great deal" or "quite a lot" of confidence in Congress. That was the lowest level of confidence measured at any time since Gallup started asking the question in 1973. Americans had slightly more confidence in banks and major corporations.[2]

This dissatisfaction with public institutions has been reflected at the ballot box. Turnout among eligible voters in national elections has dropped over past decades from 63 percent in 1960 to 57 percent in 2008 (after lows of 49 percent in 1996 and 51 percent in 2000), with particular declines among young Americans.[3] Set to compound voter cynicism about the political process, I fear, are the effects of the Supreme Court's decision in *Citizens United vs. Federal Election Commission* (2010), which loosened constraints on the participation of corporations and labor unions in politics.

These factors threaten to make us suffer the fate prophesied by former University of Chicago President Robert Maynard Hutchins, who observed that "The death of democracy is not likely to be an assassination from ambush. It will be a slow extinction from apathy, indifference and undernourishment." Indeed, the impoverished quality of American citizenship will continue to endanger our democracy unless key leaders work together to revitalize citizen participation.

Many institutions, including political parties and major media, have a role to play in arresting this civic erosion. But the two groups of Americans with the most potential to salvage citizenship—if they work together—are politicians and academicians, especially those educators in disciplines, such as political science and history, that have the most direct influence on how students view their roles as citizens.

* * *

Politicians have injured citizenship not only through fierce partisanship, bickering, and horse trading, but by undermining—or at least ignoring—the Jeffersonian standard of education. Thomas Jefferson wrote in 1818 that "the objects of this primary education" include: "To give to every citizen the information he needs . . . to understand his duties to his neighbors and country and to discharge with competence the functions confided to him by either," and "To instruct the mass of our citizens in these, their rights, interests, and duties, as men and citizens."[4] Yet as this book documents, our political leaders have not been vigilant in stopping contemporary American education from falling far short.

When I graduated from high school in 1955, I had taken the national standard of civic instruction: three years between the seventh and twelfth grades. When my oldest granddaughter graduated from a public high school in Tallahassee in 2009, she also had the national standard: one semester of civics between the seventh and twelfth grades. In less than sixty years, American students lost 450 school days of civics instruction.

This loss came after both the far right and far left of American politics concluded that civic education was being taught to their disadvantage. The two sides disagreed on the alleged bias, but effectively concurred on a solution: Cut civics from the curriculum.

As damaging as that unholy alliance was, the advent of high-stakes tests mandated by states and the federal No Child Left Behind legislation was devastating. With few exceptions, these tests ignored civics and other social sciences. Given the old educational axiom "Not tested, not taught," curricula overlooked civic education all the more. It is crucial, therefore, for politicians to reconsider how legislation like No Child Left Behind affects civic education in the classroom.

For politicians to improve civic health more generally, they could start by becoming adults in their public and private conduct. As someone who spent thirty-eight years in elective public office, I feel ill when I see elected officials behave in a manner that legitimately evokes citizens' ridicule and disdain. The US Department of Justice reports that 9,179 public officials across the nation were convicted of crimes between 1998 and 2007.[5] Between 2000 and 2010, Congress saw eight of its members convicted of major felonies like bribery, financial corruption, and manslaughter.[6]

Elected officials should establish and enforce ethical standards to help begin the huge task of restoring public confidence in elected institutions. It would be wise to study those states with the least political corruption (including Iowa, New Hampshire, and Oregon[7]) to determine how their political cultures help limit such behavior.

Politicians should also enact new campaign finance and lobbying reforms that limit the ability of special interests to unduly influence politics at the expense of national, state, or individual citizen interests. They should also closely review arcane legislative procedures to determine whether they have continued usefulness. The US Senate's filibuster, for example, was intended to ensure full and fair consideration of important national issues, but as currently used it has become a symbol of gridlock.

Regarding education policy, lawmakers should restore civic education to its traditional role as a main component of the primary and secondary curriculum, and include civics and the social sciences as subjects on which student progress is systematically evaluated. In 2010, the Florida Legislature unanimously passed legislation, the Justice Sandra Day O'Connor Civics Education Act, requiring that all students be taught and tested on civics starting in the 2013–2014 academic year.

Also crucial is adequately funding elementary, secondary, and postsecondary education so that teachers and professors charged with instructing students on their rights and responsibilities as citizens have the resources needed to succeed. Lawmakers should also provide more opportunities for secondary, undergraduate and graduate students to experience civic engagement through government or other public service. The Center for Civic Education provides one outstanding model through its Project Citizen, which helps students learn how to monitor and influence public policy.

Some of these are lofty goals, but their active pursuit by elected officials and other policymakers would be a better demonstration of civic leadership than the histrionics and partisanship that increasingly pervade government today.

* * *

While less visible than politicians, academic administrators and scholars also carry substantial responsibility to salvage citizenship.

Former Harvard University President Derek Bok has offered two reasons why political scientists and historians have shied away from active engagement in civic education in the last several decades. First, these professions became more niche-oriented, increasingly rewarding narrower and narrower slices of scholarship. Second, the professions became more insular, focusing their attention and resources inward, toward the academy. In turn, they excluded their broader responsibilities to prepare citizens for perpetuating a robust democracy.

As Bok wrote in 2005, "despite frequent references to citizenship in college brochures, faculties have paid little attention to the subject."[8] He cited Carol Schneider, the president of the Association of American Colleges and Universities, concluding after years of study that "there is not just a neglect of but a resistance to college-level study of United States democratic principles."[9]

Academics immersed in subjects related to American civic life and history should lead in establishing not simply new curricula related to civic knowledge and engagement, but a culture of citizenship throughout higher education.

They could, for example, initiate reviews of the state of citizenship on their campuses. Such reviews could identify relevant indicators of civic engagement and determine whether the student body demonstrates the skills needed for effective civic participation on campus and in the broader society. They could also evaluate whether their institution's civic values have influenced the surrounding community and the professional and philanthropic pursuits of alumni.

The academic community could also develop metrics by which the civic health of individual campuses is factored into their accreditation. Individual schools, meanwhile, can include civic engagement as a primary factor in admission to undergraduate, graduate, and professional programs.

Within academic departments, professors can encourage graduate students to consider citizenship a valued topic of research and teaching. Departments of political science and history can promote this through stipends and publication opportunities, among other methods. In addition, they can partner with colleges of education to help instruct the next generation of civics teachers and to provide additional training for current teachers.

Other partnerships can help preprofessional or preoccupational departments integrate citizenship components into their curricula. At the University of Florida, the Bob Graham Center for Public Service is working with the College of Pharmacy to help identify how pharmacists can further contribute both to the common good and to the advancement of their profession. Examples of such civic service could include pharmacists serving on state boards overseeing professional licensing, volunteering in public health units, and participating in preparing local emergency plans. To encourage such work, the profession could train more pharmacists for public health needs and require some degree of public service for recertification.

* * *

In 2005, thirty-one years after I spoke with those students in the Wolfson High School cafeteria, I spent an academic year as a senior fellow at Harvard University's Kennedy School of Government. During the fall semester, I led a group of undergraduates in a weekly seminar on the skills of effective citizenship. Even Harvard's highly motivated students, I learned, had not been exposed to basic skills of citizenship.

This situation cannot stand. The health of our democracy hinges on citizens knowing how to take an active role in shaping their communities. For all the debates over the recession, health care, Afghanistan and Iraq, none of these issues poses a fundamental risk to our democratic system. The greatest threat to American democracy today doesn't stem from any legislative measure, but from civic inaction and decay.

Democracy is at risk as long as our political and educational systems tolerate a system that teaches fewer and fewer Americans to embrace their rights and responsibilities as citizens, that leaves Americans considering democracy a mere spectator sport. Many factors have influenced the sharp decline of civic education, but the two stakeholders most able to fix the problem are elected officials and academicians. Those groups must join forces to ensure that all American students finish their educations with a clear understanding of what it means—and what it takes—to be an active citizen of the United States of America.

NOTES

With the permission of CQ Press, portions of this chapter were adapted from *America, the Owner's Manual: Making Government Work for You* (2009), by Senator Bob Graham with Chris Hand.

1. National Conference on Citizenship, "America's Civic Health Index 2009," August 2009.

2. Lydia Saad, "Congress Ranks Last in Confidence in Institutions," Gallup, July 22, 2010.

3. Michael McDonald, "2008 General Election Turnout Rates," United States Elections Project, October 10, 2010, http://elections.gmu.edu/Turnout_2008G.html.

4. Thomas Jefferson, "Report of the Commissioners for the University of Virginia," August 4, 1818.

5. Bill Marsh, "Which Is the Most Corrupt State? Not Illinois," *New York Times*, December 13, 2008.

6. Associated Press, "Members of Congress Previously Charged with Crimes," July 29, 2008.

7. Marsh, "Which Is the Most Corrupt?"

8. Derek Bok, *Our Underachieving Colleges: A Candid Look at How Much Students Learn and Why They Should Be Learning More* (Princeton, NJ: Princeton University Press, 2006), 177.

9. Bok, *Our Underachieving Colleges*, 178.

Chapter Eight

Forgetting Martin Luther King's Dream

How Politics Threatens America's Civil Rights Memory

Secretary Rod Paige

On August 28, 2011, the National Mall in Washington, DC—home to a glorious collection of monuments to individuals and events that have shaped our nation—unveiled a new four-acre memorial honoring Dr. Martin Luther King Jr. Fittingly, this tribute to the man who personifies the civil rights movement aligns with the Lincoln Memorial, where King delivered his "I Have a Dream" speech on August 28, 1963.

The creation of the King Memorial highlights the civil rights movement's enduring impact on our nation's past, present, and future—on our laws, social systems, and politics. The civil rights movement's impact reached far beyond the South, where it originated. The voting rights protests in Selma, Alabama, and the famous Selma to Montgomery marches, for example, prompted the 1965 Voting Rights Act, which dramatically altered our political landscape and national character by reenfranchising black Southerners and giving rise to the election of African Americans to local, state, and national offices.

And yet, despite its importance and place in the relatively recent past, most American students have neither an appropriate understanding nor appreciation of this great historical movement. Consider how students fare on the civil rights-related questions on the National Assessment of Educational Progress, commonly known as "the nation's report card," which is given periodically by the federal Department of Education to students nationwide. [1]

In 2006, only 43 percent of eighth graders gave an "appropriate" response when asked why marchers participated in Martin Luther King Jr.'s 1963 march on Washington. In 2001, only 34 percent could identify that the phrase "Jim Crow" refers to laws that "enforced racial segregation," as opposed to laws that made liquor illegal, restricted immigration, or protected the environment. And in 1994, only 5 percent of eighth graders presented with the text of the Fifteenth Amendment could identify what group it was designed to help, and why it was proposed in the years after the Civil War.

Then there are twelfth graders, those on the cusp of adulthood and full citizenship. In 2006, only 38 percent could identify appropriately the social policy reflected by a sign declaring "COLORED ENTRANCE" above the door of a theater. In addition, only 28 percent knew that the main issue in the Lincoln-Douglas debates of 1858 was whether slavery should be expanded into new US territories, and 40 percent failed to identify the purpose of the punitive "Black Codes" passed in the South during Reconstruction.

This deficit of understanding is a glaring educational failure that poses great risks. Without an understanding of the civil rights movement, young people cannot begin to appreciate the cost—and value—of our present freedoms, and they are ill-equipped to make wise, informed civic choices in the future.

"History is to the nation as memory is to the individual," observed the eminent historian and social critic Arthur Schlesinger Jr. In some respects, this is a frightening thought. An individual without memory cannot distinguish between friends and enemies, nutrients and poisons, safe paths and perilous ones. Unable to benefit from experience because the past is lost in a fog of forgetfulness, the individual is poised to fulfill the poet-philosopher George Santayana's warning that "those who cannot remember the past are condemned to repeat it."

* * *

One day in 2008, I was on a plane returning from Los Angeles to Houston. My seatmate was a young African American male who proudly told me that he was a senior at a Houston high school.

I was enjoying a good book that day, *Death of Innocence: The Story of the Hate Crime That Changed America*, by Mamie Till Mobley and Christopher Benson, about the 1955 murder of Emmett Till in Money, Mississippi.

The incident, which occurred not long after the 1954 *Brown vs. Board of Education* decision, sparked enormous anger in the African American community and stoked the passions that propelled the civil rights movement.

The young man seated next to me repeatedly glanced at the picture of Emmett Till on my book's cover. After some time he asked me whose picture it was, and I told him. You can guess his next question: "Who is Emmett Till?"

I was astonished, but recognized a teachable moment. So for the rest of the plane ride, I engaged the young man in a journey through the history of the civil rights movement. *Brown vs. Board of Education*. The Emmett Till saga. The Montgomery bus boycott. The Freedom Rides. The assassination of Medgar Evers and the murders of three civil rights workers in Philadelphia, Mississippi. The Selma to Montgomery march. Sit-ins by college students at segregated stores of F. W. Woolworth Company in Greensboro, North Carolina and other cities throughout the South.

The only part of civil rights history that this young man was aware of was the March on Washington, the "I Have a Dream" speech, and the assassination of Martin Luther King Jr. That was all.

I made a point of emphasizing that African Americans have made enormous progress since 1619, when we arrived on these shores as conscripted pilgrims, to the time when one of us could run for president of the United States (let alone win, which Barack Obama did in the following months).

I wanted my seatmate to know that the freedoms and rights that he, like all of us, enjoys today did not result from benevolent people motivated by the idea that all men were created equal and deserved equal opportunity. Our freedoms have resulted from hard-fought battles, agonizing sacrifices, and, too often, the deaths of heroic civil rights workers determined to make this nation live up to its ideals. Freedom is what the civil rights movement was all about—not black power, or African American privilege. It was about freedom.

The young man on the plane, like most his age, was familiar almost exclusively with the events and personalities of his generation. For him and others like him, life goes on without knowledge of the civil rights movement. For him and others like him, the benefit of understanding their forebears' experiences is unavailable.

* * *

Many have offered explanations for this tragic situation. In a report published by the Fordham Foundation, *Where Did Social Studies Go Wrong?* (2003), for example, various researchers blamed the educational establishment for embracing multiculturalism and for tolerating poorly trained teachers, ineffective teaching methods, and weak curriculum materials. Back in 1989, the Bradley Commission on History in the Schools focused on textbooks, criticizing them as "overstuffed with facts, distracting features and irrelevant graphics" and "rarely organized to clarify larger themes and questions."

To this list of reasons, I would add another that merits further analysis: politics, a problem put on particularly prominent display recently in Texas.

The Texas State Board of Education—elected from local districts, with a chair appointed by the governor—has long seen warring factions clash to influence schools according to particular political beliefs. Among the board's responsibilities is to review state curriculum standards, which publishers use for guidance in writing textbooks. The board does so every ten years, and 2010 was the year for reviewing the state's social studies standards (which include the guidelines for history instruction).

At the time, the board consisted of five Democrats and ten Republicans. Many of the Republicans believed that years of Democratic control had skewed the state's curriculum to the left. As conservative board member Don McLeroy put it, the existing standards

> paint[ed] a negative view of America; they [had] an overemphasis of multicultural issues; they [were] obsessed with the differences of race, class and gender; thus, they turn[ed] America into "E Unum Pluribus"—"Out of one, many" instead of "E Pluribus Unum"—"Out of many, one." And, most importantly, they ignor[ed] the Judeo-Christian contribution to Western civilization and they ignor[ed] the contribution of the free enterprise system.[2]

The Republican board members considered it their mission to correct this imbalance. The Democratic members, meanwhile, considered their counterparts to be right-wing extremists intent on rewriting history to reflect their particular ideology. The battle was set.

In January 2009, the board had appointed a team—consisting primarily of educators and history professors—to review the standards adopted in 1997 and to propose new ones. When the conservative members of the board obtained a working copy of the team's draft proposal and judged it unacceptable, the fireworks began.

In April 2009, the board voted to bring in a new team of six "experts" to guide the revision process. Some had no relevant academic training and were known for having extreme political views. One, Peter Marshall, an evangelical minister, had expressed the view that Hurricane Katrina, among other catastrophes, was God's punishment for America tolerating gays.[3]

After a year of deliberations, a war of amendments between board members, and a growing national outcry, the final outcome was the state board's adoption, on May 21, 2010, of a disorganized, politicized, and in some cases bizarre set of standards.

When assessed in 2011 by the conservative Fordham Institute (of which I am a trustee), Texas's standards received a "D" grade, earning only two points out of a possible seven for "content and rigor," and one point out of three for "clarity and specificity." "Texas combines a rigidly thematic and theory-based social studies structure with a politicized distortion of history," Fordham's report concluded. "The result is both unwieldy and troubling, avoiding clear historical explanation while offering misrepresentations at every turn."[4]

As the Fordham report noted, Texas's standards barely mention slavery, and they mention racial segregation only in a section on the integration of the armed forces in 1948. The standards include nothing about the Black Codes, the Ku Klux Klan, sharecropping, or "Jim Crow." Meanwhile, they attribute opposition to the civil rights movement only to Southern Democrats, while failing to mention that much of this bloc later evolved into Republicans.

In addition to downplaying aspects of US history that it found unflattering or politically unacceptable, Texas's board went to considerable lengths to revise the history of religious influence on American civic life. As the Fordham report put it, "Biblical influences on America's founding are exaggerated, if not invented. The complicated but undeniable history of separation between church and state is flatly dismissed." The standards also favor specific right-wing policy positions, criticizing federal entitlement programs such as Lyndon Johnson's Great Society, and they encourage mistrust of international treaties, portraying them as threats to US sovereignty.

As a result of these and other serious flaws and omissions, the Fordham researchers concluded that "Texas's standards are a disservice both to its own teachers and students and to the larger national history of which it remains a part."

* * *

Given that the members of Texas's Board of Education were elected to their positions, one might argue that they were simply fulfilling their duty to review state standards. The board might have been dominated by conservative Republicans, but Texas voters had elected them fair and square.

While this is true, the problem is that board members are elected from single-member districts in low-turnout elections that few Texans pay any attention to. Board members have enormous power, yet one would be hard pressed to find a Texan who knows who his or her board representative is.

It is a significant problem that a few partisan individuals possess extraordinary power to influence how students in Texas (and beyond) view the past, understand the present, and are prepared for the future. And it is a problem that the board's majority did not want to present students with an honest, though perhaps sometimes uncomfortable, view of US history. This pattern extends to other subjects too.

As the national movement toward educational accountability strengthens, and as state standards are becoming all the more important, it is imperative for Americans to address these problems. Teachers' evaluations are increasingly based on students' performance on state-mandated tests. Those tests are aligned to state standards, so teachers are motivated to teach to them, whether they are good or bad.

Because our Constitution is silent on the matter of public education and the Tenth Amendment makes clear that powers not delegated to the federal government are reserved to the states, each state has its own way of dealing with public education, including history standards and more.

Forty-nine states and the District of Columbia produce standards for the teaching of US history and social studies. As one might guess, there is wide variation among them. According to the 2011 Fordham Institute study, US history standards today "run the gamut from impressively comprehensive to uselessly vapid. Unfortunately, the latter heavily outnumbers the former: if teachers and students in much of the country are to have meaningful guidance, the standards of many states will require massive revision."[5]

The Fordham study identified a few states in which the history standards are worthy of an "A." South Carolina was one of them. The study was especially complimentary of how South Carolina's standards dealt with slavery, the state's role in the Civil War, and the history of Jim Crow. This inspired me to rush to the South Carolina Department of Education website and reach out to contacts there to learn how a Southern state that was at the very center of the Civil War could address the African American role in US history so forthrightly.

My search yielded a stunning surprise. South Carolina has legislation (S.C. Code Ann. § 59–29–55) designed to ensure that the history, culture and experiences of Africa and African Americans are integrated into the K–12 curriculum. South Carolina's most recent state standards provide explicit references to the civil rights movement and include key events of the movement as standard indicators at various grade levels.

South Carolina's fourth-grade standards, for example, specify that students should be able to summarize: the roles and accomplishments of the leaders of the abolitionist movement and the Underground Railroad before and during the Civil War; significant battles, strategies and turning points of the Civil War, including the battles of Fort Sumter and Gettysburg, the Emancipation Proclamation, the Gettysburg Address, and the surrender at Appomattox; and the role of African Americans during the war.[6]

One of South Carolina's fifth-grade standards specifies that students will be able to "explain the advancement of the civil rights movement in the United States, including key events and people, desegregation of the armed forces, Brown v. Board of Education, Martin Luther King, Jr., Rosa Parks, and Malcolm X."

Another Southern state, Mississippi, recently began requiring that every one of its public schools teach students about the civil rights era. "In many places," wrote the *Christian Science Monitor* about Mississippi's new system, "it will end a decades-old culture of silence."[7]

It also might help citizens better understand controversies that periodically arise over subjects, especially the history of slavery and segregation, that some would prefer to gloss over. In 2011 alone, for example, Mississippi Governor Haley Barbour seemed to diminish the significance of white supremacist groups during the civil rights era, and the state legislature considered creating a special state license plate to honor former Confederate general and KKK leader Nathan Bedford Forrest.[8]

* * *

As the standards in South Carolina and Mississippi so sharply contrast with those now governing schools in Texas, it is perhaps unsurprising that these states' respective processes for developing standards also differ significantly.

In both Texas and South Carolina, the State Board of Education is responsible for public education. Yet the means by which the two states' boards are formed differ dramatically. In Texas, as noted, the fifteen members of the board are elected in notoriously low-turnout local elections. In South Carolina, the seventeen members of the board are appointed: Legislators from the state's sixteen judicial circuits each appoint one member, and the final member is appointed by the governor.

The differences do not end there. In Texas, the process for reviewing and revising standards is controlled almost exclusively by the state board, which writes the standards, oversees their periodic review, selects the experts who make outside recommendations, and decides which public comments to credit and which to ignore.[9] The Texas board, in other words, gets to serve as judge, jury, and executioner.

South Carolina's process is far more multifaceted and involves participation from a broad range of entities.

Prominent among them is the Education Oversight Committee (EOC), an independent, nonpartisan group of eighteen educators, business people, and elected officials who are appointed by the legislature and governor.[10] Also involved is a panel, appointed by the State Department of Education, which includes experts in the given discipline and in academic standards and testing. There are also three external review panels, appointed by the EOC, that include national assessment experts; South Carolina parents, business leaders, and community leaders; and teachers of special education students and English-language learners.

All these various bodies meet to study South Carolina's standards and prepare proposals for revision. The EOC then votes on the proposed revisions and sends them to the State Superintendent of Education and the chair of the State Board of Education.

At that point, a comprehensive review process begins that includes public comments, discipline-based focus groups, various panels, and presentations on the State Department of Education website. The EOC, the State Department of Education, and the State Board of Education work together in a multipart collaborative process to consider and approve recommendations. Finally, the Board of Education gives its approval and enacts the revised standards.[11]

The lesson learned is that the quality of our education system depends heavily on the quality of our political system. The quality of our political structures, and of the politicians who design and act within them, are major determinants of our educational excellence.

Of course, high-quality state standards do not, in and of themselves, assure high-quality instruction. Nor do poor standards necessarily mean that all instruction in the state will be inadequate. Great teachers often find ways to succeed, notwithstanding the quality of state standards. But as a general rule, high-quality academic standards guide teachers toward higher-quality instruction.

* * *

Without a solid understanding of history, our next generation of leaders will lack the critical understanding of what brought our nation to where it is now. Failing to teach of the significant challenges and contributions of African Americans hinders all students' ability to appreciate the strengths and values of the many groups that make up America. This will further deepen the kind of balkanization and ethnic partitions that divide groups of citizens from one another.

Only by understanding our rich and complex history—with its proud and not-so-proud moments, with its great leaders and simple, everyday heroes—can we strengthen what holds us together and create "unum" from "pluribus."

Taking two crucial steps could help ensure that academic standards are not handmaidens for political ideologists, and that schools are effective purveyors of authentic US history:

First, we must limit the extent to which politicians permit nonhistorians and noneducators to influence the development of US history standards. The education system in this country is inherently political, so it is unreasonable to expect decisions to be apolitical. But we can and must reduce the extent to which politics distorts decisions about education in general and history education in particular.

States could begin to do this by devising education governance structures that are protected from political extremism. As Texas shows, state boards of education whose members are elected in low-turnout elections, and whose decision-making authority is largely unchecked, are at high risk of undue politicization. On the other hand, boards whose members are elected in high-turnout elections or are determined by some combination of appointment and senate confirmation, and whose decision-making authority is subject to checks and balances, offer greater protection from undue political influence.

Second, we need to explore the feasibility of national US history standards that would provide a strong common foundation for schools' treatment of this vital subject. A good model would enable governors to choose to commit their states to a set of national standards developed, vetted, and controlled outside the federal government. The most promising model is the ongoing Common Core State Standards Initiative of the National Governors Association and the Council of Chief State School Officers (http://www.corestandards.org).

Here too we cannot expect freedom from political influence, as is evidenced by the fierce controversy that surrounded efforts to develop national history standards in the 1990s. Nevertheless, national standards would entail fewer decision points than currently exist in our system, in which all fifty states have different state boards of education with differing structures, goals and procedures. Accordingly, with the development of national standards, one could expect fewer opportunities for decisions to be heavily swayed by political influence.

Of course, reducing the number of decision points could be risky: If those points are indeed determined by politics, then the politicized resulting standards would affect the instruction of students in all states nationwide. But a solid process of developing national standards would be carefully scrutinized by relevant experts and others committed to high-quality results. The inherent high profile of the process could yield a product that is more rigorous, thorough, and balanced than what our individual states produce today—a patchwork worthy, on average, according to the Fordham Institute study, of a "D."

NOTES

1. All question-and-answer data for the National Assessment of Educational Progress are available at http://nces.ed.gov/nationsreportcard/itmrlsx/.

2. Don McLeroy, "Teaching Our Children What It Means to Be an American in 2011" (remarks to the Education Policy Conference, St. Louis, Missouri, January 28, 2011), http://www.tfn.org/site/DocServer/McLeroy_presentation_1.28.11.pdf?docID=2301.

3. Matt Schudel, "Obituary: Peter J. Marshall, Conservative Evangelist in Texas Schoolbook Controversy," *Washington Post*, September 23, 2010.

4. Sheldon M. Stern and Jeremy A. Stern, "The State of State US History Standards 2011," Thomas B. Fordham Institute, February 2011, 141.

5. Stern and Stern, "The State," 11.

6. South Carolina Social Studies Academic Standards 2005, South Carolina Department of Education, http://ed.sc.gov/agency/Standards-and-Learning/Academic-Standards/old/cso/standards/ss/.

7. Carmen K. Sisson, "Mississippi Mandates Civil Rights Classes in Schools," *Christian Science Monitor*, October 9, 2009.

8. See Andrew Ferguson, "The Boy from Yazoo City: Mississippi's Favorite Son," *Weekly Standard*, December 27, 2010; and Associated Press, "Miss. License Plate Proposed to Honor KKK Leader," February 10, 2011.

9. Texas Education Agency, "January 2011 Committee on Instruction Item 3: Update on Texas Essential Knowledge and Skills (TEKS) Review," January 21, 2011, http://198.214.97.204/index4.aspx?id=2147493776&ekfxmen_noscript=1&ekfxmensel=e105c3e3e_620_628.

10. See South Carolina Education Oversight Committee, http://eoc.sc.gov.

11. See "Report on the Review of the South Carolina Social Studies Curriculum Standards," presented to the South Carolina Education Oversight Committee, January 2004, http://eoc.sc.gov/NR/rdonlyres/BB62352D-5D72-4A3F-803B-403E613949AE/0/SCSSCurriculum-Standards04.pdf.

Chapter Nine

Revolutionary Ignorance

What Do Americans Know of the Original Tea Party?

Bruce Cole

The American Revolution is still making headlines. Vigorous debates about the role of government in town hall meetings and among self-styled "tea party" activists demonstrate the continuing relevance of this earthshaking event. References to the revolution have made a comeback—from Glenn Beck's book *Common Sense: The Case against an Out-of-Control Government, Inspired by Thomas Paine* to the growing popularity of "Don't Tread on Me" T-shirts and meetings at Boston's Green Dragon tavern, where the revolutionary Sons of Liberty regularly met and where colonists planned the Boston Tea Party. Images and ideas that pay homage to early American history are proving to be battle cries for citizens in the twenty-first century.

Today's so-called tea partiers have found a sense of legitimacy in basing their concerns on historical precedent. Their protests against taxation, comparisons of the health-care reform law to the Intolerable Acts of 1774, and invocations of "What would the Founders do?" show that there is a popular desire to revere and be guided by American history, especially the period of the founding. But what do Americans really know about the Revolution? And why should we care?

Americans' ignorance of US history is well documented. When the American Revolution Center, which I lead, surveyed 1,001 Americans in 2009, a confident 89 percent gave themselves a passing grade on their knowledge of the Revolution and of our founding documents and principles. But on the test that followed—with questions focusing on key documents, events, people, and ideas of the revolutionary period—83 percent failed.[1]

Nearly half lacked a basic understanding of historical chronology, believing that either the Civil War, the Emancipation Proclamation, or the War of 1812 happened before the American Revolution. Indeed, more than 33 percent could not even place the Revolution in its proper century. More than 50 percent wrongly attributed the quote, "From each according to his ability, to each according to his needs" to George Washington, Thomas Paine, or Barack Obama—not to its author, Karl Marx. One-third, meanwhile, did not know that the right to a jury trial is found in the Bill of Rights, and 40 percent mistakenly thought that the right to vote is.

Contrast this with Americans' knowledge of pop culture. Sixty percent of those we surveyed correctly identified the number of children (eight) of reality television parents "Jon and Kate." And our reporting found that many more Americans know that Michael Jackson sang "Beat It" and "Billie Jean" than know that James Madison was the father of the Constitution.

And yet more than 90 percent—across all demographic categories—said that knowledge of the American Revolution and its principles is "very important" and should be taught in schools. Seventy percent said they are interested in learning more about the Revolution.

If Americans are so interested in their history, what explains their disturbing gaps in understanding? Cultural pundits often say that it is because Americans are forward-looking. But that healthy characteristic is hardly a justification for civic illiteracy—nor is it the sole cause.

* * *

Many high school history and civics classes either do not teach about the Revolutionary War period sufficiently, or they forgo doing so entirely.

Officials at North Carolina's Department of Education recommended in 2010 that high schoolers stop studying US history pre-1877. Their recommendation provoked outrage from citizens, who sent over seven thousand e-mails and letters to officials. As a result, the State Board of Education did not accept the recommendation. Rather, it created a two-year high school course covering all of American history. Unfortunately, as the Fordham Institute found in a 2011 report:

given that course's sketchy and disorganized specifics, it seems to make little difference what time span the standards purport to cover. . . . Indeed, the two-part high school course is so generalized that the thematic headings for US History I & II are identical. Only the examples differ. Each outline is barely six pages long, including the introduction, and much is empty space, both literally and figuratively. [2]

For a sense of what the new course might look like, we can look to North Carolina's last set of US history standards, set in 2006. They were poor. Only one of the twelve competency goals covered the period from 1789–1820—and that was the earliest era covered at all. Thus the standards excluded the French and Indian War, the Stamp Act, the Boston Tea Party, the Declaration of Independence, the constitutional convention, *The Federalist Papers,* and the Revolutionary War itself. [3]

Today's most widely used history textbooks, meanwhile, are diluted, dull, and politically correct. They fail to inspire students with a sense of wonder, importance, or fascination about our storied past. In her 2003 book *The Language Police*, the education historian Diane Ravitch revealed the short-comings of committees responsible for reviewing textbooks, both at publishing houses and in state departments and boards of education.

According to Ravitch, such committees are often not informed either by rigorous research or by a peer review process based on specific subject expertise. Instead, committees tend to focus on "representational fairness"—on ensuring that no group is overrepresented, underrepresented, or stereotyped. [4] "When I read the panelists' reasons for rejecting passages, I realized that their concept of bias was not the same as the common understanding of the term," Ravitch wrote. Committees do not release their bias and sensitivity reviews to the public, but, wrote Ravitch, "As far as I could tell, they did not actually find any examples of racial or gender bias as most people understand it. There were no stories in which girls or children who were members of a racial or ethnic minority were portrayed in a demeaning way. Some of the panel's interpretations were, frankly, bizarre."[5]

Making matters worse is that a large majority of Americans effectively cease their civic education once their (inadequate) schooling ends. Despite the popularity of recent books by distinguished authors such as David McCullough, only two in ten Americans report augmenting their learning with books or articles they've read on their own.[6] Most Americans stop learning about the Revolution when they leave the classroom—having not learned much there.

Learning about the American Revolution—and about our national past in general—is important because we are all direct heirs to it. This is demonstrated every time an American reads a newspaper editorial, attends a public meeting, worships at a religious institution, chooses not to worship at any religious institution, serves on a jury, expresses a dissenting opinion, and so on.

Many nations have had revolutions; some have experienced quite a few and most, unlike ours, have not ended well. But America was not a nation before the Revolution. It was a collection of thirteen little disparate seaboard colonies, each itself a miniature state. What united us, what forged the country, was the Revolution—the event that made the United States and the modern world.

The Revolution led to another earthshaking event: a constitutional revolution that created a new system of government "of the people, by the people, and for the people." The Declaration of Independence provided its creed and the Constitution outlined its form with genius. These documents enshrined the liberties and rights that Americans have exercised over the last two centuries. Knowledge of them is vital for the survival of our republic because we are united not by blood, land, or common religion, but by our founding principles—our "ancient faith," as Lincoln called it. Unlike other countries, whose origins are lost in the mist of time, the United States has a start date and a blueprint.

The Constitution outlines the purposes of the US government as establishing justice, insuring domestic peace, providing defense, promoting the general welfare, and securing the blessings of liberty to ourselves and our posterity. One of the most vital means of securing the blessings of liberty is by educating rising generations about these precious birthrights. In 1789, in his first inaugural address, George Washington stated that "the preservation of the sacred fire of liberty, and the destiny of the republican government, are justly considered as deeply, perhaps as finally stacked, on the experiment entrusted to the hands of the American people."

When the people are the primary decision makers for public matters, the virtue of the people is the virtue of the country. Civic virtue is the chief concern of a republic. And civic virtue cannot be cultivated without civic literacy. As the French enlightenment thinker Charles de Montesquieu argued, "the tyranny of a prince in an oligarchy is not so dangerous to the public welfare as the apathy of a citizen in a democracy." Citizens of a republic have not only political rights but duties as well.

Thus our historical amnesia requires immediate attention. More than ever in our increasingly diverse nation, we need well-educated citizens with a shared knowledge of our history and a common understanding of our rights and responsibilities as Americans. Students and citizens "should be educated and instructed in the principles of freedom," John Adams wrote in 1787.[7]

* * *

After September 11, when I was serving as chairman of the National Endowment for the Humanities (NEH), it became apparent that defending America requires more than a strong national defense. In September 2002, I launched "We the People," an effort to improve the teaching and understanding of American history and culture. The mission of the program was to promote knowledge of our founding principles, history, institutions, rights, and responsibilities. It was based on the principle that citizens cannot defend what they cannot define.

On September 17, only a year after September 11, President George W. Bush introduced We the People at the White House, on Constitution Day. With bipartisan support, Congress provided the NEH with more than $82 million for the program from 2002 to 2009. We used those funds to strengthen our programs in research, education, and preservation and access.

We the People included Landmarks of American History and Culture Workshops, through which more than a thousand teachers spent a week in summer studying with scholars and exploring historical sites such as Mount Vernon and Ellis Island. Another We the People program, the Bookshelf, provided thousands of schools and public libraries with free sets of fifteen classic works of literature that convey to young readers important themes of American history and culture, such as "courage," "freedom," "becoming American," "the pursuit of happiness," and "created equal."

In addition, We the People funded programs in higher education, including a program in military history at Kansas State University. As demonstrated by the abundance of books on the US military, Americans are drawn—respectfully and in large numbers—to such history. This is good, and should be institutionalized in American universities, as military history is a crucial part of our civic tradition.

We the People grants also supported documentaries, bringing history into homes across the nation. We supported Ken Burns's *The War*, which chronicled the nation's transformation as it fought the Axis powers. Another documentary, *The War That Made America*, examined how the French and Indian War moved the colonies toward revolution; others profiled Annie Oakley and Alexander Hamilton, among others.

At the beginning of 2008, the NEH made the first awards for *Picturing America*, through which more than eighty thousand schools and public libraries received forty large-scale reproductions of masterpieces of American art, from Emanuel Gottlieb Leutze's "Washington Crossing the Delaware" to Edward Hopper's "House by the Railroad." NEH staff selected the masterpieces for their quality, enduring value over time, diversity of form, and ability to convey significant information about the people, events, and places of the United States.

Millions of students in tens of thousands of communities will benefit from these programs for decades, but the NEH is a small federal agency with limited funds—and, unfortunately, its commitment to civic education has waned since I left the organization in 2009.

President Barack Obama's budget for fiscal year 2011 requested $11.5 million for We the People—a drop of $4.3 million, or 27 percent, since 2009. Meanwhile, that same budget also requested $2.5 million in first-time funds for "Bridging Cultures," a new initiative announced in 2009 by my successor as NEH chairman, former Congressman James Leach. According to the NEH, the purpose of Bridging Cultures is to "help Americans better understand our own rich cultural heritage, while enhancing public knowledge of and respect for others both here and abroad."[8]

Bridging Cultures "encourages projects that explore the ways in which cultures from around the globe, as well as the myriad subcultures within America's borders, have influenced American society. With the aim of revitalizing intellectual and civic life through the humanities, NEH welcomes projects that expand both scholarly and public discussion of diverse countries, peoples, and cultural and intellectual traditions worldwide."[9]

The NEH has traditionally understood its primary mission as celebrating American cultural achievement—and therefore funding research and projects on American culture. In 2007, for example, whereas NEH grants for projects on the history and culture of other countries totaled $27.9 million, or 23 percent, of the agency's total program dollars, support for projects on American history and culture accounted for 40 percent. (The remaining 37 percent of funds were mandated for state humanities councils and projects with no specific geographical focus, such as training libraries and museums to preserve rare collections of manuscripts, photographs and the like.) This approach is even more important when, as is increasingly the case, schools and universities tend to prioritize non-American studies. The NEH, then, can serve the public good as a counterbalance.

The Bridging Cultures initiative threatens to alter the NEH's focus for the worse. By the end of the dramatic budget politics of early 2011, Bridging Cultures had seemingly replaced We the People, which was the only program the NEH discontinued in its 2012 budget.[10] Thus, the NEH effectively assumed that Americans have sufficient knowledge of their own culture to draw comparisons with others. But this is a faulty assumption, as numerous reports and tests have already shown. If Americans are woefully ignorant of their own history and culture, how then can they be expected to sufficiently compare and understand other cultures? The NEH's changes in priorities do not bode well for its role in encouraging civic literacy.

* * *

This is one reason why the cause of preserving American memory must be taken up not just by the NEH or the government, but by colleges, universities, libraries, community organizations, and families. No one has made this case better than President Ronald Reagan, who warned of the danger of American forgetfulness in his 1989 farewell address from the Oval Office.[11]

"We've got to teach history based not on what's in fashion but what's important," he exhorted the nation.

> If we forget what we did, we won't know who we are. I'm warning of an eradication of the American memory that could result, ultimately, in an erosion of the American spirit. Let's start with some basics: more attention to American history and a greater emphasis on civic ritual. And let me offer lesson number one about America: All great change in America begins at the dinner table. So, tomorrow night in the kitchen I hope the talking begins. And children, if your parents haven't been teaching you what it means to be an American, let 'em know and nail 'em on it. That would be a very American thing to do.

It would indeed.

NOTES

I am indebted to Annie Hsiao for her help with this chapter.

1. American Revolution Center, "The American Revolution: Who Cares? Americans Are Yearning to Learn, Failing to Know," July 2009, http://www.americanrevolutioncenter.org/sites/default/files/ARCv27_web.pdf.

2. "North Carolina," in Sheldon M. Stern and Jeremy A. Stern, "The State of State US History Standards 2011," Thomas B. Fordham Institute, February 2011.

3. North Carolina State Board of Education, "Standard Course of Study—Social Studies—2006—Eleventh Grade United States History," http://www.dpi.state.nc.us/curriculum/social-studies/scos/2003-04/067eleventhgrade.

4. Diane Ravitch, *The Language Police: How Pressure Groups Restrict What Students Learn* (New York: Knopf, 2003), 20.

5. Ravitch, *The Language Police*, 7.

6. American Revolution Center, "The American Revolution."

7. John Adams, *The Works of John Adams, Second President of the United States: With a Life of the Author, Notes and Illustrations, by his Grandson Charles Francis Adams* (Boston: Little, Brown, 1856), http://oll.libertyfund.org/title/2104.

8. National Endowment for the Humanities, "Bridging Cultures: Planning and Implementation Grants for Academic Forums and Program Development Workshops," April 1, 2010, http://www.neh.gov/grants/guidelines/BridgingCultures.html.

9. National Endowment for the Humanities, "Bridging Cultures."

10. National Endowment for the Humanities, "Appropriations Request for Fiscal Year 2012," February 2011, http://www.neh.gov/whoweare/pdf/NEH_Request_FY2012.pdf. The request did note that some parts of "We the People," such as "the National Digital Newspapers Program and Landmarks of American History and Culture workshops for school teachers and community college faculty," would remain part of the National Endowment for the Humanities' regular operations at least in fiscal year 2012.

11. Gleaves Whitney, ed., *American Presidents: Farewell Messages to the Nation, 1796–2001* (Lanham, MD: Lexington Books, 2005), 459.

Chapter Ten

Core Curriculum

How to Tackle General Illiteracy and Civic Illiteracy at the Same Time

Andrew J. Rotherham

Among the United States' various education problems, two share a common solution which can, in turn, help improve civic literacy. The first problem is this book's subject: the troubling lack of civic literacy and engagement in a country that is founded on the idea of an informed citizenry and participatory government. The second problem is a more basic failure that contributes to civic illiteracy: a lack of literacy overall.

It would be unfair to blame our schools' literacy problem entirely for America's civic education problem, but the two are keenly related. As such, some strategies that will help address our civic education gap can also help address our more general literacy gaps.

* * *

Ample research demonstrates how these problems are intertwined. For instance, education levels correlate with rates of civic participation: Better educated (and more economically advantaged) citizens are more likely to participate in both electoral and governmental politics.[1] Yet today the country faces serious educational problems. High school dropout rates for minority students hover near 50 percent and are even higher in many large cities. Meanwhile, many measures show that substantial gaps in achievement separate students by race, ethnicity, and income. There is also cause for concern about how American students will fare in an increasingly globalized economy that is leading other countries to substantially improve their educational systems and economic competitiveness.

Our education problems stem partly from the poor job too many school systems and states do in teaching reading. In 2009, 33 percent of fourth-grade students read below the "basic" level on the National Assessment of Educational Progress, the national test given by the federal Department of Education to representative samples of students. (According to the assessment's performance frameworks, students reach the basic level if they can read a passage of text and make simple inferences to relate pictures to texts, recognize the main topics of articles, and describe why particular characters are important to an overall story.[2]) Only 8 percent of fourth graders read at what the National Assessment of Educational Progress considers an "advanced" level, at which students are able to generalize from age-appropriate texts and critically judge what they have read. And, as with other educational measures, there are large gaps in reading ability between students of different races and income levels.

Among eighth graders, meanwhile, about 25 percent perform below the basic level, and achievement gaps persist. For eighth graders, basic performance indicates, among other things, the ability to recognize why an author used a particular quotation, to identify causal relations between historical events, to infer the meaning of words using context, and to recognize information an author is using to persuade.

Poor reading instruction and a lack of literacy lead to a variety of problems. Students who do not read well will struggle in all subjects—science as well as history, civics, and social studies—as they advance through school. But the impact goes beyond just low academic achievement. For one, it contributes to the high school dropout problem. Schools are literacy-based communities, so students with poor reading skills often come to feel alienated from a central part of the school culture. Few people want to spend time in a place where they don't "get it."

Despite a great deal of research and a substantial evidence base, there is still not an operating consensus among educators, academic researchers, policymakers, or politicians about how best to teach reading. Debates over the subject remain highly politicized, turning on questions of ideology as much as empirical evidence. In assessing the role of content in helping students read, or debating whether and how to emphasize phonics, researchers and advocates too often abuse or ignore evidence in the service of long-running political fights.

The so-called reading wars are fought over epistemological questions— for example, about how knowledge is constructed and by whom—that are more philosophical than empirical. The result is a great deal of confusion, enduring controversy, and stasis. While large sums of federal money are intended to help with reading instruction (including much of the $14 billion appropriated in 2010 for the federal "Title I" program designed to help low-income students), there is no overarching, research-based framework guiding how this money is spent.[3]

The result of this incoherence is that states and localities are largely left to bootstrap themselves on instruction and expenditures. Although the market-place is crowded with vendors offering products of uneven quality, school board members, school administrators, and teachers often lack the training to make discerning choices. This is one reason why participation in special education programs has exploded: Teachers misuse such programs as solu-tions for students who struggle with reading. Nationally, more than half of students in special education programs have a nonspecific learning disorder, and researchers estimate that more than half of those students may indeed have no disorder other than exposure to poor reading instruction.[4]

A related problem, which more directly affects civic education, is the lack of high-quality curricula for teachers. Across the country, curricula are a patchwork. Quality varies and teachers often must fend for themselves. Meanwhile, as part of the 1965 Elementary and Secondary Education Act (called "No Child Left Behind" since 2001), which governs most federal K–12 education spending, the federal government is prohibited from activ-ities that would mandate or endorse any curricular materials. In addition to its specific statutory limitations, this prohibition tends to have a chilling effect on any ambitious federal efforts regarding curriculum.

As problematic, at the more micro level, is that the elements that compose a school's curriculum are frequently not integrated, so different departments, subjects, and grades often operate in isolated silos. Meanwhile, the school day and year are generally not structured to help teachers of different sub-jects collaborate. Thus as reading teachers try to help struggling readers, there is often no collaboration across subjects—including history, civics, or social studies—which might reinforce students' reading skills.

* * *

This state of affairs creates an opportunity for advocates of civic education. By providing schools with content—actual materials that are aligned to educational standards usable by teachers—that is engaging, relevant, and grounded in America's civic traditions, advocates can help improve general literacy and civic literacy at the same time. Reading is not merely a skill and it should not be just one subject among many. Rather, reading should be an activity woven through many parts of a school's curriculum.

This is not a novel idea. Since the 1980s, University of Virginia professor E. D. Hirsch has written several influential books about the importance of content and shared knowledge to educational improvement and civic participation. Hirsch's basic point is that reading well requires broad knowledge or a framework within which to place and synthesize new knowledge.[5] To oversimplify just a little with a familiar example: Readers who know nothing about baseball will not understand an article about a baseball game even if they can read the words. A "run"? A "hit"? "Stealing a base"? Without an understanding of baseball, those terms might as well be in a foreign language. The same is true of an article about American government, history, or contemporary politics when readers do not have relevant knowledge about those issues.

Hirsch sees shared knowledge as an essential strategy for fostering social equality in a country like the United States. Cultivating understanding of shared history, ideas, and cultural norms is vital to ensuring that all Americans can participate fully in American life, Hirsch argues. Many students gain such social capital at home or in various out-of-school enrichment activities, hobbies, and volunteer activities. But for many, especially low-income students, schools are the only place where they might be exposed to such crucial knowledge. A rich curriculum can help students become more proficient readers while exposing them to key ideas and concepts of American civic participation.

Unfortunately, this idea is too rarely acted upon, with predictably harmful implications for civic education. Because content leads to broad knowledge, advocates of civic education should be helping equip students with engaging reading material not just in social studies and history, but also in text-intensive subjects, such as English. Hirsch himself is a leader in this effort, having established the Core Knowledge Foundation in 1986. Today more than seven hundred schools use the foundation's curriculum and more than eighty schools are official Core Knowledge schools, meaning they implement the curriculum with a high degree of fidelity to the principles of Hirsch's foundation.[6] In early 2010, the foundation announced that it would begin giving its entire curriculum away for free in order to ensure that teachers have sufficient curricular support as states adopt new standards for student learning.[7]

With today's ubiquitous technology, schools should have little problem accessing content. The founding documents of the United States, for example, are now available freely at the click of a mouse—and yet students still lack for substantive exposure to foundational debates that still echo today.

The challenge, then, is organizing an abundance of content into manageable formats so that teachers can engage students. Core Knowledge does this, and some others are beginning to do so as well. In 2007, the television network NBC announced iCue (pronounced as "IQ"), a website that aligns the network's video archives with Advanced Placement curricula in subjects including US history, English, and US government. When students in participating schools study the struggle for civil rights, for example, they can use iCue to watch archival footage of key events, access additional information, and play interactive games, among other things. (iCue also provides students with supplemental content for periods that predate the advent of television.) NBC developed the $10 million program in partnership with the Massachusetts Institute of Technology's Education Arcade.

Like major television networks, major newspapers are also sitting on a treasure trove of information, and their archives stretch farther back than any video archive can. Converting that printed material so that it can be integrated into curricula and aligned with standards would create an invaluable resource for teachers and students. Indeed, with relevant support and training for teachers, newspapers might be able to monetize this content as a much-needed revenue stream. The *New York Times* already has a "*New York Times* in Education" initiative and, in the not-for-profit realm, the Library of Congress and the National Endowment for the Humanities run "Chronicling America," an effort to digitize newspaper archives for classroom use. However, while valuable, these programs do not do enough to link content with state standards or to help teachers teach specific civic skills.

* * *

Content is obviously a necessary but insufficient condition for effective civic education. Schools must also cultivate in students certain civic behaviors and skills—including the ability to absorb information about politics, to seek compromises or disagree civilly, and ultimately to make use of citizens' various means for influencing public decisions. To do this, teachers must be equipped to teach and model such behaviors and skills in interactive, engaging ways.

One impediment to this is that so few of today's teachers (and students) have themselves seen civil political behavior modeled in American public life. Consider Americans around or under the age of forty. Seminal political events in their adult lives include the Iran-Contra scandal and its aftermath, Robert Bork's rejection from the Supreme Court and Clarence Thomas's scandal-plagued confirmation to it, the 1995 government shutdown over spending, the impeachment of a president, the Florida election recount, the scorched-earth politics of the Bush years, and the poisonous politics and gridlock of Washington today. Outside of national crises, such as the response to the September 11 terrorist attacks, there are too few recent examples of government coming together to tackle big problems or challenges.

Another impediment is the harmful approach that some influential education organizations, including the National Education Association, the nation's largest teachers union, take to teaching skills. Many in the education field today stress the importance of "twenty-first-century skills," which are supposedly new and particularly important for today's times. But a close look at these allegedly new skills reveals that they are just basic hallmarks of education that have been taught by great teachers for centuries: critical thinking, problem solving, collaboration, global awareness, and even media literacy are not new. One assumes that Aristotle tutored Alexander the Great in critical thinking long ago. What is new today is the imperative to make these skills universal—not just the province of the privileged few, as they traditionally have been.

It is problematic that many advocates of "twenty-first-century skills" treat skills as more important than content, which they consider fungible. Because so much content is being created, they argue, students can't possibly know it all. That is true—but it ignores the fact that there are classic, iconic works that distill and define the essence of cultures and societies. It also ignores the cultural and pedagogical value of shared knowledge.

Such devaluing of content is a threat to civics and other subjects. Students cannot understand or value the skills of participatory American citizenship without learning—through disciplines including history, government and literature—the proud, sometimes painful, complicated, and contentious history of the United States.

But to criticize a faddish approach to skills is not to argue that schools should not teach certain important skills correctly—in a manner grounded in rich content. This is how schools should teach the skills necessary for informed citizenship and participation in politics. Some organizations, such as the Close-Up Foundation, have valuable initiatives for training teachers to model civic skills in creative and nonpartisan ways. Close-Up, which brings students to Washington, DC, for interactive lessons about government, also exposes teachers to ideas from peers and Close-Up staff about how to teach civics in engaging, substantive ways. Yet Close-Up and initiatives like it are not embedded in the basic routines or training activities of schools.

Unfortunately, schools and school districts spend professional development dollars with scant attention to quality or outcomes. Because the professional development marketplace has few useful cues about quality—for instance, evidence linking models to outcomes—administrators base decisions on factors largely unrelated to effectiveness, such as prior relationships or cost. This not only weakens professional development generally, but it marginalizes civics, which is not embedded across the curriculum in subjects such as English and language arts. Professional development in those subjects, therefore, is not only of low quality but also fails to promote a more integrated curriculum that uses subjects such as civics to help promote reading.

To improve civic education, it is essential to provide teachers not only with content but with the strategies, support, and lessons needed to model the behaviors of civil debate and political compromise. Today, students are more likely to encounter civic skills and issues as haphazard byproducts of their education than through intentional curricular effort. If we're to address this problem, that must change.

* * *

By marrying content about the great ideas, debates, and traditions that define our country with skillful teaching of the ethos and skills of citizenship, schools can improve both civic literacy and general literacy alike. Facilitat-

ing such teaching—and developing initiatives among nontraditional providers of educational services, such as media companies and nonprofit organizations—should be a primary goal of advocates nationwide.

NOTES

1. For a classic examination of participation, see Steven J. Rosenstone and John Mark Hansen, *Mobilization, Participation, and Democracy in America* (New York: Longman, 2003).

2. All performance criteria and grading scales for the National Assessment of Educational Progress can be found at http://www.nationsreportcard.gov.

3. This 2010 funding figure does not include funds from the American Recovery and Reinvestment Act.

4. Chester E. Finn Jr., Andrew J. Rotherham, and Charles Hokanson, eds., *Rethinking Special Education for a New Century* (Washington, DC: Progressive Policy Institute and Thomas B. Fordham Foundation, 2001).

5. See E. D. Hirsch Jr., *The Knowledge Deficit: Closing the Shocking Education Gap for American Children* (New York: Houghton Mifflin Harcourt, 2006).

6. Andrew J. Rotherham, "Core Convictions: An Interview with E. D. Hirsch," Education Sector, September 22, 2006, http://www.educationsector.org/publications/core-convictions.

7. Catherine Gewertz, "Core Knowledge to Link Curriculum to Core Standards," *Education Week*, February 3, 2010.

III

In the Classroom—
What Works, What Doesn't

Chapter Eleven

Fighting Civic Malpractice

How a Harlem Charter School
Closes the Civic Achievement Gap

Seth Andrew

"I ain't gonna' stand on no street corner talkin' to strangers 'bout votin'!" Nakia exclaimed. It was September 2006, and my students at Democracy Prep Charter School were participating in their first voter registration drive in our Harlem neighborhood. Nakia, who had just started sixth grade after winning admission to Democracy Prep through our random lottery, insisted: "Votin' don't matter 'cause the government don't give a s**t about me."[1]

While Nakia's language was rough and the expletive earned her an after-school detention, one can hardly blame this eleven-year-old girl—who lives in deep urban poverty in the richest nation on Earth, with both of her parents in prison—for feeling that her democracy had failed her. As her principal, my first responsibility was to hold her accountable for her language. Second was to work with her teachers to improve her grammar. Third, and most difficult, was to foster in her the understanding that our democracy is what empowers her and her peers to make the changes they seek in the world.

Nakia's negative feelings toward our political system are common among my incoming students, who come predominantly from low-income African American and Latino families. With few exceptions, the civic knowledge, skills, and attitudes of low-income Americans are spiraling downward in a vicious cycle of disengagement from American democracy. All the while, too many of our public schools contribute to the problem by effectively committing civic malpractice.

I founded Democracy Prep Charter School in 2005 to fight these problems. As of fall 2011, we have four schools serving over one thousand students from kindergarten through eleventh grade. Our mission is to educate students—whom we call "citizen-scholars"—for success in the college of their choice and a life of active citizenship. We're working to develop a replicable model for fostering virtuous cycles of civic engagement, academic and economic success, and social consciousness in American public schools. We seek to ensure that students like Nakia have the power and the disposition to look out their windows in Harlem's housing projects and believe that they have the ability to transform their communities for the better, rather than continue to be imprisoned by them.

In 2010, Democracy Prep was named the top-performing middle school and top-performing charter school in the entire City of New York.[2] Ninety percent of our citizen-scholars enter our halls substantially behind grade level, averaging third-grade reading skills at the beginning of sixth grade. By the time they reach high school, more than 95 percent demonstrate mastery on the New York State Regents exams.

But academic growth is not enough to satisfy the mission of Democracy Prep. We must also prepare our citizen-scholars for lives of active citizenship—which is, after all, the true mission of public schools.

* * *

The well-documented achievement gaps separating the English and math proficiency of low- and upper-income students are just the tip of the education crisis iceberg.

Per-pupil spending on public education (inflation adjusted) has doubled since the mid-1970s, driven mainly by a tripling in the number of teachers over the past fifty years. Yet educational outcomes have stagnated or declined. This is demonstrated by scores on the SAT and other standardized tests, high school graduation rates, college completion rates, and more.[3] The nation that pioneered public education over 150 years ago now lags behind nearly all of its global peers: When compared to twenty-nine other developed nations, the United States ranks fifteenth in reading, nineteenth in science, and twenty-seventh in math achievement.[4]

As bad as these numbers are, the reality is even bleaker for America's poor and minority children. Wide achievement gaps separate African American, Latino, and economically disadvantaged students from those who are white, Asian, and middle class. The 2005 National Assessment of Educational Progress showed that African American and Latino twelfth graders perform on the same level in math and English as do white eighth graders.[5] Only 51 percent of African American and 55 percent of Latino students graduate from high school, while 77 percent of white students do.[6]

Of those who graduate high school, only 28 percent of African Americans and 16 percent of Latinos receive a bachelor's degree.[7] Of children whose families are in the bottom quartile of earnings, fewer than 5 percent graduate from a four-year college. By contrast, about 75 percent of children from families in the top quartile do.[8]

Over the past decades, most approaches to education reform have attempted only to tinker with the traditional public school model in which the school day runs from 8 a.m. to 3 p.m., with only five hours dedicated to academic instruction, for 180 days a year. Another central part of that enduring model is a system of tenure and seniority rules that yields stasis among teachers and guarantees the jobs of even the most incompetent teachers.

Meanwhile, typical bureaucratic systems provide little if any accurate data to help educators make good decisions for their students. The lowest-performing schools often have chaotic and dangerous school cultures, and the academic expectations placed on low-income students—and which they place on themselves—are remarkably low. Valiant attempts to close the academic achievement gap while maintaining these broken school models have failed.

In recent years, however, a number of high-performing islands of excellence have proliferated among the more than six thousand public charter schools across the nation. Democracy Prep, West Denver Prep, Achievement Prep, Excel Academy, and approximately two hundred other great public charter schools have grown in the nation's lowest-income urban communities.[9] These are often called "no excuses" schools, as they commit to doing whatever it takes to get their students into college.

These excellent schools are closing achievement gaps in math, science, and literacy. They often send a higher percentage of students to college than do even their affluent suburban counterparts. Most significantly, many such schools and networks have "scaled up," growing dramatically in size and proving that the academic achievement gap can be eliminated on a large scale. They have demonstrated that, for students, demography isn't destiny.

The primary reason for these charter schools' success is that they have the autonomy to rethink educational expectations from the ground up—instead of fighting the intellectual shackles, union contracts, and vested political interests that protect the status quo in traditional public schools.

As a network of public charter schools, Democracy Prep receives government funding but operates independent of the central school district. We are therefore free from most bureaucratic regulations and barriers. In exchange for this autonomy, we are held accountable for student achievement through a five-year charter that sets explicit metrics in all subjects, including those that are unique to our civic mission. We accept all of our students based on a random lottery (there is no test to enter), and our schools are tuition-free. In addition, since we actively recruit students with special needs, we serve a higher proportion of such students than do our neighboring traditional public schools in Harlem.

Our independence as a charter allows us to implement a rigorous college prep curriculum, to have longer school days and years, and to use targeted student achievement data to drive instruction. Most importantly, we choose which teachers to hire, which to develop, and which to let go.

The crucial factor that distinguishes us from most other "no excuses" schools, however, is that we focus on the civic achievement gap that threatens our students and our future as a democracy. Even the best "no excuses" schools are rarely preparing citizens like Nakia for a life of active citizenship. This can and must change.

* * *

The demographic fault lines for civic achievement lie in the same places as those for math and reading: between white students and black and Latino students, and between middle-class students and economically disadvantaged ones. Unlike the gaps in math or reading, however, the civic achievement gap is measurable beyond test scores. The three components of excellent civic education—knowledge, skills, and attitude—all tell the same story.

Possessing civic knowledge means understanding the theory, history, and processes of American government. The National Assessment of Educational Progress tests students' civic knowledge, and the results are grim.

As table 11.1 shows, large gaps—in excess of 20 percentage points in most cases—exist along economic and racial lines. The gap is largest among twelfth graders, some of whom are already eligible to vote, as white students outperform black students by 25 percentage points. Of course, these numbers show that proficiency among all students is disturbingly low: Barely a quarter of tomorrow's voters demonstrate sufficient civic knowledge.

Meanwhile, measures of civic skills—the capacities required for participation in a democracy—show considerable gaps separating demographic groups. A 2005 survey of 2,366 California twelfth graders found that African American students took fewer civic-oriented classes (government, history, and the like) and less frequently discussed current events than did white students. Latino students reported fewer opportunities to participate in community service and civic simulations than did their white peers.[10] Such insufficient education undermines the ability of many underprivileged students to exercise the most basic civic skills—from voting to understanding current events, participating in public discourse about government policy, supporting political candidates and issues, and running for office.

As with civic knowledge and skills, there are also wide demographic gaps in measures of Americans' civic attitude, the degree to which one believes in one's ability to play a meaningful role in society. Among young people aged fifteen to twenty-five, Latinos and African Americans are far less likely than whites to agree with the statement that "I can make a difference in solving the problems of my community."[11] It's no surprise, then, that these minority groups have far lower rates of community engagement.

Another measure of civic attitude is "expectation of voting." Among students who come from homes with literacy advantages (a measure based on the number of books found in the home, which is correlated with race and socioeconomic status) and who plan to attend college, 56 percent expect to

Table 11.1.   Students Scoring "Proficient" or "Advanced" on the National Assessment of Educational Progress Civics Exam, 2006 (in percentages)

Demographic Group	Eighth Graders	Twelfth Graders
All public school students	20	27
Noneconomically disadvantaged	29	32
Economically disadvantaged	8	11
White	28	33
Black	7	8
Latino	7	11

vote. For those without literacy advantages or plans to attend college, only 18.7 percent expect to vote.[12] This is the context in which Nakia insisted to me that voting doesn't matter.

* * *

To close both the academic and civic achievement gaps, Democracy Prep goes beyond the typical "no excuses" model. For one, we focus our lottery recruiting efforts on special education, homeless, low-performing, and low-income students. We also operate our educational program exclusively with public funds, eschewing private philanthropy in order to demonstrate that our model can be replicated anywhere in the nation. (We use funds raised from private philanthropic sources only to expand our network and to pay for expensive private facilities—costs that traditional public schools do not have to incur. Once open, our schools operate on public funds alone.)

In the classroom, we provide our citizen-scholars with a rigorous civics curriculum that integrates the theory and processes of American government into social studies and debate classes. We hold students and teachers accountable through frequent student assessments. And to deepen our scholars' knowledge, we facilitate inspiring hands-on activities that demonstrate how civic skills enable them to be purposeful agents of change.

To learn about voting, our citizen-scholars participate in mock elections every year. On the ballot are candidates for city, state, and federal government, as well as Democracy Prep ballot initiatives. (Past ballot initiatives have included, "Next Tuesday, would you prefer to have opposite day or crazy hat day?" and "On our end of year trip, should we visit Boston University or Boston College?")

To be eligible to vote, scholars must properly fill out mock voter registration forms that mimic actual New York State registration forms almost exactly. (The age minimum, of course, is reduced.) As the election approaches, scholars use either teacher-created candidate guides or newspaper articles to research their choices and debate their merits in social studies classes and in Town Hall meetings.

On Election Day, when most students across the country have the day off, our citizen-scholars are required to attend school. Those scholars who have volunteered to be poll workers set up polling stations in classrooms and hallways. The others then line up to have their registrations checked. The poll workers hand ballots to those who are registered, and they deny ballots to those frustrated few who are not on the voter roll because they filled out their registrations incorrectly. Scholars then cast their mock ballots. The next day they learn the results and are able to compare them to the real outcomes in city, state, and federal elections.

Beyond voting, we teach our scholars about campaigning by having them participate in real voter registration and voter participation drives in Harlem. Each Election Day, scholars in grades 6 through 8, like Nakia, run our all-day "Get Out the Vote" campaign, standing on busy street corners wearing T-shirts and handing out flyers that read, "I CAN'T VOTE, but YOU CAN!" Over the past five years, they have encouraged over fifty thousand Harlem voters to get out the vote.

Scholars in high school participate in a phone bank, calling homes in Harlem and encouraging registered voters to head to the polls. Because our scholars have become knowledgeable about the candidates and issues, they often end up informing the would-be voters about the candidates.

The civic skill we emphasize most is that of advocating for one's rights, beliefs, and community. While our scholars do not engage in partisan political activity while at school, they are deeply passionate when it comes to advocating for excellent schools. All scholars know five other kids their age who did not win the lottery for Democracy Prep or another high-performing school—and they see the difference it has made.

That's why, when politicians hold hearings on issues that affect our ability to run and build excellent schools, we encourage students and parents to testify—and they almost always do so. Our scholars are regularly the youngest witnesses to testify before the New York City Council, State Assembly, and State Senate. Whether the subject is mayoral control of New York City's public schools or lifting the cap on the number of public charter schools in the state, our scholars research the issues, write their own testimony, and practice effective delivery. Scholars sometimes take opposite sides of the same issue, but they always produce some of the most compelling argumentation.

In addition, high school students on Democracy Prep's student council sit on the education committee of the local Community Board. The opportunity to interact with a real governing body turns a simple school assignment into an exciting, educational exercise of students' rights as citizens.

One of the most important civic skills we develop in our students is lobbying. Every year, our scholars make at least two trips to the state Capitol in Albany, where they meet with legislators to argue for school choice and funding equity. In addition, sixth graders take an annual end-of-year trip to Washington, DC, where they lobby their representatives and senators. On these trips, a scholar is selected to run each meeting, directing questions and yielding to peers to ask or answer specific ones about what it means to attend Democracy Prep and why we need more schools like ours.

* * *

The most difficult element of civic education for schools to teach is civic attitude. Democracy Prep does this by making civics exciting and meaningful in age-appropriate ways. We embrace controversy, engage with the street, encourage debate, protest loud and proud, and facilitate authentic civic opportunities whenever possible.

Every election year, my colleagues and I take all new scholars with us to vote. Sometimes the poll workers don't appreciate the fifty four-foot-tall onlookers, but many of our students would never otherwise see a voting booth—because their parents cannot register to vote, aren't registered to vote, or simply aren't civically minded. But a parent or mentor bringing a child to vote on Election Day—an experience I shared with my parents—is a foundational one for building civic attitude.

It is not obvious to kids why adults would take time out of their busy days to go pull a lever in private. To understand, a child needs to watch role models wait in line, to witness neighbors quarrelling with grumpy poll workers, to observe voters' quiet deliberation about candidates and ballot measures, and to hear mentors proudly defend their choices in conversations and debates afterward. They need to see that voting is something worth going out of the way to do.

Another way for schools to cultivate civic attitude is to leverage current events. Perhaps our biggest success in building civic attitude came surrounding the election and inauguration of Barack Obama in 2008. As his inauguration approached, it became clear that we were not going to be able to take three hundred students to Washington, DC, in the freezing cold. Instead, I enlisted a volunteer committee of forty students to create our own inauguration event. The committee of eleven- and twelve-year-olds worked with staff to identify and invite other schools, design and decorate the event space, and create the program, which included student musical numbers, dance performances and speeches.

On that January day, our scholars managed to host one of the country's largest inauguration celebrations, which was broadcast on NBC, ABC, FOX, CNN and other media on four continents. Over seven thousand friends and family members from thirty-five charter, district, and private schools packed the Harlem Armory to the rafters and watched silently as the first African American president was sworn in and addressed the nation. Following the president's speech, the crowd erupted, kids cheered, and grandparents cried.

In the front row, reserved for scholars who had earned an "All Access" pass by leading the inauguration committee, sat a beaming face filled with smiles and hope. Nakia had seen something she had not believed just two years prior: Voting does indeed matter. I can say with great confidence that's a lesson she will never forget.

* * *

Over time, Democracy Prep plans to use several metrics to track our success in fostering informed, active citizenship. As our first class of twelfth graders approaches graduation in 2013, they will have to pass the National Assessment of Educational Progress civics exam and the US Citizenship and Naturalization test before they can receive a Democracy Prep diploma. And since civic knowledge, skills, and attitude must be sustained long-term, Democracy Prep will track the civic practices of alumni over time. We plan to use several publicly available metrics, including data on voting, incarceration, philanthropic giving, civic engagement, running for elected office, political contributions, jury service, military service, and more. All such assessments will allow us to continually improve our approach to civic education for the students still in our classrooms.

In the face of the vast educational challenges facing American children in inner cities, rural towns and elsewhere, some leaders ask, "Why bother with civics?" Even many of the highest-performing schools overlook civics, relegating it to a short unit within social studies. When students are three years behind grade level in reading and math, deciding that civic education is a luxury is not absurd—but it is still wrong.

Just as students must learn the alphabet before they learn to read, they must also learn to read, write, and do arithmetic before they can master science, history, and civics. All of these skills are necessary, but public schools remain duty bound to teach civics in particular. When they fail, they commit educational and civic malpractice.

One of the clearest facts demonstrated by high-performing charter schools is that high expectations are essential to student achievement. Given that civic education is the most basic purpose of public schooling, educators should never consider it secondary, let alone foreclose on it entirely. To do so is to ignore a main lesson of the "no excuses" revolution—and to cheat students of their futures.

Effective reformers nationwide have demonstrated how schools can and must adapt to reverse achievement gaps in math and reading: by raising standards for student achievement; allowing schools to provide longer instructional days and years; allowing schools to choose, retain, and reward excellent teachers; and providing schools with the data needed to drive those decisions. Now it's time that all schools—including the highest performing, along with their justifiably growing legions of political supporters—recognize the imperative of ending civic malpractice and closing the civic achievement gap.

NOTES

I would like to gratefully acknowledge William Packer and Lana Zak for their editorial assistance.

1. "Nakia" is a pseudonym.

2. The New York City chancellor of education publishes an annual progress report that assigns a numeric score (0–100) and a letter grade (A–F) to each school based on surveys of students, teachers, and parents; attendance; performance; and value-added progress. In 2010, Democracy Prep Charter School "did better than 100% of all Middle schools citywide," and its score of 88.9 was the highest among the city's charter schools. See http://schools.nyc.gov/OA/SchoolReports/2009-10/Progress_Report_2010_EMS_M350.pdf.

3. Thomas D. Snyder, Sally A. Dillow, and Charlene M. Hoffman, *Digest of Education Statistics* (Washington, DC: US Department of Education, 2009), 98. See also, Alliance for Excellent Education, "Understanding High School Graduation Rates in the United States," July 2009, http://www.all4ed.org/publication_material/understanding_HSgradrates.

4. The Program for International Student Assessment, an international test of fifteen-year-olds in fifty countries, was last administered in 2009 (http://nces.ed.gov/surveys/international/ide/).

5. Whitney Tilson, "A Right Denied: The Critical Need for Education Reform," 34, http://www.tilsonfunds.com/Personal/TheCriticalNeedforGenuineSchoolReform.pdf.

6. Alliance for Excellent Education, "Understanding High School."

7. Tilson, "A Right Denied," 41.

8. Mary Ann Fox, Brooke A. Connolly, and Thomas D. Snyder, "Youth Indicators 2005: Trends in the Well-Being of American Youth," National Center for Education Statistics, July 2005, http://nces.ed.gov/pubs2005/2005050.pdf.

9. Building Excellent Schools, the school leadership program from which I graduated, deserves enormous credit for spreading best practices and training the individuals who lead many of these schools.

10. Joseph Kahne and Ellen Middaugh, "Democracy for Some: The Civic Opportunity Gap in High School," CIRCLE Working Paper 59, February 2008, http://www.civicsurvey.org/democracy_some_circle.pdf.

11. Cynthia Gibson and Peter Levine, eds., "The Civic Mission of Schools," CIRCLE and the Carnegie Corporation of New York, 2003, http://www.civicmissionofschools.org/site/campaign/cms_report.html.

12. Judith Torney-Purta and Carolyn Henry Barber, "Strengths and Weaknesses in US Students' Knowledge and Skills: Analysis from the IEA Civic Education Study," CIRCLE, June 2004, http://www.civicyouth.org/PopUps/FactSheets/FS_CivicKnowledge.pdf.

Chapter Twelve

The KIPP Approach

Be the Change You Wish to See in the World

Mike Feinberg

Many schoolchildren gather on the steps of the Supreme Court building in Washington, DC, each year, but few have the experience that my students from KIPP Academy Middle School in Houston, Texas had in spring 1995.

The KIPP (Knowledge Is Power Program) Houston fifth graders had taken the standard thirty-minute tour of the building, but after all they had learned about the role of the Supreme Court in US history, they were disappointed not to have seen the court in session. As I stood outside trying to augment the tour with additional details, I spotted Justice Steven Breyer walking by.

I quickly buttonholed the Justice and asked him to greet my class. As he began his polite, standard, elementary school appropriate remarks, one of our fifth graders, Ruben Garcia, shot his hand in the air with a question. "Were you here in 1966 when the court voted on *Miranda v. Arizona*?"

When Justice Breyer replied that the ruling had been before his time, Ruben continued, "Well, if you had been here, how would you have voted on that case?" Having spent three months studying the Supreme Court and its role in government, the students were all prepared to ask questions as thoughtful as Ruben's. Drawing on the three Supreme Court cases they had memorized, the students continued to pepper Justice Breyer about topics ranging from habeas corpus to the Bill of Rights.

Struck, Justice Breyer decided to ignore his packed schedule and continue speaking with the students. And for years after that point, he welcomed KIPP students to his chambers whenever they visited the nation's capital.

With my colleague Dave Levin, I founded the KIPP program in Houston in 1994 after we completed our two-year commitment to Teach For America. Today, one hundred and nine KIPP public schools—all but one of which are charter schools—serve over thirty-three thousand K–12 students in twenty US states and Washington, DC. About 80 percent of KIPP students qualify for free or reduced-price lunch, and over 85 percent of the students who have completed eighth grade at KIPP middle schools have gone on to college.

Many people attribute KIPP's success to our longer school day and academic year, or to our teachers, who commit to answering students' homework questions by cell phone after school hours. But KIPP's focus on cultivating responsible citizenship is equally important.

* * *

From KIPP's earliest days, Dave and I have worked to instill in our students the notion that freedom is not free (a saying I first came across at the Korean War Memorial on the National Mall). Throughout its history, America has had to fight to keep its freedoms, and KIPP schools help our students understand this struggle through our "culture of earning." KIPP students have to earn privileges, such as wearing jeans or going on field trips, that other schools give away as a matter of course. By working to reach academic and behavioral targets, KIPP students learn important lessons about the connection between personal responsibility and the privileges of citizenship.

KIPP's philosophy toward civic education is also based on the belief that students learn best by doing. Following the approach first articulated by early-twentieth-century philosopher John Dewey, KIPP schools build students' knowledge of history through hands-on experiences. Toward this end, a cornerstone of our civic education curriculum is the "field lesson" (known at other schools as a field trip). Field lessons include various opportunities to learn outside of school, including trips to significant sites from American history as well as visits to colleges and national parks. Across all KIPP schools, three elements unite our approach to field lessons.

First, in line with our culture of earning, KIPP students—"KIPPsters," as we call them—are not automatically included in field lessons, but rather have to earn their spots by meeting certain benchmarks for effort and behavior. (Grades are not used to determine eligibility for student trips.)

Second, we use field lessons to teach KIPPsters about their civic duties outside of the classroom. They learn, for example, to leave places cleaner than they find them. When KIPP students hike through a national park and see a half-eaten bag of chips on the trail, they are expected to pick it up and discard it. When they stay in hotels, they wipe down bathroom sinks and make their beds. These small acts build character and responsibility.

Finally, KIPPsters have to prepare rigorously before they ever get on a bus or airplane. Rafe Esquith, one of my first mentors and an internationally recognized teacher in Los Angeles, gave us a framework that guides the KIPP approach to field lessons. Esquith's principle, which is based on the standard field trip to an art museum, is that if students have to read the names on the wall next to the paintings, they did not prepare enough for the trip.

At the Vietnam War Memorial in Washington, DC, too many American students gather in large groups, trace a name from the wall on a piece of paper, and leave—having gained little understanding of what the memorial represents. KIPPsters, however, spend a long time at the memorial (as they do at Arlington National Cemetery) considering the sacrifice that American soldiers have made over our country's history.

Before they ever get to Washington, KIPP students spend months studying the Vietnam War and learning about the memorial's history and symbolism. They learn, for example, how the wall was designed to descend slowly toward the ground to represent the idea of going deeper toward the depth of a grave—and that, as one walks away, the wall rises back above ground to represent the lives that Americans are fortunate to have because of the sacrifices of those named on the wall.

* * *

Over 85 percent of the thirty-three thousand students who attend KIPP schools across the country are African American or Latino. As such, KIPP schools shape civic education programs to help students understand their ethnic and racial identities in relation to the arc of American history. In schools where African American students make up the large majority, for example, teachers place particular emphasis on the history of the slave trade and the journey toward civil rights and equality.

Following this approach, KIPP educators in two communities have worked particularly hard to design memorable field lessons that brought civic education to life for their students.

In 2005, students from KIPP WAYS (Western Atlanta Young Scholars) Academy charter school in Atlanta traveled all the way to Ghana to pursue their interest in the history of slavery in the United States. One of the history teachers from KIPP WAYS, Stephen Jones, had been to Ghana and knew the impact it had on him as an African American. Wanting to share this experience with his mostly African American eighth graders, Jones told them that if they maintained excellent academics and behavior throughout the year, he'd figure out a way to get them to Ghana. Led by Jones and KIPP Metro Atlanta executive director David Jernigan, KIPP WAYS held bake sales and car washes to raise money, and got Delta Airlines to donate roundtrip airfare for a summer trip to Africa.

The KIPP WAYS students researched Ghana intensely to prepare for the trip. In math class, they learned how to count in the cedi, the currency of Ghana, and practiced negotiating a price in the market. They also immersed themselves in the study of the slave trade to prepare for a walking tour of Ghana's infamous dungeons, where Europeans held Africans as captives before their sale in the transatlantic slave trade. For African American students, whose not-so-distant ancestors were slaves, this was an unforgettable way to experience American history.

Many other KIPP students have also ventured overseas to get an international perspective on history. Such international field lessons are part of KIPP's mission to prepare students for "college and the competitive world beyond." KIPPsters tend to return from visits abroad with a new appreciation for the freedoms they take for granted at home, and with more understanding of America's affluence relative to the rest of the world.

Back stateside, the 2009 inauguration of President Barack Obama presented civics teachers with a unique opportunity to explore the arc and impact of the civil rights movement.

Ian Guidera, who leads Los Angeles's KIPP Academy of Opportunity charter school, felt that having his students watch the inauguration on television would not suffice. But airfare and hotels were too expensive to take even one grade of students to Washington, DC. After securing a donation of twelve student tickets from Virgin American airlines, Guidera set up an essay contest to determine who would get to go. From 180 essays submitted by KIPP Los Angeles students, a panel of KIPP educators chose the winners based on their enthusiasm and their understanding of what the inauguration represented for American history.

Guidera's students readied for the trip by researching Washington, DC, and the role of presidential leadership in US history. As a culminating project, each student presented a "persuasive leadership itinerary" that detailed what he or she most wanted to see in Washington, based on the leadership lessons that could be learned at each site. The trip to DC that January, during which students witnessed the inauguration and visited nearby colleges, gave the Los Angeles KIPPsters an experience that they will share with their families and neighbors for years to come.

* * *

Although essential to KIPP's civic education, field lessons are only a part of KIPP's curriculum. In Houston, KIPP students come from over fifty different countries and five different continents, and many KIPP schools nationwide have similarly diverse populations. KIPP therefore aims to develop students who will be ethical citizens of the United States and the world.

KIPP schools operate under the philosophy that all students must understand the American political system, regardless of their ethnicity or native country. This starts with studying the American Revolution, which gives KIPP students a chance to reflect on the many countries today in which citizens struggle for freedom against repressive governments. The circumstances of the American Revolution relate to the conflicts that, in many cases, caused KIPP students' families to flee their native countries for a better life in the United States. Such understanding helps KIPP students connect to the Constitution and the Bill of Rights—and realize the unique freedom enjoyed by American citizens.

In Houston, KIPP's approach to civic education has been refined over time by two creative, longtime colleagues, Elliott Witney and Dave Crumbine. The middle school civics curriculum begins the first year, when KIPPsters are in fifth grade and engage in a study of US history that focuses heavily on the Constitution and role of democratic government. KIPP fifth graders also study the history of slavery, reading essays by Frederick Douglass and watching the miniseries *Roots*. Their English language arts curriculum ties into this exploration, as students read *Nightjohn*, a novel about a young slave girl who is taught to read by another slave.

In sixth grade, KIPP Houston students explore world civilizations and religions, including an overview of world history and an interdisciplinary unit on the European Holocaust and contemporary genocides.

In seventh grade, students study US history through the Civil War, with a focus on the history of Texas and our relations with Mexico. By exposure to artifacts and case studies, students learn about historical figures such as General Sam Houston and Frederick Douglass, along with key events of this period, including the Emancipation Proclamation and the ending of slavery. To celebrate Juneteenth, KIPP Houston students travel to Galveston, the city where Union General Gordon Granger read General Order No. 3 enforcing the federal Proclamation and freeing the slaves.

In their eighth-grade history classes, KIPP Houston students research the role of the Constitution in shaping US history. In English, students learn of more recent history through texts such as John Steinbeck's *Of Mice and Men*, Upton Sinclair's *The Jungle*, and George Orwell's *Animal Farm*. They also study various political systems from other parts of the world.

When they study the Constitution, KIPPsters take a close look at the amendment process and its uses over time. KIPP schools emphasize that students have a responsibility to leave the world better than they found it, and the constitutional amendment process shows how the framers provided an avenue for future Americans to make the country stronger, fairer, and better.

KIPP students also learn about the US political system by participating in student government and other experiential learning activities. In KIPP Houston's student government program, designed by KIPP teacher Andrew Rubin, eighth graders begin by writing an original constitution for the school. Once the "KIPP constitution" is complete, students organize their own election campaigns for leadership positions including president, vice president, senators, and representatives. Once elected, they draft legislation that, within reasonable parameters, sets policies for the school regarding dress code, lunchtime privileges, and other matters that interest them.

In 2009, KIPP Houston eighth graders amended the school constitution to allow students to wear jeans twice a month. After securing enough signatures, the amendment organizers passed it to Principal Elliott Witney who, along with the student-run Supreme Court, determined that it was fair and constitutional. With much fanfare, Elliott signed the amendment into law and KIPP Houston students earned a new freedom.

* * *

KIPP schools share a strong commitment to the social-emotional development of our students. Many of our students live in neighborhoods influenced by a street culture that values intimidation and strength over working hard and being nice. We aim to help students see that the world can be dictated by compassion, kindness, and empathy.

Simply teaching these values, however, is not enough. James Baldwin once noted that, "Children have never been very good at listening to their elders, but they have never failed to imitate them." School lessons ring hollow if teachers expect from students what they themselves do not do. Misalignments between teachers' words and deeds are noticed by students and undermine the school's mission.

For example, when teachers and administrators ask students to remain organized yet fail to clean a disheveled classroom, kids notice. When students are asked to work hard, yet faculty members race out of the building at the day's final bell, students notice. KIPP teachers, therefore, try to follow Gandhi's admonition to "be the change we wish to see in the world."

In terms of civic education, this involves modeling what it means to be a good citizen, such as volunteering in the local community and voting during election season. We encourage teachers to speak to their classes about the considerations they face on Election Day—without disclosing their own preferences.

We also ask KIPPsters to consider how they can help improve the communities that lie beyond their school walls. The KIPP Foundation, our national organization, hosts an annual retreat at which over one hundred KIPP middle school and high school students participate in two days of leadership development. Teams identify an unmet need in their community, invent a plan for addressing it, and present their plans to a KIPP Foundation panel. In 2009, for example, one winning proposal submitted by middle school students at KIPP Academy in the South Bronx conceived of a program to supply musical instruments to children in the surrounding community.

* * *

KIPP's civics curriculum and hands-on field lessons are the visible signs of our commitment to teaching students about American democracy and government. But it is the experiences that KIPPsters share—working in teams, taking responsibility for one's own actions, traveling to historical landmarks, and looking for ways to improve the world—that truly teach them what it means to be part of a democratic society.

NOTE

KIPP Houston educators and Teach For America alumni Elliott Witney and Dave Crumbine contributed extensively to this chapter, as did Andrew Rubin.

Chapter Thirteen

The Wisdom of Twenty Thousand Teachers

*Strengthen State Requirements,
Stop Marginalizing the Founders*

Jason Ross

Civic education efforts should center on the Constitution, which has afforded Americans a degree of freedom and opportunity unparalleled in history. Guided by this view, the Bill of Rights Institute has provided instruction to roughly twenty thousand teachers of US history, government, and civics since its founding in 1999. It has also provided curriculum resources that supplement the textbooks of scores of thousands of students and promote discussion of constitutional liberties, rights, and responsibilities.

Through its efforts, the institute has recognized three particular impediments to civic education: poorly conceived state requirements, a social studies discipline that sends the wrong messages about democracy and constitutional government, and civic educators' relative inability to seek crucial supplementary training.

* * *

Although the federal government has some mechanisms for influencing civic education (as documented elsewhere in this volume), the major policies that govern the teaching of US history, government, and civics are set at the state level.

Despite this decentralization, a relatively common approach toward civic education has emerged among the states. This is to require graduates to have taken three year-long units (sometimes known as "credits") of social studies. Generally this includes one unit of world history, one unit of US history, one half-unit (a semester) of state history or economics, and one half-unit of US government or civics.

Recognizing that one year is inadequate for a detailed study of US history, curriculum designers often split the subject into two full-year courses, one covering the era through the Civil War and one covering the years that followed. The common way of doing this, unfortunately, is to teach the pre–Civil War era in eighth grade and the post–Civil War era in eleventh. This division into two segments taught three years apart is an impediment to effective teaching and learning.

It is problematic that early US history—especially the Constitution and its historical origins—is relegated to eighth grade, since middle school students are less well equipped than high schoolers to understand the language and ideas of the Constitution and other founding documents. And when eleventh grade comes around, it is a challenge even for the best teachers to pick up the narrative of US history after students have had a three-year break. What's more, students nearing adulthood should be educated about their responsibilities as citizens in a constitutional republic, yet teachers of eleventh grade often have difficulty incorporating content about the Constitution into their classes about post–Civil War history.

The teaching of US government or civics is also problematic. A brief review of state policies shows that, as of 2008, forty states permit students to graduate having completed merely one semester of US government or civics (or an equivalent class, sometimes called "democratic participation"). The remaining states either do not specify a requirement in US government/civics, leave all decisions on graduation standards to local policymakers, require less than one semester of US government/civics, or mandate a mere demonstration of proficiency in the subject.[1]

Eleven states supplement their coursework requirements with mandatory examinations. Missouri, for instance, decrees that "To be eligible for graduation from high school, a student must satisfactorily pass a test or tests on the provisions and principles of the US and Missouri constitutions and in American history and institutions at some time(s) during grades 7 to 12. The design, content, and passing criteria for the test(s) are at the discretion of local school districts."[2]

Six states, meanwhile, include questions about US government and civics on their universal high school graduation tests. Georgia, for example, asks students to "describe, explain, analyze, and evaluate information related to: the Declaration of Independence; the United States Constitution; the structure, function, and purpose of the national government; civil liberties and civil rights; participation in civic life and elections."[3]

But such requirements reveal only a partial picture. Many states that mandate civics courses or testing have, at best, an incomplete approach to civic education: Only thirteen states specifically require courses in US government or civics to include instruction on the Constitution and other founding documents.[4]

What is more, required US government or civics courses typically focus on the mechanics of the political process and of civic participation.[5] This approach often fails to link those mechanics to the extended conversation among the founders—and, indeed, among generations of philosophers and citizens—regarding what institutions and practices are necessary to sustain self-government. The best teachers go beyond the standard curriculum to help students connect contemporary political issues to that extended conversation, but many are not equipped to do so.

* * *

Another impediment to effective civic education is that the social studies discipline—including those who design social studies curricula, write textbooks, and implement lesson plans—tends to address the American political system in a way that marginalizes, obscures, and even criticizes its notions of constitutional government.

Consider the 2010 national curriculum standards of the National Council for the Social Studies (NCSS). Rather than emphasize the importance of the Constitution and the enduring national debates over American self-government, the standards present a vision of "civic competence" and outline the "knowledge, skills, and attitudes" required of good citizens. The content areas in which citizens should possess knowledge, according to the standards, include: "culture; time, continuity and change; people, places, and environments; individual development and identity; individuals, groups, and institutions; power, authority, and governance; production, distribution, and consumption; science, technology, and society; global connections; and civic ideals and practices."[6]

The NCSS standards recommend that teachers address the Constitution and other founding documents in the section on "power, authority, and governance" (and some teachers might choose to do so in other content areas). But the standards make clear that instruction on the Constitution and on principles of self-government do not have a central place in the NCSS's approach to civic education.

Then there's the problem that teachers, intentionally or not, commonly discuss the Constitution and the founding era in terms set by its critics, treating the founders' supposed racism, sexism, and elitism as the subjects' essence. This approach is ahistorical, as it condemns the political culture of the late eighteenth century by modern moral standards. The generation of Americans that left us the Declaration of Independence and the Constitution was certainly not perfect. Yet the frame of government they left for the rest of us imperfect men and women still represents the greatest advance in liberty the world had ever seen.

It is particularly harmful for teachers to treat the Founding Fathers as objects of derision rather than study because by doing so, they preclude students from grounding either criticisms or defenses of our civic order in the primary sources of that order's development. Without a solid grounding in the debates of the founding era, which represented the modern world's first major experiment in self-government, students are ill-prepared to understand the challenges of preserving individual liberty under the rule of law.

There is also a strong case to be made that adolescents need to feel some positive attachment to their political community in order to complete their civic and character development. Stanford's William Damon, an expert on child development, has argued against overly critical approaches to the teaching of American history, suggesting that they undermine the goal of preparing students for citizenship. "A positive emotional attachment to a particular community," Damon wrote in 2001, "is a necessary condition for sustained civic engagement in that community."

Damon has argued: "For full participatory citizenship in a democratic society, a student needs to develop a love for the particular society, including its historical legacy and cultural traditions." Damon does not call for blind attachment to the historical legacy of our founding. He writes, "The capacity for constructive criticism is an essential requirement for civic engagement in a democratic society; but in the course of intellectual development, this capacity must build upon a prior sympathetic understanding of that which is being criticized."[7]

* * *

An increasingly common component of civic education curricula is what's known as "service learning." As defined by the NCSS, service learning "connects meaningful service in the school or community with academic learning and civic responsibility." As opposed to mere community service or volunteerism, service learning is supposed to be "integrated with academic skills and content."

According to the NCSS, quality service learning activities: "Engage students in both meaningful service and essential social studies content; Provide opportunities for reflection on the service experience and the connections between this experience, democratic values, and citizenship; [and] focus on change rather than charity, enabling students to question prevailing norms and develop new ideas for creating a more just and equitable society."[8]

"Of equal importance," advises the NCSS, "is the attempt to solve community problems, meet human and environmental needs, and advocate for changes in policies and laws to promote the common good. Through addressing real-life problems in their communities, students are challenged to work together to exercise the rights and responsibilities of democratic citizenship."[9]

Research on service learning programs has documented a number of benefits to participating students, including increased academic interest and attainment,[10] but these are not a panacea. Schools (and parents) often confuse service learning, with its requirement that service activities be embedded within an academic curriculum, with mere community service. One 2004 study found that two-thirds of schools offer community service programs, but only 28 percent of schools offer structured service learning programs.[11] Thus many classes engage students in various kinds of service that may purport to advance their civic education but do not actually amount to substantive civic learning. Such community service doubtless has value, but it risks crowding out more serious instruction.

More troublesome are service learning programs that may convey incorrect or incomplete messages about civic and political life. At the National Service-Learning Clearinghouse of the Corporation for National and Community Service (at http://www.servicelearning.org), one project offered as a model is a "Hunger Banquet." In this program, designed by OxFam America, students organize a banquet at which guests draw lots: 15 percent of guests, representing the world's rich, get to eat a full meal; 35 percent of guests eat a dinner of rice and beans; and the remaining 50 percent of guests get only a small portion of rice and water.

The stated goal of the Hunger Banquet is to ensure that students are "motivated to take action in light of the information presented." A secondary goal is for students to "celebrate the event by raising money for one of the many projects OxFam America sponsors."[12] These are valuable goals, as students should understand global problems of hunger and disease. But the banquet, like other service learning programs, encourages students to see the world in rather unsophisticated terms of injustice and inequality. Nowhere, for example, does the banquet mention the obvious fact that the world's most prosperous nations are those with constitutional governments patterned after our own.

* * *

In working with tens of thousands of social studies teachers, the Bill of Rights Institute has seen that teachers generally display deep appreciation for the liberties we enjoy as Americans. They work to connect students with American history and to help them find their place in American society. Despite their motivation and commitment to America's ideals and constitutional principles, however, many are unable to offer students a strong case for why it is important to understand the Constitution.

Some teachers report that they are intimidated by the language of colonial-era documents, and many note their reluctance to teach about documents that they themselves never properly studied. In this way, our neglect of civic education in previous generations begets a continuing neglect of civic education today.

Organizations like the Bill of Rights Institute work to enhance teachers' knowledge of the Constitution and the founding era, yet it is becoming increasingly difficult for teachers to take advantage of the professional development opportunities available to them. Civic educators are losing funding to their colleagues in the so-called STEM subjects (science, technology, engineering, and mathematics) and English. The social studies teachers who participate in our programs frequently report that their colleagues in other fields receive substantially more funding for professional development training—indeed, participants often have to pay out of their own pockets for substitute teachers to cover for them in their absence.

Civic education is not wanting for educators who desire to teach the founding documents, the liberties they protect, and the civic dispositions necessary to sustain them. The gaps we must address concern access to excellent materials and quality professional development opportunities. Preparing the next generation for responsible citizenship has always been the central mission of schools, but we will continue to falter until educators can deepen their knowledge—and break free from teaching strategies, curriculum frameworks, and testing schemes that marginalize knowledge of the founding era and its principles.

NOTES

1. Education Commission of the States, "High School Graduation Requirements—Citizenship," last modified March 2010, http://mb2.ecs.org/reports/Report.aspx?id=115.

2. Education Commission of the States, "High School Graduation Requirements."

3. Georgia Department of Education, "Georgia High School Graduation Tests: Test Content Description Based on the Georgia Performance Standards—Social Studies," September 2009, http://www.doe.k12.ga.us.

4. According to the Georgia Department of Education, those states are Alabama, Arizona, Illinois, Indiana, Kansas, Maine, Missouri, New Mexico, North Carolina, Ohio, South Carolina, Washington, and Wyoming.

5. Education Commission of the States, "High School Graduation Requirements."

6. National Council for the Social Studies, *Expectations of Excellence: Curriculum Standards for Social Studies* (Silver Spring, MD: National Council for the Social Studies, 2010).

7. William M. Damon, "To Not Fade Away: Restoring Civil Identity among the Young," in *Making Good Citizens: Education and Civil Society*, eds. Diane Ravitch and Joseph P. Viteritti (New Haven, CT: Yale University Press, 2001), 135. Damon grounds these claims in a broader approach to character education: "My argument is that consistent moral action requires commitment; commitment is a function of identity; and identity is the way a person organizes all the personal identifications, ideas, and feelings that have continuing importance in the person's life. Hence the importance of fostering a positive emotional attachment to a community, a sense that 'I care about the community in the way that I care about myself,' if we are to expect sustained moral action on its behalf."

8. National Council for the Social Studies, "Service-Learning: An Essential Component of Citizenship Education," last modified 2007, http://www.socialstudies.org/positions/service-learning.

9. National Council for the Social Studies, "Service-Learning."

10. An extensive overview of research can be found at the Corporation for National and Community Service's National Service-Learning Clearinghouse, http://www.servicelearning.org/instant_info/fact_sheets/k-12_facts/impacts/.

11. Peter C. Scales and Eugene C. Roehlkepartain, "Community Service and Service-Learning in US Public Schools, 2004: Findings from a National Survey," National Youth Leadership Council, 2004, http://www.search-institute.org/system/files/2004G2GCompleteSurvey.pdf.

12. National Service-Learning Clearinghouse, "Service-Learning Ideas and Curricular Examples: Hunger Banquet," http://www.servicelearning.org/slice/resource/hunger-banquet.

Chapter Fourteen

Teaching Political Sophistication

On Self-Interest and the Common Good

Charles N. Quigley and Charles F. Bahmueller

So drives Self-love, thro' just and thro' unjust,
To one man's power ambition, lucre, lust:
The same Self-love in all becomes the cause
Of what restrains him, government and laws.
For, what one likes if others like as well,
What serves one will, when many wills rebel?
How shall he keep what, sleeping or awake,
A weaker may surprise, a stronger take?
His safety must his liberty restrain:
All join to guard what each desires to gain.
Forc'd into virtue thus by self-defence,
Ev'n kings learn'd justice and benevolence:
Self-love forsook the path it first pursued,
And found the private in the public good.
—Alexander Pope, "Essay on Man" (1732–34)

Two principal philosophical sources of American political ideals and institutions can be termed "republicanism" and "liberalism." The former derives from ancient Greece and Rome, which emphasized the common good as the purpose of government and the necessity, therefore, for civic virtue and self-sacrifice. The latter refers to the political thought of early modern thinkers such as John Locke, who argued that the purpose of government is to protect certain fundamental rights of individuals. These rights permit and thus legitimate the pursuit of self-interest (within legal boundaries).

127

Republicanism entails a commonality principle pointing to the public (or common) good; liberalism entails an individuality principle that emphasizes the rights of individuals to pursue happiness within wide limits. The first term suggests our interdependence, the second our independence from each other; an American citizen's entitlement to fundamental rights is independent of others' consent. Republicanism and liberalism thus coexist in a state of tension. Civic education must incorporate both sets of these traditional American ideas, a defense of which is incorporated into the nation's founding documents.

Civic education curricula should foster in students the ability to evaluate alternative views of the common good and of self-interest and to decide which public policies and candidates for public office are best suited to serving them. Students should be taught to assess critically—and not to take at face value—political messages that claim to address their interests and serve the public good. Educators often speak of the need for "critical thinking" among students; evaluating political messages and what purports to be accurate, relevant information is precisely where techniques of critical thinking can be put to use.

* * *

Students cannot function adequately as citizens without being able to see how public policy affects their personal interests and the common good. Yet there is abundant evidence that portions of the American population lack the sophistication to evaluate political messages. Some are awash in outlandish conspiracy theories and other political irrationalism. A civic education reconfigured to elicit more sophisticated responses to political communications of all kinds could protect future generations from the political malaise and social distempers to which these trends—shrill, simplistic, partisan debate and occasional outright irrationality—may give rise.

Curricular programs could begin by exposing students to various thinkers' definitions of "self-interest" and "common good." Such study could begin in elementary school and become gradually more sophisticated over time.

The political scientists David O. Sears and Carolyn L. Funk have defined a self-interested approach to politics as one rooted in rationality, materialism, and egoism that focuses on a public policy's potential short- to medium-term impact on the well-being of oneself or one's family.[1]

Although self-interest is a strong force in democratic politics, the research of Sears and Funk suggests that individuals often set aside their immediate self-interest, instead taking socially rational positions in favor of other values, such as regard for the common good. Voters appear to be less selfish than writers such as Thomas Hobbes and Jeremy Bentham thought. After reviewing hundreds of studies, Sears and Funk write that the "conclusion is quite clear: self-interest ordinarily does not have much effect upon the ordinary citizen's socio-political attitudes."[2] Thus many people who are economically secure support aid for at-risk children, publicly subsidized housing, and unemployment insurance, even though such programs do not offer material benefits to themselves or to their families.

Such people may do so out of a desire to live in a compassionate society that nurtures the growth and development of young people and cares for the less fortunate.[3] Many Americans are also concerned about government budget deficits from entitlement programs, the national debt, the potential for high inflation, and the fact that much of the nation's debt is in foreign hands.[4] In such cases, Americans appear motivated by concern for the public good. As in Pope's "Essay on Man," they find "the private in the public good." Instead of narrow self-interest, as defined by Sears and Funk, other values and interests predominate.

Sears and Funk present four broad explanations for the weak effects of individual economic self-interest. First, relevance: Voters often do not see issues of government policy or candidate choices as important to them personally, "as having important personal benefits and costs."

Second, individual responsibility: Because of what Sears and Funk call "the illusion of control" or "the ethic of self-reliance," many people attribute their personal circumstances to their own behavior, over which they feel they have control, rather than to external factors such as government policy.

Third, symbolic politics: Citizens are often predisposed to respond reflexively to political symbols that influence their choices more than strict considerations of economic self-interest do. Such symbols can be words or phrases that represent political flashpoints, such as "immigration reform" or "abortion." Such symbols are prevalent and potent because politicians, activists, and even journalists have incentives to condense political issues into simplified slogans that suit their interpretation of complex issues or resonate with certain voting blocs.[5]

And fourth, public regardingness: Voters may view matters of public policy in terms other than personal self-interest because they are "politically socialized to respond to public issues in a principled and public-regarding manner." Even proponents of rational choice theory admit that, as the scholar Anthony Downs wrote, "men are not always selfish, even in politics. They frequently do what appears to be individually 'irrational' because they believe it is socially rational."[6] Sears and Funk argue: "People may have been taught to weigh most heavily the collective good when they don their 'political hats,' and to weigh their private good most heavily only when dealing with their personal affairs."[7]

These four explanations for the weak effects of individual economic self-interest might (with modifications according to age level, of course) offer a starting point for critical curricular discussions of self-interest and civic behavior.

Yet self-interest is not just a matter of individual voting behavior. As the economist Robert Samuelson has written: "We face a choice between a society where people accept modest sacrifices for a common good or a more contentious society where groups selfishly project their own benefits."[8] Groups do so principally through lobbyists and election committees that contribute money to candidates' reelection coffers. Such organized groups represent the great majority of Americans in what might be called functional or occupational representation, by which associations act in the interests of certain workers or industries. Lobbying groups have considerable influence on legislation throughout the nation. Many are designated as "special interests" because, although they frequently attempt to deny or disguise it, they act primarily for the welfare of their members, whatever the effects on the common good.

Since it frequently presses the cause of self-interest to the detriment of the common good—such as by ensuring large budget deficits—functional representation should be part of the discussion in civic education curricula.

* * *

Having introduced the concept of self-interest, civic education curricula should examine conflicting views of the common good. Such study might begin with the historical roots of the term in ancient Greece, where Plato and Aristotle agreed that a just social order and political stability are essential for the common good but differed widely on how to achieve it, and in republican

Rome, where Cicero, Cato the Elder, and others taught that the interests of the republic—the common good—should be placed above those of the individual.

After the Middle Ages, in the fifteenth and sixteenth centuries, devotion to the common good was resurrected in the civic republican culture of northern Italian city-states. Thus the ardent republican Niccolo Machiavelli found the civic autonomy of his beloved Florence essential to its common good. He insisted that the city-state could be effectively defended only by loyal citizen soldiers, not hirelings.

The civic ideals of the Renaissance greatly influenced seventeenth-century English republicanism—and the American variety that it spawned. Thus Alexander Hamilton, James Madison, and John Jay mentioned the common good (called the "public good" or similar terms) some thirty-eight times in *The Federalist* of 1788. They defined the concept in one place as "the real welfare of the people" and elsewhere as the "object of government" and "the standard of political decision."[9]

After surveying such historical understandings, curricula should examine what questions arise from different understandings of the common good. One might inquire, for example, into the moral and practical consequences of society understanding the common good as whatever promotes the well-being of 51 percent of a people, as a perhaps crude common sense notion might have it; or whatever yields the "greatest good for the greatest number of people," as argued by the utilitarian philosopher Jeremy Bentham; or another inclusive concept, such as the "good of society as a whole," which is often associated with Catholic philosophy.

As these few examples reveal, the idea of the common good is complex and contested. There is no "correct" definition to impart to students. And besides the problems of *defining* the common good, *achieving* it involves overcoming a parallel set of difficulties. Indeed, philosophers at Santa Clara University have identified a number of complexities surrounding this concept.[10]

First, different groups—religious denominations and ethical societies, for example—have conflicting views of "what is worthwhile or what constitutes 'the good life for human beings.'" The Catholic tradition, for example, conceives of the common good as "the sum of those conditions of social life which allow social groups and their individual members relatively thorough and ready access to their own fulfillment." The late political philosopher John Rawls, meanwhile, defined the common good as "certain general conditions that are . . . equally to everyone's advantage."[11]

The concept of the common good, therefore, might be "inconsistent with a pluralistic society such as ours" because "different people have different ideas about what is worthwhile or what constitutes 'the good life for human beings.'" Inevitably, if public policy choices are to be made, one notion of the common good must be adopted to the exclusion of others.[12]

Second, there is the "free rider" problem.[13] If public goods such as clean air and water are available to all, then they are available even to those who do not undertake any sacrifice of personal interest (such as paying taxes). Those evading sacrifice are "free riders." If enough people become free riders, goods depending on their support will disappear.

Third is the problem of individualism. According to the individualist mentality popular in America, society is composed of independent individuals free to pursue their own goals and interests without interference from others. Such cultural predispositions make it difficult to convince individuals to forgo some personal freedom for the common good. And forcing them to do so, of course, may constitute an abridgement of constitutionally guaranteed rights.

A final problem is that pursuing some versions of the common good requires an unequal sharing of burdens. For example, minimizing pollution may require businesses to install expensive devices that reduce profits, and making health care affordable may require insurers to charge lower premiums, thereby lowering the income of shareholders and the salaries of physicians. And any coercive public policies in the name of the common good, such as requiring those with costly diseases to forgo vital medical treatment, may lead to resistance from citizens.

The ethicists Claire Andre and Manuel Velasquez have concluded that, despite these considerable problems, citizens should continue to reflect on broad questions concerning the kind of society they desire and how to achieve it. They also challenge Americans to view themselves as members of the same community and, while respecting and valuing the freedom of individuals to pursue their own goals, to recognize and further goals shared in common.[14]

All this means that, in treating the common good, curricula should expose students to its rich historical background, various complexities, and many different interpretations by philosophers and governments. Some goods are

nearly universally accepted as part of the common good, including the pre-
vention or halting of disease epidemics, the protection of clean air and water,
the defense of the realm, and the like. But conflicting views about the common good's wider meaning, and how to achieve it, make it necessary for
students to think for themselves about how to consider the concept when
fulfilling their civic responsibilities.

* * *

In a 2009 article, University of California at Davis professor Benjamin Highton assessed "political sophistication," a term encompassing awareness, expertise, and knowledge of political matters. "Political sophistication," Highton wrote, "facilitates the development and stability of public opinion; it
enables people to connect their values and interests to their opinions and
behaviors; awareness leads to the acquisition of new information from the
political environment; and political knowledge promotes civic virtues like
tolerance and political participation."[15]

Highton decried the fact that political sophistication is found more frequently among the "better educated, the wealthy, whites, and males" than
among the "less educated, less financially secure, nonwhite, and female." He
concluded that the most important factors in generating political sophistication are "cognitive ability, parental characteristics, and pre-adult (pre-col-
lege) political engagement."[16]

Mills College researchers Joseph Kahne and Ellen Middaugh have found
that students' access to civic learning opportunities varies based on their
race, their academic track (precollege or prevocational training), and their
school's socioeconomic status. High school students who are white, college-
bound, and attend wealthier schools receive more of these opportunities than
do low-income students and students of color. And rather than helping to
equalize students' capacities for democratic participation, schools appear to
be exacerbating inequality by providing more preparation for those who are
already likely to attain a disproportionate amount of civic and political
voice.[17]

In such an environment, well-designed and implemented civic education
programs are essential for fostering sophisticated interpretation of political
messages. Such programs should seek to help youth understand the relevance
of public policy and candidate choices to their lives; evaluate the proper role
of government in society; become aware of how political symbols often aim

to displace well-founded argument; and take reasoned positions on matters of self-interest and the common good. Dealing effectively with such matters requires systematic, explicit attention throughout elementary and secondary education—much more attention than American schools have devoted over the past decades.

As the University of California researchers M. Kent Jennings and Laura Stoker have demonstrated, students who develop an interest in politics and a desire to participate in public affairs typically do so before they reach college age.[18] This finding emphasizes the urgency of providing civic education early, especially for non-college-bound youth. Those who go on to college differ markedly from those who do not, as a college education "promotes a more cosmopolitan, secular, and politically tolerant outlook"; "enhances cognitive sophistication"; "inculcates civic dispositions"; and has "salutary effects" on political participation and ideological sophistication.[19]

* * *

Although there is an increasingly vocal movement to improve civic education in the United States, no widely used programs address the development of students' abilities to: reflect upon their interests and the common good (however defined) and identify desirable public policies, candidates, officeholders, and social arrangements accordingly; resolve conflicts between their immediate private interests and the common good; or examine and evaluate a range of ideas concerning the proper role of government in society, including an identification of the implications of these positions for their individual interests and the common good.

Civic education programs should foster these capacities. But educators must acknowledge that there are widely differing views regarding matters of self-interest and the common good. Education therefore seeks to direct students not toward particular opinions or answers, but toward the ability to think critically about these important issues.

Regarding the "free rider" problem, for example, curricula could draw attention to those who refuse to sacrifice private interests (such as profit or convenience) for public goods (such as clean water and air), since they can enjoy the benefits of others' sacrifices without sacrificing in any way themselves. Students must not be preached to in these circumstances but made conscious of free rider problems and their implications for leading an ethical life.

The following are examples of questions that might be used to direct student inquiry, discussion, and debate in order to cultivate civic sophistication: What social, economic, and political benefits and/or opportunities do you think should be provided or facilitated by government? Which ones should be provided or facilitated solely by civil society? What benefits and costs may come from government providing such benefits instead of civil society? What social, economic, or political benefits would accrue to you (or your family) if your position prevailed? What benefits would accrue to society at large? How important are these various benefits to you? Does the attainment of your self-interest conflict with the common good? If so, how does this influence your decisions about public policies?

Answering such questions, students might question the *degree* of conflict between personal interest and the public good and the *relative importance* of each in particular instances. Citizens would be far more willing to sacrifice their personal interest for an overwhelmingly important public good than for something relatively unimportant.

* * *

Among the principal ideological currents that influenced the American founding, republicanism emphasizes the common (or public) good, while liberalism emphasizes individual rights and the pursuit of self-interest. The first is the *unum* of our polity; the other is its *pluribus*. As such, the critical study of both the meaning of the common good and the legitimacy of pursuing self-interest—and the inherent tension between them—requires attention in American curricula.

The goal of civic education is to foster in students the will and capacity to reflect deeply on the matter and spirit of public affairs—and, ultimately, to act accordingly as citizens. Citizens are called on to consider how to promote the policies and conditions that underwrite the nation's well-being, while not abandoning the interests of "self"—not only as individuals, but also as families and communities. And citizens do so while living amid the distractions and compromises of civic life and personal affairs.

This is a tall order. It requires extensive preparation to act not simply in light of aspiration and expediency, but under the searchlight of the animating ideas and central features of American democracy—that is, to preserve the balance between personal desire and civic conscience, and to "[find] the private in the public good."

Civic education cannot direct citizens-in-training to the "correct" answers in the tug of war we have been considering. These difficult questions are the business of civic educators to ask but not to answer. Teachers must understand that if they guide students into the stagnant waters of ideological certainty, they betray the principles of their calling and craft. But civic education can develop the intellectual tools that citizens require to practice self-defense against the toxic elements of public life that too often trigger emotive reaction instead of thoughtful consideration.

NOTES

The authors are grateful to Dr. Margaret Stimmann Branson, Dr. Suzanne Soule, John Hale, Maria Gallo, David Hargrove, Mark Gage, and Jennifer Nairne for their assistance in writing this chapter.

1. David O. Sears and Carolyn L. Funk, "The Role of Self-Interest in Social and Political Attitudes," *Advances in Experimental Social Psychology* 24 (1991): 2–5. Sears and Funk draw on the conclusions of more than 250 studies.

2. Sears and Funk, "The Role of Self-Interest," 76. The authors do qualify this finding: "We should not be taken to claim that self-interest is never important in politics and society," 78.

3. Regarding "communitarianism," see the works of political philosopher Amitai Etzioni.

4. It is notable, however, that in a 2006 poll, only 9 percent of respondents said they were willing to pay an additional tax of $2,479 to eliminate the deficit and balance the budget; 79 percent said they were unwilling. See Scott A. Hodge and Andrew Chamberlain, "2006 Annual Survey on US Attitudes on Tax and Wealth," Tax Foundation, April 5, 2006, http://www.taxfoundation.org/blog/show/1418.html.

5. Sears and Funk, "The Role of Self-Interest," 13–15.

6. Anthony Downs, *An Economic Theory of Democracy* (New York: Harper & Row, 1957), cited in Sears and Funk, "The Role of Self-Interest," 75.

7. Sears and Funk, "The Role of Self-Interest," 75–76.

8. Quoted in Claire Andre and Manuel Velasquez, "The Common Good," *Issues in Ethics* 5, no. 1 (spring 1992).

9. James Madison, Alexander Hamilton, and John Jay, *The Federalist Papers (1788)*, ed. Isaac Kramnick (New York: Penguin Books, 1987).

10. Andre and Velasquez, "The Common Good."

11. Andre and Velasquez, "The Common Good."

12. Andre and Velasquez, "The Common Good."

13. The classic work on the "free-rider" problem is Mancur Olson, *The Logic of Collective Action: Public Goods and the Theory of Groups* (Cambridge, MA: Harvard University Press, 1965).

14. Andre and Velasquez, "The Common Good."

15. Benjamin Highton, "Revisiting the Relationship between Education Attainment and Political Sophistication," *Journal of Politics* 71, no. 4 (October 2009): 1564–76.

16. Highton, "Revisiting the Relationship." See also Richard G. Niemi and Jane Junn, *Civic Education: What Makes Students Learn* (New Haven, CT: Yale University Press, 1998).

17. Joseph Kahne and E. Middaugh, "High Quality Civic Education: What Is It and Who Gets It?" *Social Education* 72, no. 1 (2008): 34–39.

18. M. Kent Jennings and Laura Stoker, "Another and Longer Look at the Impact of Higher Education on Political Involvement and Attitudes" (paper prepared for delivery at the Midwest Political Science Association Convention, Chicago, April 3–6, 2008), 18.

19. Jennings and Stoker, "Another and Longer Look," 23, 30.

IV

Among the Ivory Towers— Fighting Civic Neglect on Campus

Chapter Fifteen

Good History and Good Citizens

*Howard Zinn, Woodrow Wilson, and
the Historian's Purpose*

Michael Kazin

What kind of historical works might encourage us to become better citizens? There is no single or simple answer. Readers approach studies of the past with different levels of knowledge, sophistication, and interest. And merely being informed does not guarantee that one will put that knowledge to beneficial ends. Hitler and Stalin were both keen students of the past.

Writers and readers of history do share one characteristic: Consciously or not, they all adhere to the maxim that history is what the present wants to know about the past. Contemporaries inevitably view what happened through a lens crafted by the ideologies, events, and institutions of their own times. Thus, all worthwhile history is "revisionist": The discipline remains fresh only because historians discover something original to say about the past— either based on original research, on a new way of seeing old subjects, or both. Successful teachers, meanwhile, prepare their lessons conscious of the ideas and assumptions that students bring into the classroom. The past may be a foreign country, but when we visit it, we have no alternative but to wear the clothes and speak the language of our contemporary habitat.

After traveling into that vanished world, some historians produce works that increase readers' appreciation and understanding; others only reinforce what citizens already believe. The first group nudges Americans to empathize with people of previous generations and to debate the choices they made; the second avoids unsettling prejudices or questioning narratives that readers already have in their minds. Wise historians help to further what should be the main purpose of civic education: to revitalize democracy, to give American students a sense that self-government can be intellectually engrossing as well as the best way to serve their interests.

In the 1920s, the philosopher John Dewey and the philosophically minded journalist Walter Lippmann debated a vitally important question: Are ordinary citizens competent to understand the problems of a modern industrial society and to aid politicians in taking responsible steps toward solving them? Lippmann argued that most people thought of public life in terms of stereotypes, which made them easy prey for candidates and office holders who knew how to manipulate clichéd words and images. It would be better, he wrote, to leave governance to trained experts and those politicians willing to take their advice.

Dewey conceded that most people lacked the knowledge required to make good policy in a complex modern society. But he disagreed that decisions pivotal to their future should be made without their participation and assent. What was needed was a style of pedagogy, both in schools and beyond, that encouraged critical thinking and a vigorous debate about alternative choices. Teachers, the press, and public figures should all, wrote Dewey, "cultivate the habit of suspended judgment, of skepticism, of desire for evidence, of appeal to observation rather than sentiment, discussion rather than bias, inquiry rather than conventional idealizations."[1] In so doing, they could help construct a "Great Community" whose deliberations would lead to better governance and a more dynamic democracy.

Unfortunately, some influential historians have offered versions of the past that contain just those flaws that Dewey warned against. Consider how two enormously popular writers, Woodrow Wilson and Howard Zinn, interpreted the Civil War and Reconstruction, one of the most consequential eras in US history. During the years from 1860 to the mid-1870s, Americans suffered more than a million casualties in battle, abolished slavery, ratified three critical amendments to the Constitution, and sped the industrialization of their society. Everyone who lived through those events died long ago, but they persist in popular memory—as demonstrated by frequent reenactments of battles and ongoing debates about whether to honor the Confederacy or condemn it.

* * *

Wilson's *A History of the American People* and Zinn's *A People's History of the United States* have little in common, apart from their similar titles. Wilson's book was first published in 1892, when the future US president was a professor at Princeton University; the tome by Zinn, the long-time radical activist and professor at Boston University, came out in 1980. But each, in its own way, offered an interpretation that cheered one side in a past conflict while disparaging the other. Each work strengthened the barricades between citizens instead of generating insights that might have helped them understand the roots and implications of their differences.

For Wilson, the Civil War was a colossal misunderstanding. In his view, before 1860, most Southerners had no desire to break up the Union, and hardly any Northerners supported abolition. But Abraham Lincoln's "narrow victory" in the four-way election of that year brought to power the Republicans, a party that all of Dixie believed was "bent upon the destruction of the southern system and the defeat of southern interests, even to the point of countenancing and assisting servile insurrection." That was not Lincoln's intention, but such powerful radicals as Secretary of State William Seward refused to entertain any compromise. Then, the attack on Fort Sumter "aroused" both sides to mobilize for war.[2]

Wilson's explanation of what caused the war—hotheads on both sides had gotten their way—aligned with the prevailing wisdom of his time. Slavery, it was thought, had been no reason for Americans to kill one another. Professors from the best colleges, politicians from the major parties, and editors of the leading magazines and newspapers all agreed that most planters had treated their slaves benignly and that regional antagonisms should never have led to bloodshed.

Undergirding these views was the assumption that whites were the superior race. Wilson agreed with the influential Harvard biologist Louis Agassiz that black people were "in natural propensities and mental abilities . . . indolent, playful, sensual, imitative, subservient, good-natured, versatile, unsteady in their purpose, devoted and affectionate" and with the popular historian Ellis Paxson Oberholtzer, who wrote that slaves were "as credulous as children, which in intellect they in many ways resembled." Such statements, which we now consider crudely racist, essentially absolved slave owners of any blame for the conflict, despite Lincoln's statement, in his Second Inaugural, that slavery was "somehow the cause of the war."[3]

For Wilson, the Reconstruction process that followed the Confederate defeat was an even greater outrage than the war itself (which, for all its gore, had at least been an occasion for men to achieve glory by sacrificing their lives for their homelands and their compatriots). In his view, the radical Republicans in Congress and their white henchmen down South manipulated "the easy faith, the simplicity, the idle hopes" of newly liberated blacks to gain power and ill-gotten wealth for themselves. The keystone of their plan was the granting of suffrage to the freedmen while denying it to "the more capable white men." No wonder those white men, "aroused by the mere instinct of self-preservation," joined groups like the Ku Klux Klan "to protect the southern country from some of the ugliest hazards of a time of revolution." Wilson did not praise the Klan's "lawless work," but neither did he condemn it.[4]

There was nothing particularly original in Wilson's best-selling work, which suggests how pervasive its opinions were at the time. Deeming the Civil War and its violent aftermath avoidable helped comfort white citizens who cared a great deal about reconciling with one another and hardly at all about racial injustice. "The Birth of a Nation," D. W. Griffith's cinematically innovative and luridly racist 1915 film about the war and Reconstruction, quoted from Wilson's book. Soon after its release, then president Wilson invited his cabinet officers and their wives to attend a special screening of the film in the White House. Complaints by activists from the recently established National Association for the Advancement of Colored People went unanswered. "I'm Southern but I have very little ease with coloured people or they with me," mused Wilson. "Why is it? For I care enormously about them." On the subject of race, a highly intelligent writer and skillful politician turned into an ignorant fool.[5]

* * *

Unlike Wilson, Howard Zinn had no intention of writing a balanced study. Every work of history, he believed, is a political document. He titled his thick survey *A People's History* so that no reader would wonder about his point of view: "With all its limitations," Zinn wrote of the book, "it is a history disrespectful of governments and respectful of people's movements of resistance."[6]

That judgment, Zinn announced, set his book apart from nearly every other account that Americans were likely to read. "The mountain of history books under which we all stand leans so heavily in the other direction—so tremblingly respectful of states and statesmen and so disrespectful, by inattention, to people's movements—that we need some counterforce to avoid being crushed into submission."[7]

His message has certainly been heard. *A People's History* is the most popular work of history an American leftist has ever written. Thirty years after its first publication, it has gone through five editions and multiple printings, been assigned in thousands of college and high school courses, sold close to two million copies, and made the author a celebrity whose obituary ran in newspapers all over the United States and Western Europe.

But Zinn's vision of the Civil War era is as myopic as Wilson's, albeit with a left-wing populist mote in his eye instead of a racist one. Wilson apologized for the slave owners and sympathized with those Southerners—like his father, a Presbyterian minister—who believed that black soldiers and voters imperiled the civilized order. Zinn, a secular Jew and radical activist, viewed the war and Reconstruction almost solely through the eyes of slaves and freed people. His heroes were black abolitionists like David Walker, Frederick Douglass, and Harriet Tubman, and white radicals like John Brown, who died in a failed attempt to inspire a grand slave revolt.

Morally, Zinn's position was clearly superior to Wilson's, as he understood that slavery depended upon a regime of brutality and soulless profit making that no historian should excuse. But his analysis of the American past smacked of a conspiracy theory. According to Zinn, "99 percent" of Americans have always shared a "commonality" that is profoundly at odds with the interests of their rulers, and that phenomenon is "exactly what the governments of the United States, and the wealthy elite allied to them—from the Founding Fathers to now—have tried their best to prevent." History for Zinn is thus a painful narrative about ordinary folks who kept struggling to achieve equality, democracy, and tolerance, yet somehow were always defeated by a tiny band of rulers whose wiles were matched only by their greed. He described the American Revolution, for example, as a clever device to defeat "potential rebellions and create a consensus of popular support for the rule of a new, privileged leadership."[8]

According to Zinn, the Civil War was just another elaborate confidence game. Soldiers who fought to preserve the Union got duped by "an aura of moral crusade" against slavery that "worked effectively to dim class resentments against the rich and powerful, and turn much of the anger against 'the enemy.'" Soldiers were, in effect, brainwashed into believing that Abraham Lincoln cared deeply about the survival of the Union and the evil of slavery, when the president's true purpose, along with that of the Republican Congress, was to pass laws (such as the creation of a national bank and the funding of a transcontinental railroad) "for the benefit of the rich."[9]

Like most propagandists, Zinn measured individuals according to his own rigid standard of how they should have thought and acted. Thus, he depicted John Brown as an unblemished martyr but saw Lincoln as nothing more than a cautious politician who left slavery alone as long as possible. To explain why the latter's election in 1860 convinced most slaveowners to back secession, Zinn fell back on the old saw, beloved by economic determinists like the historian Charles Beard, that the Civil War was "not a clash of peoples . . . but of elites": Southern planters versus Northern industrialists. Pity the slaves and their abolitionist allies; in their ignorance, they viewed it as a war of liberation and wept when Lincoln was assassinated.[10] Zinn's book is history as cynicism.

But why has *A People's History* attracted so many enthusiastic readers? The unqualified directness of Zinn's prose clearly appeals to his audience. Unlike scholars who aspire to add one or two new bricks to an edifice that has been under construction for decades or even centuries, he brings verbal dynamite to the job. Frederick Douglass once wrote that "To understand, one must stand under." Although Zinn doesn't quote that axiom, the sensibility appears on every page of his book. His fans can supply the corollary themselves: Only the utterly contemptible stand on top.

While Zinn's populist perspective is valuable in a democracy, it neglects the way historical change actually occurs. Those who "stand under" usually improve their lives only when they find allies among those nearer the top (some of whom began at the bottom themselves). For example, Douglass, who was born into slavery, escaped and made himself into a leading spokesman for the abolitionist cause. During the Civil War, he persuaded Abraham Lincoln to allow black men to fight for the Union. Afterwards, he held federal office under several Republican presidents while continuing to advocate for equal rights and equal opportunity. Students who read Zinn's book learn only about Douglass as a heroic agitator against bondage. Such romantic simplicity is a form of civic miseducation, the kind of "idealization" which John Dewey abhorred.

Zinn's popular book does fill an emotional need shaped by our recent past. The years since 1980 have not been good to the American left, a group to which many history teachers, in college and high school, are broadly sympathetic. Three Republicans and two centrist Democrats occupied the White House; conservatives often controlled both houses of Congress; the phantom hope of state socialism vanished almost overnight; and progressive movements spent most of their time struggling to preserve earlier gains instead of daring to envision and fight for new ideas and programs.

In the face of such grimness, *A People's History* offers a certain consolation. "The American system is the most ingenious system of control in world history," wrote Zinn. It uses wealth to "turn those in the 99 percent against one another" and employs war, patriotism, and the National Guard to "absorb and divert" the occasional rebellion. "The people," therefore, cannot win unless and until they make a revolution. But they *can* comprehend the evil of this four-hundred-year-old order—with Zinn's help, of course. And that knowledge will, to an extent, set them free.[11]

* * *

Woodrow Wilson believed that well-born, prosperous white men were better judges of what black Americans needed than were black Americans themselves. Howard Zinn insisted that anyone who gained power in the United States could not have sincerely desired to improve the lives of his (or her) fellow citizens. Both men failed to recognize that, just as the right of free speech is meaningful only if it protects the expression of disagreeable views, so history is most valuable when it seeks to understand the motives and behavior of those whom the historian may retrospectively deplore.

Fortunately, several historians have recently offered more insightful and responsible interpretations of the Civil War and Reconstruction. Their accounts are still, necessarily, subjective. As the historian Allan Nevins observed in 1938, "Facts cannot be selected without some personal conviction as to what is truth . . . and this conviction is a bias." But these valuable works of history explain without condemning. In so doing, they capture something vital about the past as it was lived by people who were convinced that only mass killing could settle their differences.[12]

In *Upon the Altar of the Nation*, Yale University historian Harry S. Stout provides a "moral" history of the Civil War that focuses on the human toll exacted by both sides. Never flinching from describing that carnage in all its gory specificity, Stout forces readers to reflect on three moral questions raised by the Civil War and, for that matter, by all wars: Was the war justified? Was it conducted in a just way? Were other means possible to achieve the same ends?

Stout responds ambivalently to the first two questions but gives a strongly positive answer to the third: "I can only conclude," he writes, "that they [the Union veterans] supported the rightness of the war because at some profound level they believed in Lincoln's characterization of America as the world's last best hope." He adds that "an American civil religion incarnated in the war has continued to sacralize for its citizens the idea of American freedom." Without what Stout calls "a blood sacrifice," this would not have occurred. [13] Clear as this argument is, Stout does not frame his book around it. Neither does he, like Wilson and Zinn, ignore or denigrate countervailing evidence. The result is a study whose own moral seriousness matches the wrenching events it describes and analyzes.

In *What This Cruel War Was Over*, Georgetown University historian Chandra Manning examines what motivated soldiers in the Civil War, both those clad in blue and those in gray. After examining the private correspondence and published reports of thousands of soldiers, she concludes that slavery was the key motivation—on both sides. Few Union soldiers advocated racial equality, but most believed human bondage to be a sin and a threat to a society based on free labor and the promise of economic opportunity. But for Confederate volunteers, explains Manning, the fight to preserve slavery was a fight to preserve "what it meant to be a man": "A true man protected and controlled dependents, which for white Southerners meant that a man competently exercised mastery over blacks (whether or not he owned any) as well as over women and children." For most whites who fought for the Union, the war was a war for "freedom"—but not primarily for the slaves. And Southerners did not have to be slaveholders to be willing to die for a way of life anchored by human bondage. [14]

As a liberal historian writing in the twenty-first century, Manning does not need to declare her sympathy for the Union cause. Her task is to illuminate why so many men who either knew no slaves, as in the North, or who owned none, as in Dixie, volunteered to fight for or against "the peculiar institution." Her work is a model of how to educate a diverse citizenry without playing to the stereotypes offered either by neoabolitionists or by neo-Confederates.

* * *

Compared to Wilson and Zinn, Stout and Manning will reach only a small number of readers. But their works—and others, such as James McPherson's *Battle Cry of Freedom*, a magisterial narrative of the war which has sold over a million copies—combine three qualities essential to any work of history that can further civic education: balanced evidence and argumentation, a passion for making the past come alive, and empathy for actors whose actions we can no longer alter.

Empathy is the key leg on this three-legged stool, the one which makes historical understanding possible. In 1970, the cultural historian Lawrence Levine reflected on the difficulty of grasping the texture and sensibility of a vanished world. He began:

> At some point in his studies (for many historians at *all* points), the historian is faced with a situation where there is little continuity or connection between his own cultural conditioning and expectations and that of his subjects. He is faced with a culture gap that must be bridged both by painstaking historical reconstruction and by a series of imaginative leaps that allow him to perform the central act of empathy—figuratively, to crawl into the skins of his subjects. . . . It is, in fact, the primary function of the historian and gives the study of history much of its excitement and importance. [15]

There is no more useful, humane observation about our craft. Empathy is easy to proclaim but quite difficult to practice. Even with the best intentions, historians find it difficult to avoid slipping in a few paragraphs, sentences, or turns of phrase that put down our subjects for failing to think and act as they *should* have—for not being as enlightened as we imagine ourselves to be.

But empathy, both past and present, is the intellectual essence of a pluralist democracy. To apply it sincerely in scholarship and public life is to advance the ideals that Americans say they cherish.

NOTES

1. John Dewey, "Education as Politics" (1922), quoted in Robert B. Westbrook, *John Dewey and American Democracy* (Ithaca, NY: Cornell University Press, 1991), 313. Dewey was responding to Lippmann's 1922 book *Public Opinion*.

2. Woodrow Wilson, *Division and Reunion* (New York: Longmans, Green, 1923), 208. This is a reprint of sections of Wilson's original work, with additional chapters added by Edward S. Corwin.

3. Quoted in Peter Novick, *That Noble Dream: The "Objectivity Question" and the American Historical Profession* (Cambridge: Cambridge University Press, 1988), 75.

4. Woodrow Wilson, *A History of the American People: Reunion and Nationalization*, vol. 9 (New York: Harper & Brothers, 1918), 18, 50, 58, 60, 62.

5. Quoted in John Milton Cooper Jr., *Woodrow Wilson: A Biography* (New York: Knopf, 2009), 24–25. On the triumph of "reconciliation," see David W. Blight, *Race and Reunion: The Civil War in American Memory* (Cambridge, MA: Harvard University Press, 2001).

6. Howard Zinn, *A People's History of the United States, 1492–Present* (New York: Perennial Classics, 2003), 631.

7. Zinn, *A People's History.*

8. Zinn, *A People's History*, 59, 632. The next few paragraphs are adapted from my article "Howard Zinn's History Lessons," *Dissent* (spring 2004): 81–85.

9. Zinn, *A People's History*, 237, 238.

10. Zinn, *A People's History*, 189.

11. Zinn, *A People's History*, 632, 633.

12. Quoted in Novick, *That Noble Dream*, 238.

13. Harry S. Stout, *Upon the Altar of the Nation: A Moral History of the Civil War* (New York: Penguin, 2006), 458, 459.

14. Chandra Manning, *What This Cruel War Was Over: Soldiers, Slavery, and the Civil War* (New York: Knopf, 2007), 11–12.

15. Lawrence Levine, "The Historian and the Culture Gap," in *The Unpredictable Past: Explorations in American Cultural History* (New York: Oxford University Press, 1993), 14–15. The article was originally published in 1970, which accounts for its exclusive use of the male pronoun.

Chapter Sixteen

Talk Is Cheap

The University and the National Project—A History

John R. Thelin

In 1876, Harvard professor Henry Adams asked an undergraduate what had prompted him to travel from the Midwest to college in New England. The student's matter-of-fact response: "Why, a degree from Harvard is worth money in Chicago!"[1] Then as now, the student's reply strikes both a chord and a nerve in our discussions about the purposes of higher education. In the United States, going to college has long been associated with getting ahead. It is, after all, a leading source of social mobility and, in recent years, has been a hedge against downward mobility.[2] But is that all? Does the collegiate ideal in American life also present students with the rights and responsibilities of citizenship and service for the public good?

Public service and civic education—an institution's deliberate educational programs intended to foster informed participation in activities associated with citizenship—have been central to the mission of American colleges and universities since their founding. Proper civic education, in both the formal curriculum and the extracurriculum, requires students to combine thought with action. Such action might include volunteering and so-called service learning, but community service is not necessarily civic education, as it does not always cultivate the skills and sentiments of citizenship.

Civic education all too often has been a fragile part of higher education. Its fulfillment at colleges has vacillated over time as it has competed with numerous other dimensions of teaching and learning that earn the attention of faculty and students. To examine how American higher education's commitment to civic education has fared over the past century, it is useful to review how collegiate institutions have developed over that time.

* * *

The period around the turn of the twentieth century was the formative era of the modern American university. At the time, the leaders of American higher education were visibly tied to public policy and considered universities tools for serving the national interest. College and university presidents and professors were especially influential in developing the various legislative reforms associated with Progressivism.[3] They were influential and well known as public speakers on such issues as tax reform, the regulation of railroads and banks, the dissolution of industrial trusts, the extension of suffrage, and the formation of merit-based civil service systems in state and federal governments. In metropolitan areas, a university president usually chaired public commissions, served on the city school board, and executed various other responsibilities of civic leadership.

Woodrow Wilson, who taught at Princeton and served as its president before becoming governor of New Jersey and ultimately president of the United States, spoke often of the university's role in the American national project. In an 1896 address at the university, Wilson invoked the heritage of Princetonians who had distinguished themselves as leaders in creating the new United States. He said:

> America has never yet had a season of leisured quiet in which students could seek a life apart without sharp rigours of conscience, or college instructors easily forget that they were training citizens as well as drilling pupils. . . . There is laid upon us the compulsion of the national life. We dare not keep aloof and closet ourselves while a nation comes to its maturity. The days of glad expansion are gone. Our life grows tense and difficult; our resource for the future lies in careful thought, providence, and a wise economy; and the school must be of the nation.[4]

Wilson entitled his address "Princeton in the Nation's Service," which became the university's informal motto.

Some years later, in 1902, Wilson shared a similar vision upon becoming Princeton's president.[5] Noting the emergence of science and engineering as powerful and perhaps uncontrolled forces in American life, Wilson challenged universities to prepare students for roles of national leadership that reined in science and technology to appropriate ends. Undergraduate education, he argued, should not focus on training future doctoral students but on liberal arts, which provide students with the discipline, critical thinking, and values needed for citizenship. "Here in America," he said, "for every man touched with nobility, for every man touched with the spirit of our institutions, social service is the high law of duty, and every American university must square its standards by that law or lack its national title." In closing the address, Wilson said that "In days quiet and troubled alike Princeton has stood for the nation's service, to produce men and patriots. . . . The men who spring from our loins shall take their lineage from the founders of the republic."

Wilson practiced what he preached and served at the heights of public life, personifying the close fit of Progressive-era university leaders and service to country. But civic education was not central to the collegiate culture of the early twentieth century. Rather, cultural touchstones included intercollegiate football and elaborate social events. Students tended toward hedonism over purposeful study and did not aspire to fulfill civic duties.[6] As a student editor at Yale lamented in 1910, "Twenty years ago we had the idea of the lawyer, of the doctor, of the statesman, of the gentleman, of the man of letters, of the soldier. . . . Now everything has conformed to business; everything has been made to pay."[7]

Consider the historian John Davies's commentary about Princeton alumni in the years prior to World War I: "The routine thing for a new Princeton graduate was to try Wall Street—the canyons of Wall Street and the social reaches of Park Avenue offered the great opportunity to the young man on the make." One collegiate icon in the pre–World War I era was Hobey Baker, who excelled in athletics at Princeton and was voted the "most influential" member of his class. When this most influential figure filled out an exit survey upon graduation, he left blank questions about political affiliation and interests in contemporary issues.[8] As one historian observed, college in that era was "carefree, innocent, and fun. . . . Purposeful revolutionizing of society was far from most [students'] minds."[9]

The collegiate fiction of the early twentieth century reflected these characteristics. Says a young Yale graduate in F. Scott Fitzgerald's *The Great Gatsby*, "Everybody I knew was in the bond business, so I suppose it could support one more single man."[10] And in the novelist Louis Auchincloss's *The Rector of Justin*, a midtwentieth-century prep school headmaster notes that for his former students, who had gone on to graduate from prestigious east coast colleges, "Reality was the brokerage house, the corporation law firm, the place on Long Island, the yacht, the right people. . . . School is just another tape for materialism."[11]

The 1936 book *Was College Worth While?* studied the opinions and achievements of the Harvard College class of 1911, with notes on counterparts from Princeton and Yale. Written by John Tunis, a novelist and sportswriter who graduated in Harvard's class of 1911, the book profiled the graduates based on questionnaire data they submitted before their twenty-fifth reunion. Tunis concluded that Harvard, Yale, and Princeton had failed to educate pioneers, leaders, or innovators.

Few alumni had become writers, artists, or public officials; no Harvard graduate from that year had become a mayor, governor, congressman, or state legislator. There were "few who have really given to the common weal," Tunis wrote, adding that he and his classmates had "been badly educated in the fundamental problems of the modern state and few of us have taken the trouble to do anything about it. The majority have lived up to the Harvard tradition of indifference. Of this group of college-trained men, only about 13 per cent claim to have taken any part in civic and political work." Tunis concluded that "the majority of us have done little to improve the political situation except to vote once a year."[12] Roughly half of the alumni did, however, serve in the military during World War I, and six died in uniform.[13]

* * *

Necessity forced colleges and universities to focus on national service during World War I, especially through the Student Army Training Corps. Over the course of the war, 540 campuses transformed themselves into training centers, with more than 125,000 undergraduates inducted into the corps. According to the historian David Levine, this experience "transformed how the American public viewed the campus and how the campus positioned itself with respect to events unfolding outside the college walls."[14]

The timely match paired a federal government and military tooling up for entry into "The Great War" with an academy enthusiastic to help the national effort for wartime victory and peacetime renewal. One reason colleges responded eagerly to calls for service to the national war effort was that, although military enlistments depleted college enrollments, the president

(Woodrow Wilson) and Congress responded with a tune that was music to higher education's ears: Students could serve the national interest by staying enrolled and preparing to be national leaders. The Student Army Training Corps and its subsidies for student enrollments helped colleges survive financially in light of tuition dollars lost to military enlistments—and helped the American campus shed its reputation as an isolated enclave.

The campus came to be viewed as a willing partner that contributed expertise and manpower to the ongoing effort, as well as leadership for the future.

For all its initial popularity, however, the collegiate promise of national wartime service was not without shortfalls and tensions. By 1918, college administrators were concerned that the special training programs had intruded on regular college studies and had asked campuses to respond uncritically to government requests and appeals for patriotism; what had begun as a proud exercise in national service came to be tolerated by academics only as a necessary nuisance.[15]

There was little such equivocation about collegiate service during World War II, when American colleges and universities were core contributors to national efforts in numerous areas. In addition to hosting military training programs, universities contributed facilities and the expertise of their professors. Most conspicuous were the alliances between scientists, military leaders, and government officials aimed at producing new weaponry, as exemplified by the famous Manhattan Project.

Professors also proved invaluable in developing immersion courses in Asian and European languages that previously had little presence in college curricula but had become vital to worldwide military and intelligence operations. Given the great, ad hoc wartime contributions of higher education to national institutions, Congress sought to institutionalize the relationship after the war. This led to the creation of the National Science Foundation and the National Institutes of Health, which remain features of American life today.

Another crucial characteristic of the World War II–era academy was the crystallization of a culture of technical and specialized studies. As former Harvard president Derek Bok has put it, universities embraced "intellect and technical proficiency," not moral education, and they "lost their former status as an important source of moral guidance for the society."[16] In a comparable conclusion, the political theorist Benjamin Barber noted that "by the end of World War II, higher education had begun to professionalize, vocationalize, and specialize in a manner that occluded its civic and democratic mission."[17]

* * *

After World War II, university presidents generally characterized their schools' mission in uncritical terms as serving the "knowledge industry," a term made famous in the 1960s by University of California president Clark Kerr. But campaigns extolling universities' economic impact (supported by federal funding for scientific research, which boomed in the postwar years) tended to obscure—and neglect—many other contributions that universities can and should make, especially in terms of civic education and the formulation of public policy.

"Few leaders in research universities today would make [former Harvard president Charles] Eliot's claim that their fundamental mission is to serve democracy or that they are filled with the democratic spirit," wrote a large group of higher education leaders in the 1999 "Wingspread Declaration on Renewing the Civic Mission of the American Research University." The declaration's signatories noted that modern research universities seek to make themselves "more responsive to the demands of students redefined as customers. Allocations of resources are pushed toward their most remunerative uses with a slighting of other institutional values"—such as the cultivation of engaged citizens. [18]

How does this play out in the early twenty-first century? The influential activist and writer Wendell Berry observed in a 2007 commencement address that "the great and the would-be-great 'research universities,' increasingly formed on the 'industrial model,' no longer make even the pretense of preparing their students for responsible membership in a family, a community, or a polity." [19] One can understand how Berry got that impression, given the realities of university practices.

Interestingly, however, many institutions do indeed emphasize civic education—rhetorically. As one 2006 report noted,

> a recent analysis of more than 300 college and university mission statements, in fact, reveals that 95 percent stipulated social responsibility, community engagement, and public service as their primary purpose—one that recognizes higher education's responsibility to educate students to be engaged citizens of a democratic society and to generate the knowledge necessary for an optimally democratic society. [20]

Contemporary universities that stress social responsibility and community engagement in meaningful ways tend to do so in an internationalist manner, in marked contrast to the approach that prevailed from the early twentieth century through the early Cold War era. At Woodrow Wilson's alma mater, for example, the motto is no longer "Princeton in the Nation's Service" but "Princeton in the Nation's Service and the Service of All Nations."

Many universities today are developing goals, structures, and institutions to transform themselves into so-called global universities. At Columbia University, for example, president Lee Bollinger has established the World Leaders Forum, which invites notable international figures to campus, and the Committee on Global Thought, which aims to "pursue scholarship and generate new curriculum models that help students become better citizens of the world."

Another way that universities have recently tried to bolster their civic performance is by creating new administrative posts such as vice provost for engagement. (A 2008 report of the organization Campus Compact recommended that universities empower a senior administrative office to "promote engaged scholarship that addresses pressing public problems."[21]) But such bureaucratic adjustments do not necessarily lead to substantive improvement.

At the University of Kentucky, for example, where I teach, the provost's 2010 "Academic State of the University" report boasted that the Corporation for National and Community Service had recently named Kentucky to the President's Higher Education Community Service Honor Roll, "a recognition from the highest levels of federal government of the university's commitment to service and civic engagement on campus and in the nation." This sounded good, but what did it mean?

The provost explained in a public presentation that the Office of Engagement had reported over fourteen million instances of university "engagement"—then he immediately stopped his presentation to say, aloud, "That can't be right! Does anyone know what that means?"[22] Upon further consideration, the provost estimated that the Office of Engagement had vastly overcounted, probably because it had included such things as every single patient visit to a university medical clinic. Thus the university seems to have established a measure that was simultaneously everything and nothing—at best, a failed attempt at valuable reform; at worst, a vague tally of business as usual. It was an unfortunate sign of how major universities have obscured their commitments to civic education and national service.

Such a state of affairs leaves the thoughtful observer agnostic—wanting to believe universities' civic-minded claims, but left with reasonable doubt about the soundness of their approach and the efficacy of their practical accomplishments.

NOTES

1. Quoted in Laurence Veysey, *The Emergence of the American University* (Chicago: University of Chicago Press, 1964), 270.

2. Christopher Jencks and David Riesman, *The Academic Revolution* (New York: Doubleday Anchor, 1968).

3. Frederick Rudolph, *The American College and University: A History* (New York: Knopf, 1962), 355–72.

4. Woodrow Wilson, "Princeton in the Nation's Service," October 21, 1896, http://infoshare1.princeton.edu/libraries/firestone/rbsc/mudd/online_ex/wilsonline/indn8nsvc.html.

5. Woodrow Wilson, "Princeton for the Nation's Service," October 25, 1902, http://infoshare1.princeton.edu/libraries/firestone/rbsc/mudd/online_ex/wilsonline/4dn8nsvc.html.

6. Calvin B. T. Lee, *The Campus Scene, 1900–1970: Changing Styles in Undergraduate Life* (New York: David McKay, 1970), 1–22.

7. Owen Johnson, *Stover at Yale* (New York: Frederick Stokes, 1912).

8. John Davies, *The Legend of Hobey Baker* (Boston: Little, Brown, 1966), ix.

9. Lee, *The Campus Scene*, 3.

10. F. Scott Fitzgerald, *The Great Gatsby* (1925; repr., New York: Scribner, 1995), 3.

11. Louis Auchincloss, *The Rector of Justin* (New York: Houghton Mifflin, 1964), 245–46.

12. John R. Tunis, *Was College Worthwhile?* (New York: Harcourt, Brace, 1936), 86–96.

13. *Time*, "Education: Class of 1911," September 14, 1936, http://www.time.com/time/magazine/article/0,9171,756633-1,00.html.

14. David O. Levine, *The American College and the Culture of Aspiration, 1915–1940* (Ithaca, NY: Cornell University Press, 1986), 23–44.

15. Jonathan Frankel, "The Ivory Boot Camp," *Harvard Magazine*, September–October 1991, 71–74.

16. Derek Bok, *Universities and the Future of America* (Durham, NC: Duke University Press, 1990), 68.

17. Benjamin Barber, foreword to *Education for Citizenship*, ed. Grant Reeher and Joseph Cammarano (Lanham, MD: Rowman & Littlefield, 1997), xi.

18. "Wingspread Declaration on Renewing the Civic Mission of the American Research University," June 1999, http://www.compact.org/wp-content/uploads/2009/04/wingspread_declaration.pdf.

19. Quoted in Cheryl Truman, "Wendell Berry Pulling His Personal Papers from UK: Writer Protesting Coal's Influence," *The Lexington (KY) Herald-Leader*, June 23, 2010.

20. Tufts University and Campus Compact, "New Times Demand New Scholarship: Research Universities and Civic Engagement—A Leadership Agenda," 2006, http://www.compact.org/wp-content/uploads/initiatives/research_universities/conference_report.pdf.

21. Campus Compact and others, "New Times Demand New Scholarship II: Research Universities and Civic Engagement—Opportunities and Challenges," February 2007, http://la.ucla.edu/downloads/civic_engagement/NewTimesDemandNewScholarship2.pdf.

22. Report of the Provost, Academic State of the University, Lexington, KY, May 3, 2010.

Chapter Seventeen

Don't Believe the Hype

Young Voters Are Still Disengaged, and
Universities Have Few Incentives to Fix It

Mark Bauerlein

Remember "The Year of the Youth Vote"? That was the title of a January 2008 *Time* magazine story asserting that, "frustrated by feckless Washington, energized by the unscripted, pundit-baffling freedom of a wide-open race, young people are voting in numbers rarely seen since the general election of 1972—the first in which the voting age was lowered to 18."

Many analysts wrote of a growing wave of youth involvement. One February 2008 article in *Salon* carried the subtitle, "Genuinely inspired, the Facebook generation is turning out to vote in record numbers." And in a spring 2008 poll, the Harvard Institute of Politics reported that

> the youth vote (18–29) quadrupled in Tennessee, and approximately tripled in primary and caucus contests in Iowa, Georgia, Missouri, Mississippi, Oklahoma and Texas. Compared to our survey in the Spring of 2004—the year in which turnout by young voters 18 to 24 increased by 31 percent—excitement and interest in the [2008] campaign is significantly more intense.[1]

Yet when final election results came in, those bold projections did not pan out. Young voters did affect the election's outcome, but not because of their high overall turnout. Rather, it was their preference: They went for Barack Obama by an unprecedented margin of two to one. In terms of basic participation, the 2008 youth vote marked a disappointing rise from 2004. Whereas voter turnout for those aged eighteen to twenty-nine had increased from 40 percent in 2000 to 49 percent in 2004, it rose only to 51 percent in 2008.[2] This was not an unprecedented level of youth voter turnout: In 1972 the rate was 55 percent; in 1992, 52 percent; and in 1976, 1980, and 1984, just below 50 percent.[3]

Thus, in spite of preelection hype, energetic get-out-the-youth-vote efforts, critical events affecting the young (including the economy and the wars in Iraq and Afghanistan), and an unusually inspiring candidate, barely half of young voters took the time to head to a polling booth.

Young voters were even less present in state elections a year later. In November 2009, gubernatorial races in Virginia and New Jersey both drew less than 20 percent of voters aged eighteen to twenty-nine. Two months later, a senatorial election in Massachusetts attracted only 15 percent of them. "Three state elections do not necessarily make a national trend," said Peter Levine of the Center for Information and Research on Civic Learning and Engagement, "but there is clearly an issue right now with youth turnout and enthusiasm."[4]

That issue persisted through the 2010 midterm elections, when only about 22 percent of eligible Americans aged eighteen to twenty-nine voted. That was somewhat more young Americans than turned out in the 1998 or 2002 midterm elections, but it was almost identical to the share that voted in 1994 and 2006.[5]

* * *

When assessing the civic *engagement* of the young, commentators rarely mention the civic *knowledge* of the young. In 2008, for example, many reporters wrote often of how web-savvy twentysomethings used social networking tools to support candidates. But few inquired into how much young voters knew about First Amendment freedoms of organization and expression. Journalists reported on youth attitudes toward Sarah Palin but not, for instance, on their memory of other female politicians from the near and far past. Youth are regularly polled about controversial issues such as abortion, but rarely on their understanding of the separation of powers or federalism.

If commentators did measure civic and historical knowledge, they would have little cause for enthusiasm about American civic health. For, on a variety of tests, surveys, and polls administered by public and private organizations, teens and young adults display abysmal levels of learning.

Periodically, the US Department of Education's National Assessment of Educational Progress (NAEP) administers a US history exam to thousands of primary and secondary public school students across the country. When the exam was administered in 2006, only 13 percent of twelfth graders qualified as "advanced" or "proficient"—that is, possessing mastery of the knowledge and skills appropriate for their grade level. Thirty-four percent demonstrated "basic" knowledge, signifying partial mastery, and 53 percent qualified as "below basic." Thus more than half of students failed the exam, and only a few more than one in ten were as knowledgeable as they should have been. When asked to provide one reason why the United States entered the Korean War, only 14 percent provided an "appropriate" response. When shown a photograph of a theater portal with the sign "COLORED ENTRANCE," only 38 percent adequately explained the social policy it represented. And only 13 percent interpreted John Winthrop's "City upon a Hill" speech competently.

NAEP has a civics exam, too, which the government also administered in 2006. Five percent of twelfth graders qualified as having advanced knowledge, 22 percent as proficient, 39 percent as basic, and 34 percent as below basic. Asked to identify the meaning of "Federalism," 57 percent failed to do so. Fully 37 percent did not locate freedom of religion in the First Amendment. Twelfth graders, of course, are generally on the cusp of voting age.

In 2008, the education reform group Common Core surveyed the historical and cultural knowledge of seventeen-year-olds. Only 43 percent could identify the half century in which the Civil War occurred. Half knew that the purpose of *The Federalist Papers* was to win ratification of the Constitution, 51 percent knew that the McCarthy controversies focused on communism, and 67 percent knew that freedom of speech and freedom of religion are guaranteed in the Bill of Rights.[6]

Since 2006, the Intercollegiate Studies Institute has periodically administered a Civic Literacy Test to college students. The test asks about important historical events and civic concepts, the documents of the founding, historical figures such as Susan B. Anthony, and speeches such as Martin Luther King's "I Have a Dream." In 2006, of fourteen thousand college freshmen and seniors across the country, 52 percent of freshmen and 53 percent of seniors failed. "At many colleges, including Brown, Georgetown, and Yale," the 2006 report stated, "seniors know less than freshmen about America's history, government, foreign affairs, and economy."[7]

In a July 2006 study of Americans aged eighteen to twenty-nine by the Pew Research Center for the People and the Press, only 26 percent recognized the name Condi Rice and only 15 percent identified Vladimir Putin.[8] A little more than half, 52 percent, knew that the GOP held the majority in the House of Representatives. All told, only about 15 percent qualified as "attentive" to political, international, and business news. A later study, from October 2009, found that only 40 percent knew that the "public option" is something that refers to health care.[9]

What's worse, youth demonstrate not only ignorance of history and current events but disregard for their study. On the Constitutional Rights Foundation's 2005 California Survey of Civic Education, only 47 percent of twelfth graders agreed that "being actively involved in state and local issues is my responsibility."[10]

In its 2008 American Freshman Survey of 240,000 freshmen or first-time students at 340 colleges, the University of California, Los Angeles's Higher Education Research Institute found that only 36 percent talked "frequently" about politics in 2008—the so-called Year of the Youth Vote. When asked how important it is to keep up with political affairs, only 37 percent answered that it is "essential or very important." In surveys of freshmen conducted by the Higher Education Research Institute in the late 1960s, that figure was in the mid-fifties.[11]

Such findings cast doubt on the civic health of American youth, but they are often overlooked in public commentary. Too many analysts—journalists, politicians, researchers—fail to draw firm connections between civic engagement and civic knowledge. They thereby suggest that it is unimportant for citizens to understand the workings of government or the seminal highs and lows of American history.

* * *

This suggestion is harmful because civic knowledge begets civic engagement. This fact was demonstrated in a 1991 journal article by the political scientist William A. Galston (who later served as a domestic policy advisor to President Bill Clinton). Drawing on data collected by the federal government, the Corporation for National and Community Service, RAND, and other organizations, Galston demonstrated how "civic knowledge promotes political participation." "Unless citizens possess a basic level of civic knowledge—especially concerning political institutions and processes—it is difficult for them to understand political events," he wrote. "The more knowledge citizens have of civic affairs, the less likely they are to experience a generalized mistrust of, or alienation from, public life." [12]

More recent evidence supports the claim that civic knowledge fosters civic engagement. The 2007–2008 Civic Literacy Survey of the Intercollegiate Studies Institute, for instance, found that "students who gain more civic knowledge during college are more likely to vote and engage in other civic activities than students who gain less."

Another important driver of civic engagement is the sense that such engagement is one's duty as a citizen. As CIRCLE reported in 2006,

> young people are also much more likely to vote if they see voting as a duty. Of those ages 20 to 25 who say that voting is their responsibility as citizens, 41% claim *always* to vote and only eight percent say they *never* do. On the other hand, of those who say they vote when it may affect the outcome of an election, 26 percent rarely or never vote. [13]

In a sense, the nonvoter's calculations are understandable. Strictly speaking, one person's vote rarely if ever makes a difference in itself, even in Florida in 2000 or Minnesota in 2008. So why bother—especially since voting takes time and it's cold in November?

Often people vote because they admire (or dislike) a given candidate, or because of how a candidate's policies would affect their paycheck or local schools. But such circumstances come and go. Consistent voters have additional motivations, especially a moral feeling of duty—that voting is the right thing to do, as the CIRCLE study demonstrates. Consistent voters feel a moral impulse to vote; if they don't vote, they feel guilty.

Here is where civic and historical knowledge play a fundamental role. They erect a body of memories, values, and exempla that form an imperative in the minds of citizens. Action follows study. The more people know— about the suffrage movement and the Nineteenth Amendment; the impact of the Berlin Wall; the ruling in *Brown vs. Board of Education*; Benjamin Franklin's statement that the 1787 Constitutional Convention created "a republic . . . if you can keep it"—the more they will consider voting a privilege and a duty. Understanding the American system's achievements, and its peculiarity in world history, heralds the value of liberty and reminds young people that proper citizenship carries abiding responsibilities.

One responsibility is to be knowledgeable of the past and of the principles on which the United States was founded. If the nation is "dedicated to a proposition," as Lincoln said—rather than being only a collection of people within set borders—then those who do not know the proposition are lesser citizens than are those who do.

Another responsibility is to keep watch of elected officials. Because the institutions of federal and state government in the United States are so long-standing and generally stable, young Americans often take their conditions for granted. With broad prosperity and seemingly guaranteed freedoms, young citizens can overlook the policies and officeholders that foster this state of affairs.

James Madison underscored the necessity of a vigilant citizenry in *Federalist No. 51*: "A dependence on the people is, no doubt, the primary control of the government," he wrote, and if the people don't exercise their control responsibly, then government inevitably arrogates too much power to itself. Only the people can check its development and force accountability. This was why the founders guaranteed freedom of the press—not because they admired journalists (they despised them), but because a free press allows citizens to be aware of what happens in the halls of influence.

* * *

If young people are disengaged from their communities and the political process, they are licensed to shirk their duties and form opinions from the unprecedented volume of largely unedifying youth programming that surrounds them today.

Back in 1975, a thirteen-year-old watching television had viewing options that would appear to a contemporary thirteen-year-old as cruelly limited. On the six or seven television channels available were just a few afternoon shows such as *The Electric Company* and a rerun or two of a favorite prime-time show such as *Star Trek*. In the evenings, hardly anything appealed to the teen sensibility. Today, however, with Nickelodeon, PBS for Kids, MTV, the Disney channel, Cartoon Network, and so on, kids always have numerous shows to choose from. Of course, there are also "On Demand" programs and the Internet. Today's adolescent fare crowds out newspapers and news shows, preventing the informal civic learning that took place when youths more frequently overheard Walter Cronkite or listened to their parents discuss the day's news.

Because of their immersion in digital tools, young people are routinely described as tech savvy, as if their facility with the iPhone signals advanced intelligence. In truth, however, several studies report the opposite. In November 2006, for example, the Educational Testing Service surveyed the online research abilities of high school and college students and concluded that "few test takers demonstrated key ICT [information and communications technology] skills."[14]

Another study, published in spring 2010 in *Psychological Science*, found that boys age six to nine who own videogames perform less well on reading and writing tests than those who do not own videogames.[15] Researchers did not attribute the finding to anything debilitating about videogames themselves, but rather to the displacement of time they cause—away from activities that are intellectually stimulating (and more likely to have civic value), and toward hours at the videogame console.

* * *

Unfortunately, universities offer little corrective to the American civic knowledge deficit.

When the American Council of Trustees and Alumni charted general education at one hundred leading colleges and universities in 2009, it discovered that only eleven required students to take a course in US history or government.[16] The absence of US history and government from curricula parallels the decades-long slide of liberal education into preprofessional and vocational training. This is best exemplified by the exploding popularity of the undergraduate business major: From 1997–1998 to 2007–2008, the number of bachelor's degrees in business awarded in the United States rose about 45 percent, from about 232,000 to 335,000. In 2007, degrees in business and management accounted for 21.4 percent of all bachelor's degrees awarded—while the entire "social sciences and history" category collected only 10.7 percent.[17]

Given the correlation between civic knowledge and civic engagement, college professors and administrators underserve students and society if they allow civic learning to wane. Public funds, student loan programs, and federal research monies should obligate those in higher education to plant a citizenship sense in undergraduates, for in most cases young people will never have another opportunity to absorb the materials of the American heritage. And yet governments, both federal and state, fail to devise effective levers for pushing higher education toward that goal.

The result is that administrators, professors, and students have too few incentives to pursue rigorous civic learning. By and large, students and parents seek a concrete monetary payoff after graduation—they focus more on how to land a job and pay bills, than on the Bill of Rights. Employers, for their part, generally seek applicants with particular communications and numeracy skills.

University administrators, meanwhile, have incentives to boost minority enrollment, create more study abroad programs, procure ever more federal research dollars, and raise their school's standing in the annual *US News & World Report* rankings. Improvements in the civic knowledge of undergraduates are difficult to quantify and sound rather pedestrian in an environment that values cutting-edge innovation in itself.

And since professors' salaries and promotions typically depend on published research, they too are generally uninterested in addressing the civic knowledge deficits of undergraduates. Professors face constant pressure to minimize their time with students; every minute spent explaining *Federalist No. 10* to a confused sophomore is a minute taken from finishing that article or book chapter.

* * *

But if Americans do not understand the ideas and principles, heroes and villains, triumphs and catastrophes of the past, they judge the present on present concerns alone. When the time comes to exercise their freedoms, they think only, "Is this good for me? Do I like it?" That is the outcome of civic illiteracy—the opposite of civic duty.

NOTES

1. Harvard University Institute of Politics, "The 14th Biannual Youth Survey on Politics and Public Service: Executive Summary," April 2008, http://www.iop.harvard.edu/Research-Publications/Survey/Spring-2008-Survey/Executive-Summary.

2. Emily Hoban Kirby and Kei Kawashima-Ginsberg, "The Youth Vote in 2008," CIRCLE, August 17, 2009, http://www.civicyouth.org/PopUps/FactSheets/FS_youth_Voting_2008_updated_6.22.pdf.

3. Mark Hugo Lopez et al., "The Youth Vote 2004: With a Historical Look at Youth Voting Patterns, 1972-2004," CIRCLE Working Paper 35, July 2005, http://www.civicyouth.org/PopUps/WorkingPapers/WP35CIRCLE.pdf.

4. CIRCLE, "Massachusetts Senate Election: Youth Turnout Was Just 15%, Compared to 57% for Older Citizens; Young Voters Favored Coakley," January 20, 2010, http://www.civicyouth.org/massachusetts-senate-election-youth-turnout-was-just-15-compared-to-48-for-older-citizens-young-voters-favored-coakley/.

5. CIRCLE, "Reweighted Exit Poll Data Suggest Youth Turnout May Have Reached 22.8%," November 17, 2010, http://www.civicyouth.org/reweighted-exit-poll-data-suggest-youth-turnout-may-have-reached-22-8/?cat_id=6.

6. Frederick M. Hess, "Still at Risk: What Students Don't Know, Even Now," Common Core, 2008, http://www.aei.org/docLib/20080226_CommonCorereport.pdf.

7. Intercollegiate Studies Institute, "Our Fading Heritage: Americans Fail a Basic Test on Their History and Institutions," ISI American Civic Literacy Program, 2008, http://www.americancivicliteracy.org/2008/summary_summary.html.

8. Pew Research Center for the People and the Press, "Online Papers Modestly Boost Newspaper Readership," July 30, 2006, http://people-press.org/2006/07/30/online-papers-modestly-boost-newspaper-readership/.

9. Pew Research Center for the People and the Press, "What Does the Public Know?" October 14, 2009, http://pewresearch.org/pubs/1378/political-news-iq-quiz.

10. California Campaign for the Civic Mission of Schools, "Educating for Democracy: The California Survey of Civic Education," 2005, http://www.civicsurvey.org/civic_survey_final.pdf.

11. Higher Education Research Institute at UCLA, "The American Freshman: National Norms for Fall 2008," research brief, January 2009, http://gseis.ucla.edu/heri/PDFs/pubs/briefs/brief-pr012208-08FreshmanNorms.pdf.

12. William Galston, "Political Knowledge, Political Engagement, and Civic Education," *Annual Review of Political Science* 4 (2001): 217–34.

13. Mark Hugo Lopez et al., "The 2006 Civic and Political Health of the Nation: A Detailed Look at How Youth Participate in Politics and Communities," CIRCLE, October 2006, http://www.civicyouth.org/PopUps/2006_CPHS_Report_update.pdf, 16.

14. Educational Testing Service, "2006 ICT Literacy Assessment Preliminary Findings," 2007, http://www.ets.org/Media/Products/ICT_Literacy/pdf/2006_Preliminary_Findings.pdf.

15. Robert Weis and Brittany C. Cerankosky, "Effects of Video-Game Ownership on Young Boys' Academic and Behavioral Functioning: A Randomized, Controlled Study" *Psychological Science* 21, no. 4 (April 2010): 463–70.

16. American Council of Trustees and Alumni, "What Will They Learn? A Report on General Education Requirements at 100 of the Nation's Leading Colleges and Universities," 2009, https://www.goacta.org/publications/downloads/WhatWillTheyLearnFinal.pdf.

17. US Department of Education, National Center for Education Statistics, "The Condition of Education 2010," June 2010, http://nces.ed.gov/pubs2010/2010028.pdf, table A-41-1.

Chapter Eighteen

Donor Intent

Strategic Philanthropy in Higher Education

Admiral Mike Ratliff

Having risked their lives, fortunes, and sacred honor in a successful effort to achieve self-government, many of America's Founding Fathers spent their postrevolutionary years as part-time educators.

To ground the new country's future leaders in the ideas that had shaped the US founding and the design of its constitutional order, the Founding Fathers built institutions of higher education including Franklin & Marshall College, Dickinson College, the University of Virginia, and more than ten others. They also redesignated and reshaped existing campuses to address the new country's needs: Among others, King's College emerged as Columbia College, and the College of Philadelphia became the University of Pennsylvania. Benjamin Franklin, Thomas Jefferson, Benjamin Rush, and other successful revolutionaries believed that, like themselves, future American leaders needed to appreciate the ideas of John Locke, David Hume, Adam Smith, Montesquieu, and their Greek and Roman predecessors.

In 1998, representatives from colleges and universities that date back to the revolutionary era gathered in Carlisle, Pennsylvania to consider civic education in the twenty-first century. Dr. Lee Fritschler, then president of Dickinson College and later US assistant secretary for postsecondary education, opened the conference by quoting Benjamin Rush. "The business of education has acquired a new complexion by the independence of our country; the form of government we have assumed, has created a new class of duties to every American," said Rush in 1786. "It is only by rendering knowledge universal," Rush said on another occasion, "that a republican form of government can be preserved in our country."[1]

Today, unfortunately, too few Americans appreciate the link between university education and citizenship. For one, many believe that the time for future leaders to receive their civic education is in their K–12 years. Indeed, elementary and secondary education are essential to introducing students to the structure of government and the basic issues of civic life. But there are many reasons why civic education is a necessary element of higher education. First, and perhaps most simply, the knowledge, skills, and sentiments needed to be an informed and engaged citizen must be learned repeatedly, at increasing levels of sophistication and depth, throughout a student's education.

Second, colleges and universities are where the country's future civic and professional leaders concentrate in high numbers, complete their preprofessional education, and begin to establish their adult habits, including civic ones such as voting.

Third, strengthening civic education in higher education will, over time, reshape elementary and secondary education as well. Colleges and universities educate our future K–12 teachers. Those teachers who have experienced a meaningful, serious, high-quality civic education will not only be more likely to teach the subject themselves, but will also be better able to convey the importance of civic education to their peers and their students.

* * *

To be wise and engaged participants in the political process, citizens need a firm grasp of American history—broadly conceived to include our roots in the Judeo-Christian experience, including ancient Greece and Rome—and of political and economic institutions.

In terms of the university curriculum, this translates to the study of history, economics, and political science. (Of course, important education also comes from the study of literature, philosophy, and social sciences.) As former Harvard President Derek Bok concluded in his 2006 volume, *Our Underachieving Colleges*: "The least that colleges can do . . . is to offer their students an intellectual foundation that will enable them to vote and participate in public life as wisely and thoughtfully as possible." Unfortunately, noted Bok, "Barely one-third of undergraduates ever complete an introductory course in American government and politics. Fewer than one in ten study political philosophy or international affairs. More than 40 percent do not even take a basic course in economics." All in all, he wrote "college-educated students today possess only approximately the same levels of political knowledge as high school graduates achieved in the late 1940s."[2]

On campuses across the nation, too few professors teach, and too few students take, courses that cultivate citizenship. As a result, noted the American Political Science Association's Task Force on Civic Education in 1998, "current levels of political knowledge, political engagement, and political enthusiasm are so low as to threaten the vitality and stability of democratic politics in the United States."[3]

Fortunately, there are many people—in the general population and within universities—who are not only concerned that young Americans are inadequately prepared for citizenship, but who are acting to fix the problem. Donors (such as Jack Miller, who founded the center that I lead) are enhancing collegiate civic education by, among other things: providing seed money for new campus programs; supporting young professors seeking to build careers that will offer effective civic education to undergraduates; and creating opportunities for professors, nonprofit leaders, and others to build effective networks dedicated to imparting knowledge and appreciation of the American project. These donors understand that today's campuses are, in some senses, a free market. Courses compete for students, and students can be drawn to demanding courses that will ground them in American history, politics, and economics.

* * *

A growing number of programs provide students with strong civic education—and demonstrate that student interest in such study outstrips current course offerings.

At the University of Virginia, for example, professor James Ceaser and a number of graduate fellows have developed the regularly oversubscribed seminar course the American Political Tradition. Beginning with readings from Aristotle, Plutarch, and Montesquieu, the course focuses on *The Federalist Papers*, Tocqueville's *Democracy in America*, and other central texts. Matthew J. Sitman, a fellow who taught the course in 2009, explained to the *Chronicle of Higher Education*, "We're trying to get the students to think about American politics in a very particular way. . . . The fundamental questions are, What is the nature of the regime? Who rules? What principle sustains the regime? And how is the regime sustained by the sentiments of the people?"[4]

Sidney M. Milkis, the former chair of University of Virginia's Department of Politics, told the *Chronicle*, "When we reviewed the student evaluations, they made clear that students love the course, but also that it's a difficult course. You don't always see that combination." Ceaser has called the course a national model and, indeed, it has recently been taught at the Johns Hopkins University and Amherst College, among other schools.

The University of Texas presents a similar success story. Established by professor Robert Koons and currently directed by professors Lorraine and Thomas Pangle, the university's Thomas Jefferson Center for the Study of Core Texts and Ideas emphasizes major works—of philosophy, religion, history, literature, art, science, and social science—that have distinguished themselves by their influence on subsequent thought or history. Before this new course of study was introduced, University of Texas administrators doubted that there would be significant student demand for such courses. As word of the program spread, however, its courses filled rapidly and demand rose for new ones.

Today, the Thomas Jefferson Center offers about twenty courses each semester, a major in the Great Books, and a six-course certificate program in core texts and ideas that is available to all students at the university. In addition, the center operates a lecture series; an undergraduate book club; Great Books discussion groups for adults in Austin, Dallas, and Houston; and a postdoctoral fellowship that sponsors young scholars committed to the interdisciplinary study and teaching of the core texts.

The University of Virginia and University of Texas are just two of more than one hundred and seventy campuses on which the Jack Miller Center works with professors seeking to enrich education in American history and the ideas that shape our free institutions. Gratifying as these efforts are, however, they are small relative to the size of American higher education; there are thirty-two hundred institutions of higher education in the United States, including approximately twenty-four hundred that award baccalaureate degrees.

Since it is impossible to work on every campus, our center has adopted a strategic and targeted approach to leveraging our limited resources. A basic guiding principle is that, to promote efforts that universities might not have vigorously pursued on their own, it is best to support specific individuals and programs with specific allocations and sustained engagement—strategic philanthropy that recognizes that the higher education landscape is shaped as much by scarce resources as by politics.

The first part of our approach is to invest in talented scholars capable of making a large impact in their fields and institutions. Our primary means of making this investment are by hosting professional development institutes for young faculty and graduate students, and by sponsoring postdoctoral fellowships.

The two-week-long institutes, which take place in summer, are led by renowned faculty from across the country. They give promising young academics an opportunity to participate in seminars on American history, government, and political theory, and to attend workshops that guide them in developing courses, securing tenure, and publishing.

Our postdoctoral fellowships, meanwhile—which are directed by senior scholars from Harvard, Yale, Brown, Georgetown, Emory, Texas, and elsewhere—go to promising academics in the humanities who have recently earned their doctorates and are dedicated to strengthening the teaching of America's founding principles and history. Fellows gain valuable teaching experience and work with some of the leading scholars in the country. Combined, these efforts function as a career development pipeline that is unique in the academic environment.

Because individual professors can only do so much, however, the Miller Center also provides support, including initial seed money, to establish and grow "academic centers" that provide campuses with permanent institutional homes for the study of America's founding principles and history. By drawing on the talents of various faculty members from diverse disciplines, centers can reach a broader range of students than can any single professor or class.

* * *

The Jack Miller Center has adopted strategies for promoting civic education at a wide range of campuses, from the country's great research and public universities to its liberal arts colleges, regional universities, and leading tech campuses.

At top research universities, one of our goals is to revitalize scholarship and programs that prepare the next generation of professors. For example, at Yale University, professors Keith Wrightson and Stephen Smith are seeking

to revitalize the study of the history and theory of Anglo-American constitutional democracy. As they have written, the study of Anglo-American consti-
tutionalism has "lost the central place it once enjoyed in the American academy." Meanwhile, "the study of the constitutional history of early modern
Britain, an essential prologue to the foundation of the American republic, has
become a rarity."[5]

Thus we are supporting the establishment of a pilot center for the study of
representative institutions at Yale. The center's research focus will be the
three civil wars that formed the American conceptions of rights, property,
trade, and liberty: the English parliamentary crises and civil war of the mid-
seventeenth century, the American Revolution of 1776, and the American
Civil War, which culminated in what some call our second founding. The
center will host postdoctoral fellows to teach and conduct research; sponsor a
series of conferences for Yale faculty, Miller postdoctoral fellows, and invited scholars from other campuses; and provide grants for undergraduate and
graduate student research. Taken together, these efforts will encourage scholarship, advance the careers of young scholars, and enrich the environment of
undergraduate and graduate study at Yale and other research universities.

Given their particular educational focus, liberal arts colleges can play a
special role in civic education. They remain the standard bearers for the
approach that views education's aim as the preparation of young citizens to
be wise, engaged participants in free societies. Liberal arts colleges generally
eschew professional education and maintain their focus on the humanities,
including history, politics, economics, and literature.

Many liberal arts colleges offer a so-called Great Books curriculum. One
of the more famous is at St. John's College, which has campuses in Annapo-
lis and Santa Fe and caps enrollment below five hundred students at each.
Another campus that has flourished by highlighting the importance of Great
Books is Pennsylvania's Ursinus College, especially under the leadership of
President John Strassburger, who passed away in 2010. He championed the
Common Intellectual Experience, a two-semester course in which all freshmen read Aristotle, Shakespeare, Adam Smith, Thomas Jefferson, and others. In the course, students learn not just about the ideas that undergird our
political and economic institutions, but they also acquire invaluable skills of
analysis by grappling with important and challenging primary texts—rather
than the broad and superficial summaries too often found in such courses.

This approach has proved extremely popular. During Strassburger's 1995–2010 tenure as president, Ursinus's enrollment grew from eleven hundred to seventeen hundred, *Newsweek*/Kaplan named it one of "America's 25 hottest colleges," and it is rightly considered a model for effective civic education at liberal arts institutions.[6]

Similarly, Christopher Newport University (CNU), in southeastern Virginia, is a model for regional public universities. Thanks to the leadership of its president, Paul Trible, CNU recently enacted Vision 2010, a transformation of its core educational curriculum that included the establishment of a Center for American Studies and Civic Leadership. Vision 2010's goal, says the university, is to prepare "students to lead lives of significance and responsibility in a free, democratic society" and to "connect liberal learning to ethical conduct and civic responsibility."[7] CNU has also redrafted its liberal arts Core Curriculum to reflect this focus on civic responsibility in a democratic society and created a new major and minor in American studies.

CNU's American studies major, first offered in 2006, is the school's first interdisciplinary major. The major's five core courses center on the great "American experiment" in democracy, capitalism, and self-government, allowing students to examine the philosophical and cultural foundations of American life and identity (under the instruction of postdoctoral fellows from the new Center for American Studies and Civic Leadership). The center also organizes an annual conference on civic engagement, a guest speaker series, programs for training and recertifying K–12 teachers, and a Junior Fellows Program for the best undergraduates at CNU.

A particular challenge and opportunity for educators and philanthropists is to design civic education suited for students who study science and engineering, not the humanities or social sciences. Science and engineering programs are often so demanding that they leave little time for study outside of a given technical specialization. Yet scientific progress is so far-reaching that to grapple with it thoughtfully, one must be able to consider matters of law, politics, philosophy, and history.

Professor Bernhardt Trout of the Massachusetts Institute of Technology has taken on this challenge with MIT's Benjamin Franklin Project. As Trout explains, the program includes a lecture series, a working group, and a series of courses focused on fundamental questions of the Founding Fathers that endure today. His first course, Philosophical History of Energy, cross-listed in the departments of chemical engineering and philosophy, will study the writings of Aristotle, Descartes, Newton, and other great thinkers. Trout is planning similar courses on the social, political, and ethical significance of science and engineering. The long-term objective, he says, is to develop a fully sustainable program through which all MIT students can "investigate fundamental issues behind science and technology with an emphasis on the Founding Fathers' vision of science and technology for America."[8]

* * *

We have hardly scratched the surface of what can and must be done. The eighteenth-century gentlemen who gathered in Philadelphia and debated how the new republic should be governed can seem alien to students in the twenty-first century. Even Abraham Lincoln can seem distant and irrelevant. And these figures' grappling with principles such as rule of law, property rights, equality, limits on government, and separation of powers can seem vague and obscure. Professors have a tough task, then, in helping their students connect with America's ongoing experiment in liberty, a conversation that dates back to colonial Philadelphia and before.

Yet it can be done. As Lincoln said in one of his 1858 debates with Senator Stephen Douglas,

> We run our memory back over the pages of history for about eighty-two years, and we . . . find a race of men living in that day whom we claim as our fathers and grandfathers; they were iron men; they fought for the principle that they were contending for. . . . We have—besides these, men descended by blood from our ancestors—among us, perhaps half our people, who are not descendants at all of these men . . . but when they look through that old Declaration of Independence, they find that those old men say that "We hold these truths to be self-evident, that all men are created equal" and then they feel that . . . is the father of all moral principle in them, and that they have a right to claim it as though they were blood of the blood, and flesh of the flesh, of the men who wrote that Declaration.[9]

Helping our future leaders feel that kinship requires the best of our colleges and universities. Of course, some citizens may thrive without a college degree (as Lincoln did). But our leaders will come predominantly from among graduates of colleges and universities—and we must ensure that they graduate as well prepared for citizenship as for their first job.

NOTES

1. Benjamin Rush, "Of the Mode of Education Proper in a Republic," in *The Selected Writings of Benjamin Rush,* ed. Dagobert D. Runes (New York: Philosophical Library, 1947), 87.

2. Derek Bok, *Our Underachieving Colleges: A Candid Look at How Much Students Learn and Why They Should Be Learning More* (Princeton, NJ: Princeton University Press, 2006), 182.

3. American Political Science Association, Task Force on Civic Education in the 21st Century, "Expanded Articulation Statement: A Call for Reactions and Contributions," *PS: Political Science and Politics* 31, no. 3 (September 1998): 636–37.

4. David Glenn, "Private Effort to Create Courses Draws Praise—and Charges of 'Buying' Curricula," *Chronicle of Higher Education*, July 13, 2009.

5. Keith Wrightson and Stephen Smith, writing in a proposal submitted to the Jack Miller Center, 2010.

6. Ursinus College, "Biography of President John Strassburger," http://career.ursinus.edu/ netcommunity/page.aspx?pid=2934. See also Pranay Gupte, "Lunch at the Four Seasons with: John Strassburger," *New York Sun*, April 13, 2006.

7. Christopher Newport University, "Vision 2010," http://www.cnu.edu/about/leadership/ vision2010/index.asp.

8. Bernhardt Trout, writing in a proposal submitted to the Jack Miller Center, 2010.

9. Abraham Lincoln, "Speech in Reply to Douglas at Chicago, Illinois. July 10, 1958," in *Abraham Lincoln: His Speeches and Writings*, ed. Roy P. Basler (Cambridge, MA: Da Capo, 2001), 401.

V

A Vision for the Twenty-First Century

Chapter Nineteen

After the Digital Explosion

Education and Civil Liberties in the Internet Age

Harry Lewis

On July 25, 2009, the secretary of the state of Washington State received a petition signed by 138,500 Washingtonians. Responding to a law that the state legislature had recently enacted, the petition called for a referendum on whether the state should grant certain rights to same-sex domestic partners. In short order, opponents of the petition stated their intention to publish on the web the names of those who had signed it—in an attempt, among other things, to cause petitioners to have "personal and uncomfortable conversations" with fellow citizens.[1] Saying they felt threatened, a group of petitioners sued to block the publication of their names.

The case raised serious questions about constitutional principles and the functioning of American democracy in the twenty-first century. Opponents of the petition argued that publishing the petitioners' identities was in line with principles of open government, for if a petition is a public document then the public should be able to see it. Petitioners argued that representative democracy would be jeopardized if the modest act of signing a petition subjected citizens to the same devastating loss of privacy that already afflicts politicians. Both sides claimed that their freedom of speech lay in the balance.

In June 2010, the Supreme Court ruled by an 8–1 margin that, as a general rule, disclosing the names of petitioners does not violate their freedom of speech. In their opinions on the case, the Court's two most conservative justices, Antonin Scalia and Clarence Thomas, reflected dramatically different viewpoints on the civic impact of the Internet. Scalia called for "civic courage, without which democracy is doomed," and added that he does "not look forward to a society which . . . exercises the direct democracy of initiative and referendum hidden from public scrutiny and protected from the accountability of criticism." Thomas, meanwhile, held with equal conviction that to routinely publish the names of petitioners would chill free speech unacceptably and threaten citizens' "associational right to privacy."[2] The substantial gulf between these two arguments demonstrates how the Internet can upend traditional categories of thought about basic constitutional institutions.

Such debates occur because the Internet has changed the world. Never before could an ordinary citizen publish 138,500 names instantly, at virtually no cost, to be read by anyone—in the state of Washington or anywhere else. In the era of the printing press, a long list of names was impractical to publish and difficult to analyze. Today, publication is essentially free and anyone can search and sort lists of great length.

Although the names and addresses of contributors to presidential campaigns have been public information for decades, contributors today are startled to discover that, thanks to the Internet, anyone in the world can instantly see not only their name and contribution, but a neighborhood map showing exactly where they live.[3] When extremists will post an ominous online list of doctors who perform abortions—using gray font for those who have been wounded in vigilante reprisals and a strikethrough for those who have been killed—politically active citizens can be forgiven for worrying about the new transparency.[4] The Internet expands opportunities for both freedom of information and fear of information. Although it can democratize knowledge and foster civic engagement, it can also facilitate defamation, intimidation, and violence.

Across the world—in Washington State and far beyond—the Internet is forcing governments and citizens to reconsider the meaning of public information in ways that will affect the basic principles of knowledge, speech, and privacy on which the democratic process depends. It is vital, therefore, that Americans understand the Internet not only as a tool, but as a shock to the foundations of civic life and democratic governance.

* * *

The basic ideas of American democracy relate to the role of information and knowledge in society. Among our core principles are that the government should not prevent the people from learning facts and expressing opinions; that the people should be secure against unreasonable searches of their persons, houses, effects, and papers; and that the people should know enough about their government to judge its effectiveness and hold its officials accountable for their conduct of public affairs.

These principles—which amount to the view that the people should know a lot, and the government no more than necessary—motivated a revolution that was as much about access to information as about control of territory.[5] That revolution, and the new nation it created, relied heavily on the printing press, a scarce technology with meager output. Printed words were expensive to produce and to distribute. But in the late twentieth century, with the advent of the personal computer and the Internet, words became ubiquitous, cheaply and instantaneously conveyed across oceans and national borders.

As words have become less expensive, the average quality of public speech has declined. Authors' communications are largely disintermediated; writers blog or tweet directly to curious readers, without assistance from editors or quality control by publishers. The constraints of the printing press once applied pressure to prioritize the good over the bad and the important over the trivial. Such editorial restraint is much weaker today.

Disintermediation has many benefits, not least when it undermines the efforts of censorious governments, such as those in China and Iran, to control information. Diffusion of information lends strength to dissidents. And in the United States, advocates of government transparency have made remarkable progress in publishing on the web information previously accessible only with difficulty. For example, citizens today can easily learn which lobbyists for foreign governments have been meeting their elected representatives (and when and how often).[6] In earlier eras, such information would have been expensive to print, hard to find once recorded, and, given our biennial elections, too quickly stale. Indeed, the mere fact that citizens in their homes can find and read the laws to which they are subject would surely have brought joy to the hearts of Jefferson and Adams.

Yet the same information technologies are also affecting, for the worse, the way we understand the richness of available information. Deep reading of texts—slow, deliberate, noninteractive, immersive reading—seems to be on the decline. In 2009, the National Endowment for the Arts conducted a survey of reading and cheerfully entitled it "Reading on the Rise." But reading was on the rise only over the preceding six years; over the past quarter century, the proportion of young adults reading literature had actually dropped by more than 13 percent.[7] It's possible, of course, that youth today are reading computer screens as intensely as their elders once read bound volumes.[8] Perhaps, while bouncing from link to link, today's readers compensate for diminished profundity with gains in satisfied curiosity. But in 2010, teenagers spent, on average, eight hours per day using online media— and only forty minutes viewing any text.[9] A 2008 British study describes the reading style of today's young scholar: "horizontal, bouncing, checking . . . promiscuous, diverse, and volatile. . . . It almost seems that [readers] go online to avoid reading in the traditional sense."[10]

Yet certain texts are special and require focused study. The US Constitution is one of them. And without the cognitive tools to comprehend the harmonies and tensions implicit in our founding documents, Americans risk being ill-equipped to consider important issues of life and liberty about which self-governing people need a shared understanding.

* * *

Digital technologies raise many questions that place different American values in tension. When the Fourth Amendment protects one's "papers" from unreasonable government searches, for example, does that protection apply to the searches one conducts on Google?

The FBI has in recent years asked Internet service providers (such as Comcast and Verizon) to retain information about users' web browsing for potential government use. If companies were required to keep such information, the FBI argues, authorities could more successfully investigate crimes such as child pornography.[11] Would such an arrangement represent the prudent conduct of law enforcement, or an unconstitutional overreach by the state? And if Internet service providers decided on their own to keep that information, using it to target advertising while simultaneously assisting law enforcement, would the Constitution have any bearing on the matter? The Internet demands thoughtful consideration of such questions,[12] even as it threatens to erode citizens' abilities to address them in an informed fashion.

Another example: The government wants the authority to demand that cellular service providers (such as Sprint and AT&T) hand over data about customers' cell phone locations, even if investigators do not have a warrant.[13] According to the government, this would not be an unreasonable search because individuals freely decide to walk around with cell phones, splattering radio waves all about them. As one US attorney argued, "one who does not wish to disclose his movements need not use a cellular telephone."[14] In a case like this, should citizens push back against government officials, applaud them, or ignore them and let the courts decide?

What about email? Since email resembles both postal mail and telephone calls, it would seem that the government could not retrieve it from service providers without a warrant. Yet a series of federal court cases have come to the opposite conclusion. In March 2010, for example, the US Court of Appeals for the Eleventh Circuit ruled that a person "loses a reasonable expectation of privacy in emails, at least after the email is sent to and received by a third party."[15]

The digital age has not only diffused information but also centralized it, creating bottlenecks that corporations or the government can monitor. One's life would be an open book if the data held by Internet service providers, cellular carriers, and Google were retained and made available to prying eyes. What does the Fourth Amendment dictate in this environment—and should ordinary, law-abiding citizens care? Will the next generation of American citizens have enough critical capacity, knowledge of constitutional principles, and understanding of civil rights to judge such actions of public officials and private corporations?

And as the world becomes increasingly interconnected, will Americans have the understanding necessary to distinguish appropriate US practices from those of other countries with lower standards of privacy? Americans generally have little sense that the state takes note of their actions online. That's not the case in other countries. It takes much less to win a defamation suit in the United Kingdom or Australia than in the United States. In Italy, a court convicted three Google executives of violating privacy laws because in 2006 a group of teenagers beat up a mentally disabled boy and posted a recording of their act on the Google video service.[16]

Seeing this, some American students may think that their country's legal system lacks compassion. That would be understandable if students considered such issues emotionally, empathizing with the victims of verbal or video ridicule and judging that governments should do something to punish the abuse. But what of free speech rights? As the US Supreme Court stated in the 2010 *Citizens United vs. Federal Elections Commission* ruling, the First Amendment is "premised on mistrust of governmental power."[17] Students should understand, then, why those Google executives would not have been convicted of a crime in the United States: The US Constitution, unlike European constitutions, is biased toward protection against abuses of governmental power (like those documented in the Declaration of Independence). [18]

Over time, if neither secondary schools nor colleges preserve historical memory as they educate young citizens, the United States will have great difficulty reconciling its principles and norms with those of other states. Without an understanding of history, citizens will have no way to judge which compromises to make and which to resist.

* * *

Preserving historical memory is especially hard since the written word is in decline as the authoritative means of communication. Video is ascendant.

Visual images hit the brain more directly than written words, which require a two-step process to convey reality: First a writer reduces an experience to symbols, and then a reader uses the symbols to reconstruct the experience. The ascent of video began with the birth of television and accelerated greatly with the Internet, which now allows anybody to be a cinematographer or animator. In the past, amateurs could only write, sketch, or paint. With YouTube at the ready, however, anyone can be a video producer and distributor.

This new dynamic has yielded much admirable creativity, and yet visual communication threatens to crowd out verbal reasoning in the experience of American youth. As of March 2010, US Internet users were watching 31 billion videos per month. YouTube watchers alone—who number 135 million in the United States—averaged about seven hours of YouTube watching per month. [19] This already exceeds the time that the average teenager spends reading, online or offline. [20] And YouTube watching has grown at a rate of about 40 percent annually from a base of essentially zero in 2005.

Words have a special place in the American democracy. The Constitution was the product of a long process of reducing ideas to words, as the founders distilled normative principles from centuries of experience and political philosophy. Almost uniquely in the world, the United States is defined by ideas, not ethnic bonds. Those ideas—let alone the structures of government—cannot usefully be reduced to visual imagery.

America's core ideas are best understood by remaining informed about legislation, voting, engaging neighbors to advocate for change, serving on school boards, and the like—in other words, by engaging with republican government. But educational institutions increasingly characterize civic responsibility and engagement in other terms. Schools—from primary schools to universities, including Harvard, where I have taught since 1974—tend to characterize engaged citizenship in terms of building buildings for the destitute, volunteering in shelters, and generally "making a difference" in the community. Such volunteerism surely benefits all parties, and in the days of No Child Left Behind, we do well to encourage young people to pursue successes more tangible than scores on test papers. Cooperating with peers toward a common social goal broadens students' civic understanding.

However, to the extent that physical activity displaces intellectual engagement with the principles and dilemmas of American democracy, we may regret the hours devoted to hammering nails and organizing charity events instead of to reading and debating. Indeed, there is reason to fear that exactly that displacement is occurring in high schools. A 2003 report of CIRCLE and the Carnegie Corporation showed that "school-based civic education is in decline" at the same time that there is "an increase in the number of young people involved in community service and volunteering."[21]

One can argue that volunteering and service learning enhance students' civic sensitivities. By that standard, community service is not a poor substitute for civic education, but is itself civic education. Yet the decline in students' civic knowledge may suggest that schools have another motivation for substituting service for civics: doing so helps them avoid the complexities of discussing civic matters in the classroom. Regrettably, school boards have become ideological battlegrounds, as in Texas, where the state-approved American history curriculum downplays the role of Thomas Jefferson and fantasizes that the United States was founded as a "Christian nation." One cannot help but sympathize with schools tempted to teach fewer ideas and, instead, to send their students to help in the community; Habitat for Humanity is not as potentially agitating as the Establishment Clause.

But teachers and schools should overcome such complications, not avoid them at the cost of students' civic knowledge. They are educating young American citizens, and part of their mandate from taxpayers is to create a common civic infrastructure in the minds of students.

* * *

The decline in civic education is especially troubling today because the Internet has, despite the utopian predictions of some, contributed to a splintering of society. In 1938, H. G. Wells declared that the advent of microfilm "foreshadows a real intellectual unification of our race. The whole human memory can be, and probably in a short time will be, made accessible to every individual."[22] The spread of the Internet in the late twentieth century led to similar utopian visions of a coming global unity. Yet neither the world nor the United States is more united today than it was two decades ago, when the Internet was still the province of a few geeks. Quite the opposite.

It turns out that when information flows instantaneously everywhere, people don't want to settle on consensus versions of truth and falsehood or right and wrong. Instead, they use the technology to locate others who share their particular views, however errant or extreme, and they stay away from those who would disagree. Thus nonpartisan news outlets are in trouble, but the *Drudge Report* and the *Huffington Post* are thriving.

People seem to be naturally homophiliac: They love to talk with others who think as they do and to avoid those who do not. Yet a healthy pluralistic democracy is xenophiliac, full of citizens who take joy in discussion and debate. Disagreements don't threaten civic culture; homophily does.[23] As Barack Obama said in a commencement address at the University of Michigan in April 2010, reading alien political opinions "may make your blood boil; your mind may not often be changed. But the practice of listening to opposing views is essential for effective citizenship."[24]

The United States is large, it contains multitudes. To be a citizen means understanding the Constitution's words, wisdom, and applicability to daily events. And educating youth for citizenship has never been more important than it is today, when technology has made it so easy to learn the facts and so easy to avoid unwelcome interpretations.

NOTES

1. Brief of Appellant Washington Coalition for Open Government, Doe v. Reed, 586 F.3d 671 (9th Circuit 2009).

2. Doe v. Reed, 130 S. Ct. 2811 (2010). The Court's 8–1 vote affirming the general principle that petitioners should expect their names to be public may not signal how the court would rule in any specific case.

3. See, for example, fundrace.huffingtonpost.com.

4. James Bopp Jr., the attorney who spearheaded the challenge to the disclosure of petitioners' names, is also challenging the disclosure of campaign contributors in the state of Washington, where the threshold for disclosure is lower than the federal level of $200. For more on the so-called Nuremberg files, see Hal Abelson, Ken Ledeen, and Harry Lewis, *Blown to Bits: Your Life, Liberty, and Happiness after the Digital Explosion* (Boston: Addison-Wesley, 2008), 250–51.

5. In an 1822 letter to W. T. Barry, Madison wrote, "A people who mean to be their own Governors, must arm themselves with the power which knowledge gives." And Washington wrote in his farewell address, "In proportion as the structure of a government gives force to public opinion, it is essential that public opinion should be enlightened."

6. See, for example, the Foreign Influence Lobbying Tracker produced by Pro Publica and the Sunlight Foundation.

7. National Endowment for the Arts Office of Research and Analysis, "Reading on the Rise: A New Chapter in American Literacy," January 2009, http://www.nea.gov/research/Readingonrise.pdf.

8. See Matthew Kirshenbaum, "How Reading Is Being Reimagined," *Chronicle Review*, December 7, 2007.

9. Kaiser Family Foundation, "Generation M^2: Media in the Lives of 8-18 Year-Olds," January 2010, http://www.kff.org/entmedia/upload/8010.pdf. Many other studies are cited by Mark Bauerlein in *The Dumbest Generation: How the Digital Ages Stupefies Young Americans and Jeopardizes Our Future* (New York: Penguin, 2008), especially chapters 2 and 3.

10. British Library and University College London, "Information Behaviour of the Researcher of the Future," January 2008, http://www.ucl.ac.uk/infostudies/research/ciber/downloads/ggexecutive.pdf.

11. Declan McCullagh, "FBI Wants Records Kept of Web Sites Visited," *CNet News*, February 5, 2010.

12. For example, are Internet packets themselves protected? They contain both addressing information, which is analogous to postal addresses or telephone numbers, and payload, which is analogous to letters or telephone calls.

13. Andrew Cohen, "Cell Phone Tracking: The Most Important Case You've Never Heard Of," *The Atlantic*, February 12, 2010, http://www.theatlantic.com/national/archive/2010/02/cell-phone-tracking-the-most-important-case-youve-never-heard-of/35827/. See also the amicus briefs filed by the American Civil Liberties Union, the Electronic Frontier Foundation, and the Center for Democracy and Technology, http://www.aclu.org/files/assets/FiledCellTrackingBrief.pdf.

14. Letter from Roslynn R. Mauskopf to Judge James Orenstein, October 11, 2005, http://www.docstoc.com/docs/3546197/Case-mj-JO-Document-Filed-Page-of-U-S-Department.

15. Rehberg v. James P. Paulk, 611 F. 3d 828 (2010).

16. Stephen Shankland, "Execs Convicted in Google Video Case in Italy," *CNet News*, February 24, 2010.

17. Citizens United v. Federal Election Commission 558 U.S. 1 (2010).

18. Adam Liptak, "When American and European Ideas of Privacy Collide," *New York Times*, February 26, 2009.

19. comScore, "comScore Releases March 2010 US Online Video Rankings," April 29, 2010, http://www.comscore.com/Press_Events/Press_Releases/2010/4/comScore_Releases_March_2010_U.S._Online_Video_Rankings. The figure of about seven hours is derived from two reported numbers: 95.6 videos per viewer and 4.3 minutes per video. This number is almost the same as that reported in the Kaiser Family Foundation report "Generation M^2."

20. The average for time spent reading online is about three minutes per day, according to "Generation M[2]." The average for time spent reading offline is about ten minutes per day, or five hours per month, according to the Bureau of Labor Statistics, "American Time Use Survey 2009," http://www.bls.gov/news.release/atus.nr0.htm.

21. Cynthia Gibson and Peter Levine, eds., "The Civic Mission of Schools," CIRCLE and the Carnegie Corporation of New York, 2003, http://www.civicmissionofschools.org/site/campaign/cms_report.html.

22. H. G. Wells, "The Idea of a Permanent World Encyclopaedia," in *World Brain* (London: Methuen & Co , 1938), 60–61.

23. See the blog of Harvard University's Ethan Zuckerman, "My Heart's in Accra," especially the post "Homophily, Serendipity, Xenophilia," April 25, 2008.

24. Barack Obama, "Remarks by the President at the University of Michigan Spring Commencement," May 1, 2010.

Chapter Twenty

How School Choice Enhances Civic Health

Vouchers and Informed Politics

Jay P. Lefkowitz

Opponents of publicly funded education vouchers claim that private schooling undermines the fostering of civic values.[1] While theoretically plausible, this claim has not been substantiated by the empirical studies conducted on the topic to date. To the contrary, these studies indicate that school choice and private schooling generally have a significantly positive impact on the realization of civic values among students.

In 2007, Patrick Wolf, a professor of education policy at the University of Arkansas, examined the results of twenty-one quantitative studies relating to the effects of school choice on seven different civic values, which he defined as an individual's capacity to act as an effective citizen in society.[2] Wolf considered the impact of school choice on political tolerance, volunteerism, political knowledge, political participation, social capital, civic skills, and patriotism. His conclusion: Private schooling and school choice often strengthen students' civic values, with the strongest correlations in the areas of political tolerance, volunteerism, political knowledge, and political participation.

One study in Washington, DC, found that nearly half of the students who had switched from a public school to a private school said that they would allow a member of a group they disliked to live in their neighborhood.[3] This finding is in marked contrast to just over one quarter of the students in the public school control group who gave the same answer.[4] Similarly, a study of eighth graders in New York City and Dallas–Fort Worth concluded that students in private schools are 21 percent more likely to volunteer than are their public school counterparts.[5]

Particularly noteworthy is the impact of school choice among ethnic minorities. One study, by the University of Arkansas education scholar Jay Greene, found that any type of private schooling, religious or secular, increased political tolerance among Latinos.[6] The study concluded that Latinos who received all of their primary and secondary education in private school were 16 percent more likely to report that they had voted in the last presidential election than their Latino counterparts who were educated entirely in the public school system.

Given this and other studies, Wolf concluded that school choice promotes civic values particularly among ethnic minorities in places with great ethnic diversity. These are the particular groups and areas that school voucher programs are typically designed to help.

David Campbell, a political scientist at Notre Dame University, compared the civic attitudes and behavior of students in public and private schools by analyzing data from a large national telephone survey of parents and their adolescent children.[7] Defining civic education as that which "facilitates future participation in political activity," Campbell identified four objectives in particular: (1) participation in public-spirited collective action, (2) the capacity to be involved in the political process, (3) an understanding of the nation's political system, and (4) respect for the civil liberties of others.[8]

According to Campbell, students in private schools are more likely than their counterparts in public schools to engage in community service, have training in civic skills, be confident in their ability to use civic skills, and display political knowledge and political tolerance. Based on these findings, Campbell concluded that, when compared to their publicly educated peers, "students in private schools generally perform better on multiple indicators of civic education."[9]

What particular aspects of school choice and private schooling account for these findings? What is it about private schooling that fosters greater realization of civic values among students?

Wolf offered several theories. One is that private school teachers have more freedom to integrate moral lessons into their classes than do public school teachers, who may shy away from discussing controversial issues.

According to Wolf, students who are trained to encounter "value-based claims and perspectives" regularly and respectfully may acquire greater tolerance for others whose value-based opinions differ from their own. [10]

Another theory to explain the positive effect of school choice on civic education is that private schools generally have more discipline and order than do public schools, particularly in urban areas. As Wolf explained, "a well ordered and nonthreatening education environment likely contributes to students' feelings of security and confidence." Wolf suggested that these feelings may be "a necessary precondition for young people to develop a willingness to tolerate potentially disruptive ideas and political groups and to venture out into the community to promote social causes." [11]

Terry Moe, a political scientist at Stanford University, views the positive correlation between private schooling and civic education differently. According to him, the reason that public schools are unable to serve as models of democratic deliberation may be because they are so entangled in bureaucracy, which is the antithesis of democratic deliberation. [12] "A bureaucratic 'community,'" writes Moe, "is artificial, built on formally specified relationships, rights, and responsibilities that literally obstruct the development of a true community." [13] Moe contends that changing the education system to promote school choice would "tend to promote the emergence of schools as true communities. As parents choose their schools, they are more likely to identify with them, to share their values and missions, to trust one another, to participate, and to have respect for teachers and principals." [14] As Campbell explained, "Moe implies that these schools' organizational structure will serve as a model for democratic involvement, enhancing their ability to prepare students for civic engagement." [15]

* * *

The religion clauses of the First Amendment provide: "Congress shall make no law respecting an establishment of religion, or prohibiting the free exercise thereof." The first of the two clauses is the establishment clause, and the second is the free exercise clause. While the two clauses express complementary values, they often exert conflicting pressures. [16] The Supreme Court has repeatedly recognized that the establishment clause raises difficult issues of interpretation, and cases arising under it "have presented some of the most perplexing questions to come before [the] Court." [17]

The doctrine of separation of church and state is generally traced to a letter written by Thomas Jefferson in 1802 to the Danbury Baptists, in which he referred to the First Amendment of the Constitution as creating a "wall of separation" between church and state.[18] Jefferson's sentiment is often understood to be an authoritative interpretation of the establishment clause. In 1947, the Supreme Court quoted Jefferson's language to justify its holding that the First Amendment guarantees a separation of church and state.[19] "This powerful metaphor, once employed," wrote the historian Edwin Gaustad, "became even more familiar to the American public than did the constitutional language itself."[20]

And yet, popular sentiment aside, the doctrine of separation of church and state is not a constitutional one; the phrase does not appear at all in the Constitution. Indeed, separation of church and state is only one of several possible interpretations of the establishment clause. Legal scholars have suggested numerous alternatives, including "no discrimination in favor of religion" and "no support on the basis of religion,"[21] both of which seem to be derived more clearly from the actual language of the establishment clause.

The phrase "separation of church and state" is not and should not be interpreted to be synonymous with the establishment clause, when it is nothing more than one possible and not especially persuasive interpretation of the First Amendment. In the past twenty years, as the constitutionality of Jefferson's principle has been questioned, the Supreme Court has gradually withdrawn from—but not overruled—its earlier interpretation of the First Amendment.

* * *

The Supreme Court's modern establishment clause jurisprudence stresses two bedrock principles: (1) the importance of neutrality on the part of the government, and (2) the need for the government to avoid direct funding of religion. Supreme Court case law has now firmly established that government programs that provide benefits to sectarian and nonsectarian institutions alike, and do so only indirectly, do not have the "primary effect" of advancing religion, and therefore do not violate the establishment clause.

The Supreme Court has long stressed the importance of government neutrality toward religion.[22] It has also repeatedly emphasized the absence of direct government aid or direct government control over the destination of funds. In *Everson v. Board of Education* (1947), its first decision applying the establishment clause to the states, the Court upheld a program that reimbursed parents for the cost of transporting their children to and from sectarian schools.[23] When the Court next considered government aid to sectarian schools, in *Board of Education v. Allen* (1968), it upheld New York's policy of loaning textbooks free of charge to students in sectarian schools.[24] In approving this textbook loan program, the Court specifically noted that "no funds or books are furnished to parochial schools, and *the financial benefit is to parents and children, not to schools*" (emphasis mine).[25]

In *Mueller v. Allen* (1983), the Court established that a neutral program providing only indirect funding to private sectarian schools does not have the "primary effect" of advancing religion, and thus does not run afoul of the establishment clause.[26] In that case, the Court approved a Minnesota statute that permitted parents to deduct expenses related to their children's education—including expenses attributable to private sectarian schools. In upholding the statute, the Court emphasized that "under Minnesota's arrangement public funds become available only as a result of numerous, private choices of individual parents of school-age children."[27] The Court concluded that "the historic purposes of the clause simply do not encompass the sort of attenuated financial benefit, ultimately controlled by the private choices of individual parents, that eventually flows to parochial schools from the neutrally available tax benefit at issue in this case."[28]

The Court reaffirmed the importance of individual choice and indirect aid in *Witters v. Washington Department of Services for the Blind* (1986).[29] *Witters* upheld the state of Washington's grant of money to a blind student so that he could receive theological training at the Inland Empire School of the Bible. Justice Thurgood Marshall, writing for a unanimous Court, stressed: "Any aid provided under Washington's program that ultimately flows to religious institutions does so only as a result of the genuinely independent and private choices of aid recipients."[30] The Court observed that when individuals, rather than the government, determine whether (and how much) money flows to a sectarian organization, the effect is no more constitutionally troubling than when a government employee donates his paycheck to his church or synagogue.[31]

The Court again emphasized the bedrock principle of indirection in *Zobrest v. Catalina Foothills School District* (1993), which upheld the government's direct provision of an interpreter for a student in a Catholic high school.[32] The Court characterized the statute at issue as "a neutral government program dispensing aid not to schools but to individual handicapped children,"[33] even though, as a formal matter, the government, not the parents, directly paid for the cost of the interpreter.[34] The dispositive factor in *Zobrest* was that the sectarian school would not have received any benefit but for the parents' intervening choice. "Any attenuated financial benefit that parochial schools do ultimately receive from the [statute] is attributable to 'the private choices of individual parents.'"[35]

Rosenberger v. Rector and Visitors of University of Virginia (1995) reaffirmed both the indirection and the neutrality principles.[36] In ruling on the case, the Court first noted that "a significant factor in upholding governmental programs in the face of Establishment Clause attack is their neutrality towards religion."[37] Second, all nine justices reaffirmed that government funding that reaches sectarian institutions indirectly through a neutral program does not raise establishment clause concerns.[38]

This line of cases—*Mueller, Witters, Zobrest,* and *Rosenberger*—stands for a critical proposition: The intervening autonomous choices of individuals eliminate the constitutional difficulties raised by direct government aid to sectarian schools. Factors that have proven fatal to direct government aid to schools lose their significance when government money flows to sectarian schools only as a consequence of the individual choice of a "third party."

Any doubt as to the ascendancy of the neutrality and indirection principles was erased by the Supreme Court's decision in *Agostini v. Felton* (1997), when it expressly acknowledged that "Establishment Clause law has '[significantly changed]'" in recent years and that in particular "what has changed . . . is our understanding of the criteria used to assess whether aid to religion has an impermissible effect."[39] In particular, the Court—citing *Witters* and *Zobrest*—noted that it had discarded the rule that "any and all public aid that directly aids the educational function of religious schools impermissibly finances religious indoctrination, even if the aid reaches such schools as a consequence of private decisionmaking."[40]

The Court also observed in *Agostini* that its recent establishment clause decisions focused on whether state aid "[creates] a financial incentive to undertake religious indoctrination," or whether, instead, "the aid is allocated on the basis of neutral, secular criteria that neither favor nor disfavor religion, and is made available to both religious and secular beneficiaries on a nondiscriminatory basis."[41] The Court explained that, pursuant to this principle of neutrality, it had repeatedly "sustained programs that provided aid to all eligible children, regardless of where they attended school."[42]

Finally, in 2002, the Supreme Court directly considered the constitution-ality of voucher programs in *Zelman v. Simmons-Harris*.[43] In that case, the challenged program allowed income-qualified parents in Cleveland to apply state-funded school vouchers toward their children's tuition at private sectar-ian schools.[44] Finding that the constitutionality of the Cleveland program was controlled by the holdings in *Mueller*, *Witters*, and *Zobrest*, the Court concluded that it did not violate the establishment clause. The court con-firmed that indirect public aid to sectarian education is constitutionally per-missible when the financial assistance program has a valid secular purpose, provides benefits to a broad spectrum of individuals who can exercise genu-ine private choice among religious and secular options, and is neutral toward religion.[45]

The Supreme Court has thus clearly confirmed that (1) government aid to sectarian institutions passes constitutional muster when it is provided on a neutral basis and only as a result of private decision making and (2) vouchers can be one such form of aid.

* * *

The religion clauses of the First Amendment, and their relevance to the debate over school vouchers, provide an object lesson in civic values. Toler-ance—be it religious, political, or cultural—is a core civic value, and the religion clauses provide a perfect illustration of the constant struggle neces-sary to cultivate that value, like any other. The conflicting pressures exerted by each of two clauses necessitate a careful balancing of the protectionism of the establishment clause, on one hand, and the high regard and even support for religion of the free exercise clause, on the other. In the debate over school vouchers, this balance is easily upset and is often completely ignored.

A proper interpretation of the Constitution, as underscored by the Su-preme Court, supports the view that a voucher program, when used for sec-tarian education and allocated on a neutral basis and as a result of private decision making, meets the constitutional obligations imposed by the First Amendment. To claim otherwise is to champion the establishment clause at the expense of the free exercise clause, and to disrupt the careful and precise balancing of the clauses that the Constitution's framers intended.

Opponents of school vouchers, in their haste to stand up for what they perceive as a violation of the establishment clause, may thus unintentionally trample on the protections guaranteed by the free exercise clause. No constitutional clause can be understood independently of its peers, and when two clauses speak to a common topic they must be read and interpreted as a coherent and cohesive unit. To disregard the constitutional support for carefully crafted voucher programs is to focus all the attention on the establishment clause and effectively read the free exercise clause out of the Constitution.

To apply both constitutional and civic values to the school vouchers debate, both clauses must be understood and their interaction, tension, and ultimate balance must be respected. To do otherwise is to threaten both constitutional integrity and civic responsibility.

* * *

The public debate over vouchers is itself affected by the quality of civic education in America and, in turn, by the degree of civic literacy—and illiteracy—among Americans. As Stanford's Moe observes, while almost all Americans have had some interaction with schools, far fewer have ever considered the issue of school choice. In theory, people who are dissatisfied by the public school system should be among the strongest and most active proponents of school vouchers. But most such people do not have firsthand experience with any sort of voucher program or proposal. The concept is, in Moe's words, "an abstract idea about how to transform public policy." Many citizens are therefore "unable to connect their underlying opinions and interests to the voucher issue."[46]

In 1995, according to a study conducted by Moe, only 35 percent of Americans had ever heard of the concept of school vouchers.[47] In 1999, according to a survey conducted by the firm Public Agenda, 63 percent of the general public claimed to know "very little" or "nothing" about vouchers.[48] And in a 1996 study of registered voters, who are presumably better informed about policy issues, when asked which party generally favors government vouchers, 49 percent (correctly) said Republicans, 36 percent (incorrectly) said Democrats, and 13 percent said that they did not know.[49]

Perhaps Americans remain uninformed about school vouchers because they feel that they have insufficient incentive to become informed. It can be costly or time-consuming to collect information, and individuals might have difficulty seeing what personal gain comes from doing so. Policy changes are effected through a collective democratic process, after all, and once a policy is implemented it benefits all who qualify, regardless of whether they had been knowledgeable of and engaged with the issue.

But ignorance may be explained, not justified—and it is itself a sign of insufficient civic education. One of the primary goals of civic education is to help voters realize the value and importance of being informed, even though an individual voter cannot alone dictate policy outcomes. When voters don't feel a sense of obligation to participate in the political process, participatory government becomes less participatory—and individual voters risk becoming not only statistically insignificant, but altogether disenfranchised.

NOTES

I acknowledge the assistance and excellence of Devora Allon, an associate at Kirkland & Ellis LLP, in preparing this chapter.

1. In dissenting from the majority decision in *Zelman v. Simmons Harris* (2002), Justice John Paul Stevens predicted that government funding for private schools will "weaken the foundation of our democracy." See also Amy Guttman, *Democratic Education* (Princeton, NJ: Princeton University Press, 1999).

2. Patrick J. Wolf, "Civics Exam," *Education Next* 7, no. 3 (Summer 2007), 66–72.

3. Wolf, "Civics Exam," 68.

4. Wolf, "Civics Exam," 68.

5. Wolf, "Civics Exam," 69.

6. Wolf, "Civics Exam," 70.

7. David E. Campbell, "The Civic Side of School Choice: An Empirical Analysis of Civic Education in Public and Private Schools," *Brigham Young University Law Review*, no. 2 (2010): 487–524.

8. Campbell, "The Civic Side of School Choice," 489–90.

9. Campbell, "The Civic Side of School Choice," 489.

10. Wolf, "Civics Exam," 72.

11. Wolf, "Civics Exam," 72.

12. Terry Moe, "The Two Democratic Purposes of Education," in *Rediscovering the Democratic Purposes of Education*, ed. Lorraine M. McDonnell, P. Michael Timpane, and Roger Benjamin (Lawrence: University Press of Kansas, 2000), quoted in Campbell, "The Civic Side," 494.

13. Moe, "The Two Democratic Purposes."

14. Moe, "The Two Democratic Purposes."

15. Campbell, "The Civic Side," 495.

16. See Locke v. Davey, 540 U.S. 718 (2004): "These two Clauses . . . are frequently in tension." See also Walz v. Tax Comm'n of the City of N.Y., 397 U.S. 668–69 (1970): "The Court has struggled to find a neutral course between the two Religion Clauses, both of which are cast in absolute terms, and either of which, if expanded to a logical extreme, would tend to clash with the other."

17. Comm. for Pub. Educ. and Religious Liberty v. Nyquist, 413 U.S. 756, 760 (1973); see also Mueller v. Allen, 463 U.S. 388, 392 (1983); Lemon v. Kurtzman, 403 U.S. 602, 612 (1971).

18. Daniel L. Dreisbach, "'Sowing Useful Truths and Principles': The Danbury Baptists, Thomas Jefferson, and the Wall of Separation," *Journal of Church and State* 39, no. 3 (1997), quoted in Philip Hamburger, "Separation and Interpretation," *Journal of Law and Politics* 18, no. 1 (2002): 7–64.

19. Everson v. Board of Educ., 330 U.S. 1, 13 (1947), quoted in Hamburger, "Separation and Interpretation," 7.

20. Edwin S. Gaustad, "Religion," in *Thomas Jefferson: A Reference Biography*, ed. Merrill D. Peterson (New York: Scribner, 1986), quoted in Hamburger, "Separation and Interpretation," 7.

21. Hamburger, "Separation and Interpretation," 11.

22. See, e.g., *Everson*, 330 U.S. at 18; Board of Educ. v. Allen, 392 U.S. 236, 243 (1968).

23. See *Everson*, 330 U.S. at 17–18.

24. See *Board of Educ. v. Allen*, 392 U.S. at 243–44.

25. *Board of Educ. v. Allen*, 392 U.S. at 243–44.

26. *Mueller*, 463 U.S. 388.

27. *Mueller*, 463 U.S. at 399.

28. *Mueller*, 463 U.S. at 400.

29. Witters v. Svcs. for the Blind, 474 U.S. 481 (1986).

30. *Witters*, 474 U.S. at 488, at 490–91 (Powell, J., concurring), at 493 (O'Connor, J., concurring).

31. *Witters*, 474 U.S. at 486–88.

32. Zobrest v. Catalina Foothills Sch. Dist., 509 U.S. 1 (1993).

33. *Zobrest*, 509 U.S. at 13.

34. *Zobrest*, 509 U.S. at 13–14 and n.11.

35. *Zobrest*, 509 U.S. at 12 (quoting *Mueller*, 463 U.S. at 400).

36. Rosenberger v. University of Va., 515 U.S. 819 (1995).

37. *Rosenberger*, 515 U.S. at 839.

38. *Rosenberger*, 515 U.S. at 838–40, at 880–81 (Souter, J., dissenting).

39. Agostini v. Felton, 117 S.Ct. 2016, 2010 (1997).

40. *Agostini*, 117 S.Ct. at 2010–12.

41. *Agostini*, 117 S.Ct. at 2014.

42. *Agostini*, 117 S.Ct. at 2014 (citing, inter alia, *Mueller*, *Witters*, and *Zobrest*).

43. Zelman v. Simmons-Harris, 536 U.S. 639 (2002).

44. *Zelman*, 536 U.S. at 644–46, 663.

45. *Zelman*, 536 U.S. at 662–63.

46. Terry Moe, *Schools, Vouchers, and the American Public* (Washington, DC: Brookings Institution, 2001), 172.

47. Moe, *Schools*, 173.

48. "On Thin Ice: How Advocates and Opponents Could Misread the Public's Views on Vouchers and Charter Schools," Public Agenda, as cited in Moe, *Schools*, 175.

49. Moe, *Schools*, 174.

Chapter Twenty-one

Education versus Indoctrination

What Separates Sound Policy from State Overreach?

Glenn Harlan Reynolds

If you've read this far, you already understand why civic education is important. But there is a danger in trusting important (or unimportant) things to the state: Those in charge of the state may abuse that trust in order to secure their own power, or to marginalize efforts to hold them accountable, rather than acting for the public good. What, then, distinguishes healthy civic education from unhealthy, inappropriate indoctrination of students by the state?

Undemocratic societies, after all, have their own sort of "civic education" that usually features ubiquitous images of the Great Leader; children's choirs singing his (it's generally "his") praises; tedious books of "wisdom" authored, or at least allegedly authored, by the leader; and often an elaborate theory, promulgated by obsequious academics, of why the *fuhrerprinzip,* or some variation thereon, is the culmination of human governance.

Whether we are talking Mao's China, Qaddafi's Libya, or any of a number of comic-yet-brutal dictatorships, there is always an elaborate structure of civic "involvement" and "education." The involvement and education is directed from the top down and operates for the benefit of the existing power structure, not the citizenry.

Even in societies that have not reached this level of autocracy, there is always the danger of opportunistic propaganda on the part of educators—the small-scale despotism of the classroom. Educators have always known that while some students see through efforts at indoctrination, many others do not and remain influenced for life. So the value of classroom indoctrination, to those who want to shape society at large in ways that serve their own interests, is significant, and the temptation to abuse that power in service of educators' favored ideology is always present.

In a dictatorship, teaching children how to please their rulers probably counts as useful civic education in a peculiar sense. But in a democracy—or, more accurately, in a federal republic based on representative democracy—such as ours, the people themselves are supposed to be the rulers, and appropriate civic education thus involves teaching them how to exercise that rule effectively and responsibly.

The question, thus, is whether a particular approach to civic education is preparing citizens to be obedient subjects, or preparing them to be responsible rulers. This is a question that cannot be answered simply by looking at the nominal form of the government, since even in a representative democracy, government officials tend—always for the highest possible motives, of course—to want to accumulate power to themselves, while minimizing their accountability to the Great Unwashed. Such is human nature, and few indeed are the politicians who can rise above it.

That being the case, the citizenry—and particularly that portion of the citizenry composed of parents and students—must be particularly vigilant to ensure that civic education doesn't become just another tool for keeping the powers that be in being. Following are some things to watch for, both good and bad.

* * *

The easiest and least controversial part of civic education involves a basic description of our system of government. As we know, this part isn't going very well. The simple outlines of our system—the three branches of the federal government, the relationship between them, how bills become law, and how the Constitution is amended—aren't well understood by Americans, and popular press accounts seem woefully uninformed.

The good news is that there's a lot of low-hanging and uncontroversial fruit out there in the area of basic governmental literacy, and there's not much room to argue that facilitating such literacy represents abusive indoctrination. Even those who believe that students should be taught to take a primarily critical stance toward their own country's institutions presumably have no objection to students learning what those institutions are: Ignorance, in fact, makes critique impossible. One cannot critique what one does not understand, and ignorance about how government works makes criticism less, not more, likely. Ignorance, in our society, at least, is not strength.

So one thing to look for in a civic education program is simple, straightforward instruction about how the government is structured, and how it is supposed to work. A program based on providing this sort of information is—to that extent, at least—one that is about education, not indoctrination. And, more significantly, a civic education program that does not provide that sort of information can be little more than indoctrination, since it fails to provide students with the basic knowledge that they need to think for themselves.

Of course, even in these areas, there's some wiggle room. Teaching about the relationship of the branches, or the roles of the states and the federal government, inevitably involves touching on contested issues: Is federalism obsolete? Are courts more or less trustworthy than legislatures? Is our constitution a "living" document, or does it have fixed meaning?

How are we to evaluate the treatment of these issues? How can we tell indoctrination for the benefit of the state from education for the benefit of the citizenry?

The short answer is, by exercising judgment. Indoctrination is typically one-sided. Opposing or inconsistent views are ignored or marginalized. Independent thought is discouraged. The universe of discourse is closed.

On the other hand, although a few constitutional issues are pretty much closed—thirty-four-year-olds need not apply for the presidency, for example—in the discussion of most issues that go beyond pure structure, there are respectable views from a variety of perspectives. A class that is aimed at informing and educating will present them—and without ridicule.

The presence of ridicule in more than the tiniest degree is itself a highly useful warning sign of indoctrination. Not only does it suggest a teacher's effort to undermine ideas with which she disagrees. But a teacher who behaves this way models an attitude of contempt for those who disagree that is inconsistent with the notion of education for civil society. When ideas or their proponents are ridiculed, the message to students is that they don't have to think about those ideas at all for they are, quite literally, ridiculous. A message not to think about ideas is far more likely to serve the interests of indoctrinators than educators.

On the other hand, a teacher who explains different viewpoints on their own terms—and who notes that some people who held views that were unpopular in their day were, in fact, leading thinkers of their time who looked at the world incisively—is a different sort of model: One of respect and openness toward ideas, and toward one's fellow citizens.

Likewise, a teacher's choice of materials may offer some insight. The more that a course uses original documents—the Constitution, the Declaration of Independence, the Emancipation Proclamation, *The Federalist Papers*—rather than modern summaries or commentaries, the less that it is open to the imposition of a particular point of view.

It is not that the framers lacked their own point of view, of course. But the framers' point of view, precisely because it is the framers' point of view, stands independently of contemporary politics. Understanding the framers' intentions does not force us to follow those intentions, but it represents a very useful starting point for understanding how present-day institutions fit into our scheme of government. It also—precisely because the framers' views are "out of date"—provides a helpful counterpoint to contemporary ideologies.

Some might object to privileging the framers' views, but why shouldn't they be privileged? The views of our society's founders should occupy a central place in any discussion of the society they founded. Indeed, efforts to downplay the importance of the framers' views, or to dismiss them as obsolete, are themselves another warning sign that educators may be trying to make room for their preferred modern narrative. The framers' views may or may not be correct, but they are, at least, something other than the latest fad or directive.

Another source of insight is localism versus uniformity, though here it's not as clear which way the balance tilts. On the one hand, a locally developed curriculum for civic education is unlikely to reflect the demands of an overweening nation-state: You can bet that the curriculum was centrally directed in Orwell's Oceania, where Big Brother reigned.

On the other hand, it is often the case that localities—particularly large cities or small rural communities—tend to be political monocultures, meaning that a locally developed civics curriculum may tend more toward the one-sided. That risk is present whether in Berkeley, California or Pulaski, Tennessee (though probably more pointedly in the former than the latter).

So it's hard to say whether a system of locally controlled curricula is more likely to lead to indoctrination than a system involving one national curriculum. On the one hand, as Madison noted in *The Federalist*, small republics are more prone to factional capture than large ones. In any given community, whether Berkeley or Pulaski, a particular view is likely to pre-dominate. Nationally, many different approaches contend.

A national curriculum, on the other hand, if captured and turned into indoctrination, becomes uniform indoctrination for the whole nation. It may not be clear which approach is more likely to lead to indoctrination, but it does seem that a single national curriculum, if captured, produces a more dangerous result. That seems like a pretty strong argument for local control of education, at least in this regard.

* * *

Implicit in any discussion of civic education is the assumption that the edu-cating will be done by, well, educators—that is, chiefly by the public schools. That assumption is understandable, but maybe there is another way.

A friend who is a lawyer recently told me that his best civic education came from a college internship with the Tennessee State Senate. He learned a lot about politics and government, he said, and with no indoctrination. The people he worked for—committee chairs and staff in a part-time legisla-ture—were too busy to try indoctrination even if the idea appealed to them, and they were too focused on their real jobs to care. Yet he learned a lot by seeing them in action.

This is a good argument for moving at least some civic education outside the public schools and into the real world—for adopting an apprenticeship model to supplement the classroom model. Given the mushrooming size of government at all levels, there should be plenty of opportunities for high school and college students to intern with all sorts of government officials and agencies, and the experience is at least as likely to encourage a skeptical attitude as it is to breed infatuation. Otto von Bismarck famously said that those who like laws or sausages should not look too closely into how they are made; that certainly suggests that firsthand exposure will foster knowledge, but not a slavish devotion to government or party.

An apprenticeship approach could also make indoctrination (conscious or unconscious) harder to pull off by dividing up students and getting them out of schools. As we are often told, there is strength in diversity, and an appren-ticeship model exposes students to a much more diverse assortment of indi-viduals, settings, and experiences than can a purely school-based approach.

Apprenticeship is probably not the best way to teach the basic what-the-government-does stuff, but it certainly offers a lot of potential in terms of building a broader and deeper store of knowledge.

In addition, an apprenticeship model teaches students to think of themselves as part of the political system, rather than as outsiders looking in. Someone who has witnessed citizens groups lobbying a state senator is far more likely to think of himself or herself as a political actor, not merely as the subject of political actions. And that sort of attitude is likely to encourage political involvement over a lifetime in a way that no classroom experience can duplicate.

There might be benefits flowing the other way, as well. The framers of our Constitution wrote incessantly about "corruption," but they were not simply talking about crude, bags-of-cash-for-votes transactions. Rather, corruption occurred when institutions became systematically biased in favor of insiders at the expense of the public good. One major contributor to such corruption is insularity—when the "ins" become sufficiently distant from the "outs" that they lose perspective on their own actions, even as the "outs" lose the ability to provide the oversight and supervision that voters in a democratic system are expected to provide.

An influx of apprentices from high school and college might help with that, by reminding the insiders of how things look to outsiders. What's more, it might deter some misbehavior simply by providing a steady flow of outside witnesses to what goes on.

* * *

Of course, it will take more than civic education to preserve the republic, and more than apprenticeships to save civic education. Structural approaches can help guard against indoctrination, but—as with the Constitution itself—if the will to resist indoctrination or tyranny fails, structure will not provide sufficient protection. Structural approaches can promote good behavior and retard the bad, but only to a degree.

If the preservation of the Constitution depends on maintaining a spirit of liberty within the larger society—and I feel quite sure that it does—then the real lesson is that we need to promote such a spirit not only within the educational system, but everywhere else. Ultimately, civic education is a process, not an event, and it isn't just for schoolchildren, but for all of us.

Chapter Twenty-two

Letter to President Obama

A Policy Approach for the Federal Government

Peter Levine

Previous chapters in this volume have examined what forms of civic education students should experience in their classrooms and schools. No package or sequence of experiences will be appropriate for every young person, and we must be sensitive to differences in culture and local context, as well as to students' backgrounds, dispositions, and interests. Still, rigorous research has shown certain experiences to be effective. Unfortunately, those opportunities are rare and unequal, and the forms of civic education that would most benefit poor, immigrant, and minority youth are the least likely to be offered in their schools.

The most challenging question is not what students should experience but how to ensure through public policy that students all receive the opportunities we know to be valuable. Analyzing a survey of one hundred thousand high school students by the Knight Foundation, some colleagues and I were unable to find any state policies that had substantial impacts on what students knew, despite considerable variation in the policies.[1] That result provides an important caution: State policy is a blunt instrument, and even the best-intentioned and most ambitious mandates may not affect what happens in schools or classrooms.

Our study did not assess the impact of federal policy, but Washington is even more distant from students and teachers, and therefore less likely to influence learning. It is not impossible for federal or state governments to improve civic education, but the effort requires modesty, flexibility, and a willingness to experiment, revise, and try again. No solutions are simply waiting to be imposed on the nation's schools.

* * *

Concerned outsiders to the civics field often suggest that all states and localities should require their students to study various civic and political topics, from the Constitution to current events. But all fifty states and Washington, DC, already require some teaching in civics and/or government.[2] States already require that mandatory courses cover a whole range of specific topics and subjects—for instance, the Bill of Rights and the separation of powers. The prevalence of civics and social studies courses is fairly high and has risen in the past twenty years at the high school level.[3] Many schools and districts and one whole state (Maryland) require service learning.

Yet outcomes are inadequate and highly uneven, even within states that have strict requirements. That is evidence that more course mandates may not work. Long lists of required topics may actually be part of the problem, making the mandatory courses incoherent and superficial. As the late Paul Gagnon of the National Council for History Education wrote in 2003, "the most common failure is not deciding on priorities." History and social studies offer "mountains of content." "Rather than battle over what to put in and leave out, writers [of state standards] put in everything, either in the form of endless specifics or vast headings that could 'cover' any and all unnamed essentials."[4]

It is certainly possible that better course requirements would help. More instructional time could be required: The typical high school "civics" mandate is just one semester. State standards for courses could be streamlined to emphasize shorter lists of essentials, and states could experiment with mandating a new course that emphasizes civic action and experience.

Such experiential courses used to be common. Before World War II, more than half of all American ninth graders took "civics," a class that emphasized the active roles that individuals play in their communities. This course was designed to complement student governments, school newspapers, service projects, and other opportunities for active engagement. Just after the war, more than 40 percent of American high school students took a semester of "problems of democracy," which typically involved reading and debating stories from the daily newspaper.[5]

Those two courses are now very rare, although service learning programs (offered in about 24 percent of schools[6]) fill some of the same purposes for the students who take them. Most students still take a different class, called "American government." This is typically political science for high school students, emphasizing the formal processes of national politics and treating government with academic detachment rather than exploring ways that students can personally engage.

A modern version of the old "civics" and "problems of democracy" course would include some combination of studying and discussing current events, creating public documents or presentations, and service learning. There is much more evidence for the positive impact of such courses than there is for political science in high school.[7]

Federal policy could be used to encourage experiential civics. The Obama administration has already made $4.35 billion in education grants to states through the Race to the Top competition, and it intends to hold additional competitions for federal grants. As it does so, it could give advantages to states that require experiential civics courses.

* * *

Thirty years ago, people who favored almost any form or aspect of education, regardless of their position on the ideological spectrum, would have argued for funding it. That strategy is less influential today because both conservatives and liberals doubt that schools will use such funds well. Given a proposal to provide a large urban public school system with money for experiential civics classes, conservatives would worry about waste and poor quality in the schools, and progressives would worry that only relatively advantaged students and schools would benefit from the funds.

Nevertheless, civics needs investment, especially funds for developing and testing new tools and curricula. In 2011, amid its substantial budget cuts, Congress cut all federal funding for civic education. (It preserved funding for some other relevant programs, such as Teaching American History grants.[8]) Before 2011, over the first decade of this century, federal funding for civics had totaled less than $70 million per year and had gone almost exclusively to two programs.

First, Washington gave the Center for Civic Education "congressional directed grants" to provide textbooks and professional development for civics. In 2010, the center's appropriation was $26.5 million.[9] Meanwhile Congress gave money to Learn & Serve America, a program of the Corporation for National and Community Service, to fund service learning. Its budget in fiscal year 2010 was \$36.5 million.[10] Much of Learn & Serve America's spending, in turn, took the form of noncompetitive allocations to states and small competitive grants to nonprofit organizations and colleges and universities that supported service learning for K–12 students. Few of its grants or subgrants involved rigorous evaluation.

In the future, it would help to have more federal funding, of which more is allocated for rigorous pilot tests of new interventions.

Given the small federal role in funding civic education, it was not strategic to reserve almost half of the funds for a program that provided the same set of textbooks to some students every year, especially since outside evaluations of the Center for Civic Education have been methodologically weak.[11] (I should acknowledge that the Center for Civic Education's executive director, Charles N. Quigley, a cocontributor to this volume, has responded substantively when I have made this critique in public forums.[12]) As for Learn & Serve America, its reliance on uncompetitive state grants and small subgrants with insufficient oversight did not maximize innovation.

A more effective strategy would allocate funds on a highly competitive basis to school districts or organizations that propose to achieve substantial increases in students' civic skills, knowledge, and values through innovative approaches that could be rigorously tested and then widely imitated if they worked.

Today's main education reform strategy, however, is neither to require courses nor to fund experimental programs. It is to impose assessments of educational outcomes and hold schools, teachers, and/or students responsible for them.

In the case of civics, that poses a dilemma. On one hand, unless a subject is tested, it may not be taught—at least not as a priority. Neglecting to test civics when we make so much of tests in reading, mathematics, and science presumably communicates the message that civics is not important. On the other hand, if we add a new test with consequences for students, we add a new way for individuals to fail when the high school dropout rate is already about one in three. That is not a general argument against testing, but it is a caution about adding a new test when schools are struggling with the existing ones.

Further, a high-stakes exam cannot test values or habits, so the tested material is reduced to facts and concrete skills, like interpreting a cartoon. To the extent that such tests affect the curriculum and teaching, they may increase the time spent on learning facts and practicing concrete, individual skills. Students need to learn facts, but there is no reason to think that they will retain facts about politics or use their factual knowledge wisely and effectively in civic life unless they have experience with discussion and collaboration. If time for discussion and problem solving is reduced to make room for more facts, the net impact will be undesirable.

Considering the balance of arguments for and against testing, I would endorse the position of the Campaign for the Civic Mission of Schools, which calls for new, mandatory federal assessments of civics and history with no net increase in the total testing burden on students. That implies that the number of tests in other subjects would have to be cut, or new assessments could be developed that measured civics along with reading/language arts.

* * *

Two other policies deserve consideration, although there is no data that assure they would work. Each policy could be imposed by a school, a school district, or a state; the federal government could encourage them by adjusting criteria for federal aid. I would recommend starting with changes at the school level, with voluntary policies adopted by school administrators. Such local experience could suggest how effective the policies are.

First, students could report anonymously on the civic engagement opportunities offered in their schools (not on their opinion of these opportunities, but on which ones exist).

Beginning in 2010, all students in Boston public schools completed a questionnaire about the quality of learning in each of their courses; I recommend similar surveys (or survey items) focused on civic learning. For example, students would report whether there is a school newspaper, whether and how often they discuss current events in their social studies classes, whether they perform community service, and if so whether they study the issues related to their service. Such student reports would offer valuable (although not conclusive) evidence about which students experience which kinds of opportunities.

Schools would be held accountable for offering civic learning opportunities equitably across their student bodies. In voluntary, pilot cases, school administrators and teachers would simply use the data for their own self-review. Later, school districts, states, or the federal government could give recognition to schools that scored well. The same governmental bodies could provide support to those that performed badly and could impose sanctions for failure to improve. For example, a school that had no student newspaper would be eligible for funding and technical support to start one, but if it failed to do so, a note would be made in the principal's personnel file. Also, if only honor roll students reported talking about current events, the school would have to work to expand such opportunities to everyone.

A second policy: Hold students individually accountable not for passing a conventional test, but for performing well on a simulation of civic action that involves knowledge of principles and facts, collaboration with others, and advanced skills. For instance, within a computer game, students could perform as legislators or as members of a community (like newspaper editors, pastors, or other civic leaders) responding to a crisis. They could write emails within the game that are scored for quality of writing, application of concepts from social studies, use of factual evidence, relevance to the issue, and so on.

CIRCLE, the Center for Information and Research on Civic Learning and Engagement, which I lead, has worked with a Wisconsin-based company called Community Knowledgebase, LLC to develop and test such a game—with promising results. The first version, called CivNet, simulated the role of community activists in Baltimore, Maryland. The second version, called Legislative Aide, simulated a Congressperson's district staff office in Tampa, Florida. These projects were conducted as research and the games are not commercially available, but similar games could serve as authentic assessments of students' skills and knowledge. [13]

These two proposals both raise difficult questions, especially about what consequences should follow from failure. But both have promise to drive better educational performance. If schools or school districts tried them on a voluntary basis and had success in improving students' civic learning experiences, these approaches could then be written into state law and/or encouraged with federal subsidies. [14]

* * *

Ultimately a wide range of factors shape students' experiences, including requirements, opportunities, standards, evaluations, curricula, textbooks, materials, local civic associations, and teacher quality. Therefore, rather than expect any particular national reform to solve our civic education problem, we should change the way that the government addresses civics going forward.

At the federal level, civic education should no longer be the responsibility of a suboffice within the Department of Education's Office of Safe and Drug-Free Schools. The subject should have a prominent new office with a director empowered to convene representatives from other federal agencies involved with civic learning, including the Corporation for National and Community Service, the Corporation for Public Broadcasting, the National Park Service, and others.

Using civic literacy data, evidence about effective practices, and principled arguments about what outcomes are most important, the new office would address the complex issues involved with improving civics nationwide. Preferably, its work would be informed by an expanded National Assessment of Educational Progress in civics: Unlike its assessments in reading and mathematics, its assessment in civics is currently based on a national sample that does not permit state comparisons.

We can never stop working to improve the quantity, quality, and equality of "civics"—understood not just as a course, but as a whole range of experiences—in our rather autonomous communities. Reforming civics is a marathon, not a sprint. The proposals I lay out here have promise, but more important is to create institutions, in government and in our communities, that will continuously improve civic education into the future.

NOTES

1. Mark Hugo Lopez, Kenneth Dautrich, David Yalof, and Peter Levine, "Schools, Education Policy and the Future of the First Amendment," *Political Communication* 26, no. 1 (January–March 2009): 84–101.

2. Tiffani Lennon, "ECS Policy Brief: Civic Education," Education Commission of the States and National Center for Learning and Citizenship, July 2006.

3. Peter Levine, Mark Hugo Lopez, and Karlo Barrios Marcelo, "Narrower at the Base: The American Curriculum after NCLB," CIRCLE special report, December 2008, http://www.civicyouth.org/PopUps/Narrowing_Curriculum.pdf.

4. Paul Gagnon, *Educating Democracy: State Standards to Ensure a Civic Core* (Washington, DC: Albert Shanker Institute, 2003), 6–7.

5. Richard G. Niemi and Julia Smith, "Enrollments in High School Government Classes: Are We Short-Changing Both Citizenship and Political Science Training?" *PS: Political Science and Politics* 34, no. 2 (June 2001): 282.

6. Kimberly Spring, Robert Grimm Jr., and Nathan Dietz, "Community Service and Service-Learning in America's Schools," Corporation for National and Community Service, Office of Research and Policy Development, November 2008, http://www.icicp.org/ht/a/GetDocumentAction/i/10498.

7. Richard G. Niemi and Jane Junn found that the effect of taking a standard civics course was the equivalent of an extra four points on the National Assessment of Educational Progress in civics—a statistically significant finding but not a large one. See Richard G. Niemi and Jane Junn, *Civic Education: What Makes Students Learn* (New Haven, CT: Yale University Press, 2005). Using similar cross-sectional surveys, David E. Campbell found much larger effects from discussions of controversial issues. See Campbell, "Voice in the Classroom: How an Open Classroom Environment Facilitates Adolescents' Civic Development," CIRCLE Working Paper 28, February 2005, http://www.civicyouth.org/PopUps/WorkingPapers/WP28campbell.pdf. One program that involves discussion of current events and public speaking is Kids Voting USA. It was found, in a rigorous longitudinal study, to raise students' knowledge of politics, to reduce gaps in knowledge between the most and least knowledgeable students, and to increase the consistency between students' opinions on issues and their own voting behavior. See Patrick C. Meirick and Daniel B. Wackman, "Kids Voting and Political Knowledge: Narrowing Gaps, Informing Votes," *Social Science Quarterly* 84, no. 5 (2004): 1161–77. A large longitudinal study of students in Chicago Public Schools found that service learning, discussions of public issues, and use of news media raised students' commitment to civic participation. See Joseph E. Kahne and Susan E. Sporte, "Developing Citizens: The Impact of Civic Learning Opportunities on Students' Commitment to Civic Participation," *American Educational Research Journal* 45, no. 3 (2008): 738–66. In a clever natural experiment, Edward C. Metz and James Youniss demonstrated that a mandatory high school service requirement built lasting habits of engagement. See Metz and Youniss, "Longitudinal Gains in Civic Development through School-Based Required Service," *Political Psychology* 26, no. 3 (2005): 413–37. (This is a sample of a much larger literature.)

8. See chapters 5 and 6 for more on the Teaching American History Grant Program.

9. Larry Gerston, "Opinion: Cutting Some 'Earmarks' Would Be a Real Loss to Nation," *San Jose Mercury News*, March 19, 2011.

10. Corporation for National and Community Service, "Budget Chart," http://www.nationalservice.gov/pdf/2011_budget_chart.pdf.pdf.

11. Ardice Hartry and Kristie Porter, "We the People Curriculum: Results of a Pilot Test," MPR Associates, July 2004, http://www.civiced.org/pdfs/pilot.pdf. No evaluations have been truly longitudinal or have used randomization. The most recent and extensive evaluation of the center's Project Citizen program asserts that the program enhances students' "civic knowledge, civic discourse skills, and public policy problem solving skills." But the treatment group classrooms were selected for evaluation by coordinators of Project Citizen, and the comparison classrooms were selected by Project Citizen teachers. Thus, no inferences can be drawn about Project Citizen classrooms in general. See Susan Root and Judy Northrup, "Project Citizen Evaluation," RMC Research, June 2007, http://www.civiced.org/pdfs/PC/pcOnePager2007.pdf.

12. See, for example, this June 30, 2009, exchange on my blog: http://www.peterlevine.ws/mt/archives/2009/06/reforming-civic.html.

13. See chapter 1 for Justice Sandra Day O'Connor's description of digital civics-learning games that her organization, iCivics, has developed.

14. Such federal subsidies—and various other potential federal measures—could be enacted through the reauthorization of the No Child Left Behind law, through annual appropriations, or through a separate civic education bill that would then be reconciled with the regular appropriations bills. Various strategies should be considered, depending on the situation in Congress.

Index

About the Editor and Contributors

David Feith is an assistant editorial features editor at *The Wall Street Journal*, where he edits op-eds and writes mainly about foreign policy and education reform. He was twice a Robert L. Bartley Fellow at *The Wall Street Journal* and later an assistant editor at *Foreign Affairs* magazine. Feith chairs the Civic Education Initiative, which he cofounded while in college to promote a national agenda for strengthening civic knowledge. He graduated Phi Beta Kappa with a BA in history from Columbia University in 2009.

* * *

Seth Andrew founded Democracy Prep Public Schools in 2005. As of fall 2011, Democracy Prep is a network of four high-performing public charter schools in Harlem, including the top-ranked public middle school in New York City, serving more than one thousand students in kindergarten through eleventh grade. Mr. Andrew received his AB from Brown University and a master's degree from the Harvard Graduate School of Education, where he teaches school leadership as an adjunct lecturer.

Charles F. Bahmueller has been director of special projects at the Center for Civic Education since 1986. He has taught at Harvard University, the University of California at Santa Cruz, and the University of California at Los Angeles, among other universities, and he has authored or edited eight books and more than one hundred articles on political science, European and American history, and civic education.

Mark Bauerlein is professor of English and founder of the Program in Democracy and Citizenship at Emory University. From 2003 to 2005, Dr. Bauerlein was director of the Office of Research and Analysis at the National Endowment for the Arts. His scholarly publications have addressed nineteenth-century American literature and philosophy, and American civil rights history. His latest book is *The Dumbest Generation: How the Digital Age Stupefies Young Americans and Jeopardizes Our Future* (2008).

John M. Bridgeland served in the White House from 2001 to 2004, first as director of the Domestic Policy Council and then as assistant to the president overseeing the USA Freedom Corps and the Office of Faith-Based and Community Initiatives. He is currently CEO of Civic Enterprises and national advisory chair of the National Conference on Citizenship. He is the author of a forthcoming book on his post–September 11 experiences.

Bruce Cole is president and CEO of the American Revolution Center, which is establishing the first national museum to commemorate the American Revolution in Philadelphia, Pennsylvania. Dr. Cole served from 2001 to 2009 as chairman of the National Endowment for the Humanities and was awarded the Presidential Citizens Medal "for his work to strengthen our national memory and ensure that our country's heritage is passed on to future generations." A scholar of Renaissance art, Dr. Cole was a distinguished professor at Indiana University and has authored fourteen books. In 2008, he was decorated Knight of the Grand Cross, the highest honor of the Republic of Italy.

Alan M. Dershowitz is Felix Frankfurter professor of law at Harvard Law School. He is one of the nation's foremost appellate lawyers and defenders of individual liberties. He has published hundreds of articles in national magazines and journals, and is the author of twenty-seven books. His recent titles include *Preemption: A Knife That Cuts Both Ways* (2007), and *Finding Jefferson: A Lost Letter, a Remarkable Discovery, and the First Amendment in an Age of Terrorism* (2007).

Mike Feinberg is cofounder of the KIPP (Knowledge Is Power Program) national charter school network and an alumnus of Teach For America. Founded in 1994 as a program for fifty students at Garcia Elementary

School in Houston, Texas, KIPP now serves thirty-three thousand low-income students in one hundred and nine schools across twenty states and Washington, DC. Mr. Feinberg's work was the subject of the 2009 book *Work Hard, Be Nice: How Two Inspired Teachers Created the Most Promising Schools in America*. He currently serves as superintendent of KIPP's Houston schools and as a member of the KIPP Foundation board of directors.

Senator Bob Graham was governor of Florida from 1979 to 1987 and a US senator from 1987 to 2005. While serving in Florida's State Senate, before serving as governor, he taught civics for a semester at Miami Carol City Senior High School. In 2008, he founded the Bob Graham Center for Public Service at the University of Florida. He is coauthor of *America, the Owner's Manual: Making Government Work for You* (2010).

Chris Hand is a Florida attorney and former press secretary for Senator Bob Graham. A graduate of Princeton's Woodrow Wilson School of Public and International Affairs, he is coauthor of *America, the Owner's Manual: Making Government Work for You* (2010).

Frederick M. Hess is director of education policy studies at the American Enterprise Institute. He is author of the *Education Week* blog "Rick Hess Straight Up" and of books including *The Same Thing Over and Over: How School Reformers Get Stuck in Yesterday's Ideas* (2010), *Common Sense School Reform* (2004), and *Revolution at the Margins: The Impact of Competition on Urban School Systems* (2002). He serves as executive editor of *Education Next*, on the review board for the Broad Prize for Urban Education, and on the boards of directors of the National Association of Charter School Authorizers and the American Board for the Certification of Teaching Excellence. A former high school social studies teacher who has taught at the University of Virginia, the University of Pennsylvania, Georgetown University, Rice University, and Harvard University, Dr. Hess holds his MEd in teaching and curriculum and his MA and PhD in government from Harvard University.

Eugene Hickok served as deputy US secretary of education from 2003 to 2004, and as under secretary of education from 2001 to 2003. In those positions, he was an architect of the No Child Left Behind Act and was responsible for its implementation. A former professor of political science and law, Secretary Hickok was the secretary of education of Pennsylvania from 1995 to 2001.

Michael Kazin is professor of history at Georgetown University and coeditor of *Dissent* magazine. He has authored many books, including *American Dreamers: How the Left Changed a Nation* (2011), *A Godly Hero: The Life of William Jennings Bryan* (2006), *America Divided: The Civil War of the 1960s* (1999, with Maurice Isserman), and *The Populist Persuasion: An American History* (1995). He also has edited *The Princeton Encyclopedia of American Political History* (2009).

Senator Jon Kyl is a US senator from Arizona and the Republican Whip, the second-ranking member of the Senate Republican leadership. First elected to Congress in 1986, Senator Kyl is completing his third term in the Senate. A lawyer by training, he serves on the Senate Finance Committee and on the Judiciary Committee, where he chairs the Subcommittee on Terrorism, Technology and Homeland Security.

Jay P. Lefkowitz is a senior litigation partner at Kirkland & Ellis LLP and an adjunct professor at Columbia Law School. Mr. Lefkowitz has served in government as US special envoy on human rights in North Korea, deputy assistant to the president for domestic policy, general counsel of the Office of Management and Budget, and White House director of cabinet affairs. In the mid-1990s, he represented the state of Wisconsin in landmark litigation upholding the constitutionality of the nation's first-ever school voucher program.

Peter Levine is director of CIRCLE, the Center for Information and Research on Civic Learning and Engagement, at Tufts University's Jonathan Tisch College of Citizenship and Public Service, where he is also research director. He previously served as deputy director of the National Commission on Civic Renewal and he co-organized the 2003 study "The Civic Mission of Schools." He is author of, among other books, *The Future of Democracy: Developing the Next Generation of American Citizens* (2007).

Harry Lewis is Gordon McKay professor of computer science at Harvard University, where he served as dean of Harvard College from 1995 to 2003. He is the author of *Excellence without a Soul: Does Liberal Education Have a Future?* (2007) and a coauthor of *Blown to Bits: Your Life, Liberty, and Happiness after the Digital Explosion* (2008).

Justice Sandra Day O'Connor served as an Associate Justice of the United States Supreme Court from 1981 to 2006. After leaving the Court, Justice O'Connor launched iCivics.org, a website offering free interactive civic resources for students and teachers. She is chancellor of the College of William & Mary and serves on the board of trustees of the National Constitution Center in Philadelphia.

Secretary Rod Paige was US secretary of education from 2001 to 2005. Previously he was superintendent of the Houston Independent School District. Among other books, he is coauthor of *The Black-White Achievement Gap: Why Closing It Is the Greatest Civil Rights Challenge of Our Time* (2010).

Charles N. Quigley is executive director and founder of the Center for Civic Education. The author of *Civitas: A Framework for Civic Education* (1991), he has developed the Civitas International Programs to link leading civic education programs in twenty-eight US states with educational leaders in more than seventy developing democracies throughout the world.

Admiral Mike Ratliff (Vice Admiral, retired, US Navy) is president of the Jack Miller Center for Teaching America's Founding Principles and History. He was previously executive director of the National Civic Literacy Board, and until 2000 he served a distinguished thirty-year naval career, retiring as director of Naval Intelligence.

Glenn Harlan Reynolds is Beauchamp Brogan distinguished professor of law at the University of Tennessee College of Law. He hosts "InstaVision" on PJTV.com and blogs at Instapundit.com. He has published in the *Columbia Law Review*, *Virginia Law Review*, *University of Pennsylvania Law Review*, *Harvard Journal of Law and Technology*, *New York Times*, *Washington Post*, *Washington Times*, *Los Angeles Times*, and the *Wall Street Journal*, among many other publications.

Jason Ross is vice president of education programs at the Bill of Rights Institute, where he leads curriculum development, teacher-program development, and student-program development. Dr. Ross earned his PhD in political theory from the Department of Government at Georgetown University and his master's in public policy from Pepperdine University. He is the recipient of the Richard M. Weaver Fellowship sponsored by the Intercollegiate Studies Institute, the Humane Studies Fellowship sponsored by the Institute for Humane Studies, and the Civitas Fellowship sponsored by the Center for Public Justice, among others. He has published reviews and essays in the *Review of Politics*, the *Journal of Religion and Society*, and the *University Bookman*. He serves as an adjunct professor of history at Pepperdine University's Washington, DC, campus.

Andrew J. Rotherham is a co-founder and partner at Bellwether Education, a non-profit organization working to improve educational outcomes for low-income students. Mr. Rotherham leads Bellwether's thought leadership, idea generation, and policy analysis work. He also writes the weekly "School of Thought" column for TIME.com as well as the blog Eduwonk.com. He previously served in the Clinton White House as special assistant to the president for domestic policy, and he is a former member of the Virginia Board of Education. In addition to Bellwether, Mr. Rotherham has founded or co-founded two other influential education reform organizations including Education Sector.

John R. Thelin is university research professor at the University of Kentucky. A Phi Beta Kappa alumnus of Brown University, he received his MA and PhD from the University of California, Berkeley. Professor Thelin has served as president of the Association for the Study of Higher Education and has received the College of William & Mary's Phi Beta Kappa Award for Faculty Scholarship. He has contributed to *The Encyclopedia of American Social History* and is author of many books, including *A History of American Higher Education* (2004).

Juan Williams is an author and a political analyst for the Fox News Channel. His books include *Eyes on the Prize: America's Civil Rights Years, 1954–1965* (1988), *Thurgood Marshall: American Revolutionary* (2000), and *Enough: The Phony Leaders, Dead-End Movements, and Culture of Failure That Are Undermining Black America—and What We Can Do about It* (2007).

CPSIA information can be obtained at www.ICGtesting.com
Printed in the USA
267945BV00002B/4/P